Baseball at the Dawn
of the Seventies

ALSO BY PAUL HENSLER
AND FROM MCFARLAND

*Bob Steele on the Radio: The Life of
Connecticut's Beloved Broadcaster* (2019)

*The American League in Transition, 1965–1975:
How Competition Thrived When the Yankees Didn't* (2013)

Baseball at the Dawn of the Seventies

The Major Leagues in Transition, 1970–1971

PAUL HENSLER

McFarland & Company, Inc., Publishers
Jefferson, North Carolina

Unless otherwise noted, all photos are from the National Baseball Hall of Fame and Museum, Cooperstown, NY.

ISBN (print) 978-1-4766-9531-0
ISBN (ebook) 978-1-4766-5590-1

LIBRARY OF CONGRESS CATALOGING DATA ARE AVAILABLE

Library of Congress Control Number 2025037230

© 2026 Paul Hensler. All rights reserved

No part of this book may be reproduced or transmitted in any form or by any means, electronic or mechanical, including photocopying or recording, or by any information storage and retrieval system, without permission in writing from the publisher.

Front cover illustrations: (clockwise, from top left) Los Angeles Dodgers third baseman Dick Allen, Oakland Athletics pitcher Vida Blue, Cincinnati Reds manager Sparky Anderson (Adobe Firefly)

Printed in the United States of America

McFarland & Company, Inc., Publishers
Box 611, Jefferson, North Carolina 28640
www.mcfarlandpub.com

Table of Contents

Acknowledgments vii
Preface 1
Introduction 3

1. The Business of the Game 7
2. Notable Exits 39
3. Fresh Faces at the Helm 59
4. Teams in Transition, Mostly for the Better 85
5. Teams in Transition, for the Worse 106
6. The Trading Post 126
7. All-Stars and Hall-of-Famers 143
8. There Used to Be a Ballpark Here 168
9. Trends and Current Events 189

Chapter Notes 215
Bibliography 231
Index 237

To Jean Ardell

Acknowledgments

My journey in baseball writing has had the benefit not only of allowing me to contribute to the history of the national pastime but also of meeting colleagues and fellow historians with similar interests. This latest project is a perfect example of the ever-widening network of scholars that has inspired me and influenced my work.

My sincerest thanks to Andy McCue, Bill Ryczek, Lee Kluck, Dave Bohmer, Willie Steele, Leslie Heaphy, Steve Gietschier, and Charles DeMotte—authors and scholars all—for collectively reviewing the narrative and providing important commentary that hopefully smoothed out the rough spots. It has been an honor and a pleasure to have connected with each of them through the Cooperstown Symposium on Baseball and American Culture, the NINE Spring Training Conference, and the annual convention of the Society for American Baseball Research (SABR).

Of course, these literary journeys can't begin without the gathering of resource material, and there is no finer starting place than the A. Bartlett Giamatti Research Center at the National Baseball Hall of Fame in Cooperstown, New York. Research manager Cassidy Lent is always courteously quick to provide assistance and is further aided by Rachel Wells and Helen Stiles. Archivists Claudette Scrafford, on the manuscript side of the house, and John Horne, with photographs, round out the services necessary to tie the entire package together. As has been the case with my projects in the past, I greatly appreciate their attention to my requests.

I give a tip of the ballcap to Kevin Johnson and Ron Selter of the SABR Ballpark Committee, as well as John Dahle for his comments on his days in Boston during the mid-1960s.

Instrumental to this mix of personalities is the inclusion of several of "the usual suspects" who make conference and symposium attendance a joy, especially at the important end-of-day debriefing sessions that are held at a preferred location such as the Cooperstown Distillery or the Doubleday Cafe just down Main Street. Bob Cullen, Jim Gates, the Hall of Fame's librarian emeritus, and Tim Wiles, the Hall's past research director, are no strangers to such gatherings. What's not to like about discussing baseball business over a beverage?

But a select handful of people deserve special recognition in getting this particular book off the ground. David Krell, for whom I had the pleasure of contributing essays to a pair of his recent projects, is an endless source of encouragement and stick-to-it-iveness, and the aforementioned Bill Ryczek connected me with editor Gary Mitchem at McFarland, where my proposal quickly gained favor in his sight. There would not have been a springboard for this book, let alone a finish line, without their efforts.

Lastly, none of my work, whether in baseball writing or other endeavors that keep me gainfully occupied, would be possible without the support of a loving spouse. Thanks and love to you, Donna, always.

Preface

My journey as a baseball writer began in 1989 when I started work on an article for the Society for American Baseball Research's annual *Baseball Research Journal*. It was a very proud occasion for me when "Twenty Years of Playoffs and the Home-Field Advantage" was accepted and published in Volume 18 (1990) of the *BRJ*, although by modern-day standards and the profusion of analytics, that piece might impress as being a bit quotidian. Nevertheless, it was my first contribution to the scholarship of the national pastime, and since that breakthrough I've written other essays and book reviews for SABR and *NINE: A Journal of Baseball History and Culture*. While strictly an avocation, this venture has also resulted in my authoring six books, the latest of which you are now reading.

The first of those volumes, *The American League in Transition, 1965– 1975: How Competition Thrived When the Yankees Didn't*, was published in 2012, and this work set me on a course to probe deeper into the timeframe in that book's subtitle. Subsequent works built on the experience of the first, not least of which was *The New Boys of Summer: Baseball's Radical Transformation in the Late Sixties*, which has a narrow focus on the seasons of 1968 and 1969. This newest book, *Baseball at the Dawn of the Seventies*, is a companion volume to *New Boys*, although there were some challenges in writing it besides those of the usual enterprise of authorship.

Having covered a lot of ground in previous books put me at risk of repeating myself as I sought to create a narrative with the limited timeframe of 1970 and 1971. I wanted to keep this latest effort as fresh as possible while at the same time avoiding the pitfalls of rewriting what I had done in earlier works. It is my sincere hope that I have succeeded in doing so. May I also assure you, the reader, that artificial intelligence had no part in the creation of this book. Although AI continues to play a burgeoning role in the twenty-first century world, I'm a Luddite who has not gone down that path.

Finally, I dedicate this book to Jean Ardell, who passed away in the autumn of 2022. An enthusiastic fan of the Los Angeles Angels, as am I,

Jean became an instant friend upon my meeting her and her husband Dan at the first Cooperstown Symposium on Baseball and American Culture that I attended back in 2009. Early in 2022, she edited a book I wrote about my high school baseball team (for which I did not play), and *Pride of the Greyhounds: Ray Legenza and 64 Straight Wins by Connecticut's Best High School Baseball Team* was a marvelous if localized success, thanks to her professional touch. The baseball community and I will always remember her fondly.

Introduction

Historians frequently note that the dividing line between decades does not necessarily follow a sharp and true mathematical protocol, the events, politics, and cultural phenomena of the earlier period easily blending into the next. Several years can pass before the once-prevailing forces of the prior era diminish and at last give way to a new identity that the succeeding decade can call its own. Put in perspective and with the benefit of hindsight, we can interpret that life in America, as it segued from the 1950s into the '60s, generally speaking, did change but with little dramatic shifting.

The specter of the Cold War, punctuated in a most suspenseful way by the Cuban Missile Crisis of 1962, was the continuation of an existential threat created when the Soviet Union was discovered to have developed its own nuclear capability shortly after the end of World War II. Despite the jolt to the senses brought about by the assassination of President John F. Kennedy in November 1963, the country was still experiencing the rhythms of a post-war economy that brought consumerism to many American homes while suffering the periodic effects of downturns and recessions that forced the adjustment of the nation's business landscape. The struggle for civil rights, always a flashpoint, continued its long, tedious arc that endures to the present day. In the world of culture, when The Beatles deplaned at New York's JFK International Airport in February 1964, popular music on this side of the pond took a turn in a new direction, and the expansive medium of television provided a visual narrative to all of these signal events.

Yet, the above points could easily have been identified with the 1950s. The situation in Cuba grew as an outcropping of the Soviets' launch of *Sputnik*; Kennedy's death followed a pattern of similar and recent political upheaval that claimed the lives of several other world leaders; the murder of Emmett Till, the Montgomery bus boycott, and school integration resulting from the decision of *Brown v. Board of Education* segued to the Freedom Rides, the 1964 Civil Rights Act, and the Voting Rights Act of

1965; and the Fab Four, although British-born, were the latest in the line of path-breaking entertainers like Elvis Presley and James Dean.

But in the wake of the Gulf of Tonkin Incident in August 1964, the subsequent bombing campaign launched by the United States against North Vietnam, and the landing of United States Marines at Da Nang in March 1965, the tide had turned through the shedding of an innocence not since recovered. The war in Vietnam, seriously impactful, became a touchstone of what marked the onset of the "real" 1960s even though American military advisors had been involved in Southeast Asia—broadly speaking—for several years. Once President Lyndon Johnson put boots on the ground, a new chapter in U.S. history unfolded, and so too was the demarcation of a fresh point in history not constrained by a conveniently numbered decade.

As antiwar protests grew in number and the counterculture evolved, defiance of authority gained currency and was on heated display during the 1968 Democratic National Convention in Chicago. The dethroning of LBJ, accomplished months before the Windy City gathering through his announcement he would not seek re-election, spoke volumes about the seismic shift caused by a conflict that was surreptitiously chronicled by the U.S. government. Johnson's successor, Richard Nixon, had campaigned on his purported ability to end the war and bring law and order to domestic streets, yet little relief was obtained. When the war persisted through 1969—the final toll of American casualties that year was surpassed only by the number of dead in 1968—the public at large had reason to wonder what had become of Nixon's peace plan.

The 1960s may have concluded in the numerical sense, but the transition into the 1970s, which some may think of as a post–Woodstock era, was marked by few soothing changes. Respite was nowhere in sight in the late winter and early spring of the first year of the new decade: NASA's climactic moment of landing a man on the moon in the summer of 1969 was countered by the accident and near-loss of the crew of *Apollo 13*; the revelation by the Nixon Administration to expand the war into neighboring Cambodia prompted massive protests across the country, notably on college campuses, which in turn led to the deaths of four students at Kent State University; as campuses exploded, the Hard-Hat Riot in New York City found blue-collar construction workers enforcing their vision of patriotism on the youth who demonstrated against the killings in Ohio; and even the break-up of The Beatles, as well as the untimely deaths of Jimi Hendrix and Janis Joplin in the late summer and early autumn, colored the world of popular culture with a sullen shade of blue. Indeed, the calendar pages indicated 1970, but the content and context of new happenings could easily have been mistaken as backdated by a few years.

Introduction

Among other notable occasions in 1970, Earth Day was celebrated for the first time, the Women's Strike for Equality staged a parade in Manhattan, *Monday Night Football* debuted—other television programs, *The Odd Couple* and *The Mary Tyler Moore Show*, also joined the airwaves with popular ratings—and a pair of films with starkly contrasting plots, *Love Story* and *M*A*S*H*, drew the attention of movie-goers. In the world of business, the Penn Central Transportation Company, created in January 1969 in an effort to rescue, through merger, the once mighty and proud New York Central System and Pennsylvania Railroad, distinguished itself ingloriously by declaring bankruptcy a mere 18 months after it came into existence.

Such roiling was thankfully attended by a steep decline in American war casualties. By 1971, the death toll would drop to its lowest level in six years after U.S. troops first arrived en masse, as the program of Vietnamization, which was intended to turn over the bulk of the war's responsibilities to the South Vietnamese government and military, began. Headlines during that second year of the 1970s contained calm and controversy in varying doses: The south tower of New York's World Trade Center was completed and joined its northerly companion as the two tallest buildings in the world; Walt Disney World opened in Orlando, Florida; Jim Morrison, the lead singer and spiritual guide of The Doors, joined Hendrix and Joplin through his own untimely passing; a riot at the Attica Correctional Facility claimed the lives of 33 inmates and 10 correction officers, most of whom perished at the hands of law enforcement teams that stormed the prison; the Pentagon Papers, the term used to describe a secret study commissioned by the Secretary of Defense to examine the militaristic and political aspects of the Vietnam War, were printed in *The New York Times*. And the 26th Amendment to the U.S. Constitution was ratified, thereby lowering the voting age from 21 to 18, a privilege for Baby Boomers now given the franchise.

Meantime, the affairs of Major League Baseball found the game at a crossroads between old and new in the earliest years of the 1970s. The tenure of the game's latest commissioner was barely beginning, and the business aspects of the national pastime were in flux as the players' union was gaining increased bargaining power. Club ownership grappled with financial matters as forces beyond baseball's reach were impacting its once uncontested status as the most popular sport in the country. Players, managers, and even entire teams were in transition in terms of the clubs they played for, the teams they managed, and where those clubs might be located, to say nothing of how successfully they performed on the diamond. At the same time that baseball was shedding some of its antiquity, such as older stadiums and flannel uniforms, the sport found that it was not immune to controversies or the turbulence of current events that were part of American society and the human condition.

In early January 1971, a new situation comedy, *All in the Family*, made its debut on CBS to critical acclaim and belly-laughs—in addition to raised eyebrows. Produced by Norman Lear and Bud Yorkin, the show cast Carroll O'Connor as Archie Bunker, an unvarnished, working-class bigot who, in most politically incorrect terms, skewered not only those closest to him—a particular target was his live-in son-in-law portrayed by Rob Reiner, usually referred to as "Meathead"—but went about his life expressing constant disdain for anything he perceived to be out of line with his conservative, chauvinistic world view. Each episode began with a duet performed by Bunker and his oft-clueless wife Edith, who, as a "dingbat" in Archie's eyes, was played by Jean Stapleton.

Seated at a piano in the living room of their modest Queens, New York, residence, the couple sings the show's opening theme, with Edith's screeching vocals reminiscent of fingernails scraping a chalkboard, while her crooning husband also gestures with his cigar. The lyrics reference a simpler time in America, when the prior generation pulled itself up by the bootstraps during the Great Depression and persevered during World War II, the memories of which are fond to both of them. "Those were the *days*," they harmonize, drawing out the final word of the coda while evincing no small degree of wistful longing.

Moving away from some of the past, baseball was adapting to its next phase of modernity. The earliest part of the new decade held its own significance as the national pastime readied to usher in, sometimes in fits and starts, the changes that became emblematic of a new age. The 1970s had begun.

1

The Business of the Game

The baseball world had reason to be optimistic at the dawn of the 1970s. Defending their title as World Series champions, the New York Mets had completed an unusual journey from the depths to the pinnacle of the Major Leagues, with no complaint from their euphoric fans. Several new stadiums were slated to debut as the age of modernity inexorably caught up with the Grand Old Game and allowed for the vacating of several decrepit legacy ballparks. Teams newly formed in the latest round of expansion delivered, albeit with varying degrees of success, big league action to three new markets and backfilled another recently abandoned. And having just celebrated its centennial as a professional sport, baseball appeared poised to move forward under the guidance of its latest commissioner, who, as a knowledgeable and enthusiastic fan, was a far cry from his predecessor.

However, the veneer of these glad tidings masked several crucial issues lurking not far below the surface: Labor disputes, image problems, and slippage of the game's hold on the American spectator drew notice in league offices and among the ranks of baseball club ownership. Several players created controversy through willful misconduct or by confronting the mores that guided—that is to say, dictated—how players were expected to act or otherwise conform to the policies of the sport's establishment. Each of them ended up confronting the commissioner and thus added to the growing list of issues he now faced.

The opening of the 1970s brought the latest episodes in the unceasing struggle between Major League Baseball's work force—the players and umpires—and the team magnates. The director of the Major League Baseball Players Association (MLBPA) was still in the early stages of gaining the confidence of his constituency. For the umpires' part, the attempt by two arbiters to organize their own union in 1968 resulted in their dismissal by the American League as well as subsequent legal action that the pair undertook before the National Labor Relations Board.

Disputes with the hired hands notwithstanding, the upper offices of baseball also contended with the ongoing bureaucratic side of running the enterprise, affairs of public relations meant to keep the best possible face on the national pastime, and maintenance of the status quo with regard to the reserve clause. This agenda was, at the very least, ambitious.

Major League Baseball was in a new phase of adjusting to the times in which the cost of doing business was increasing each year, and the encroachment of pro football on territory once thought to be the sole domain of the American and National Leagues was cause for alarm. The Leagues' combined two dozen franchises were not in danger of folding their tents, but their pre-eminence faced challenges from the gaining popularity of the National Football League, which itself was newly restructured as a 26-team entity in the wake of a merger with its former rival, the old American Football League.

Baseball moguls recognized that changes were necessary in order to freshen their game and bolster its image, all the while hoping that the traditional way of catering to its employees—that is, especially the players—would hold firm.

Having brokered a two-year collective bargaining agreement for the 1968 and 1969 seasons, MLBPA leader Marvin Miller had put in place another nascent building block that helped him earn in methodical fashion the trust of the players. As indicated in the tables below, there was a steady overall rise in total union membership (accounting for fluctuations among members who were classed as active, inactive, vested, non-vested, and retired) as well as payments for retirement, disability, life insurance, health care, and widows' benefits.[1]

These enrollment numbers and payment amounts seem trivial by twenty-first century standards, yet the figures were unquestionably on the rise, all to the betterment of players and increasingly of concern to team management. To provide another bit of financial perspective, for the fiscal year ending October 31, 1970, the commissioner's office noted distribution of World Series and league championship series receipts in the amount of over $3.6 million.[2]

Table 1.1 MLBPA Members

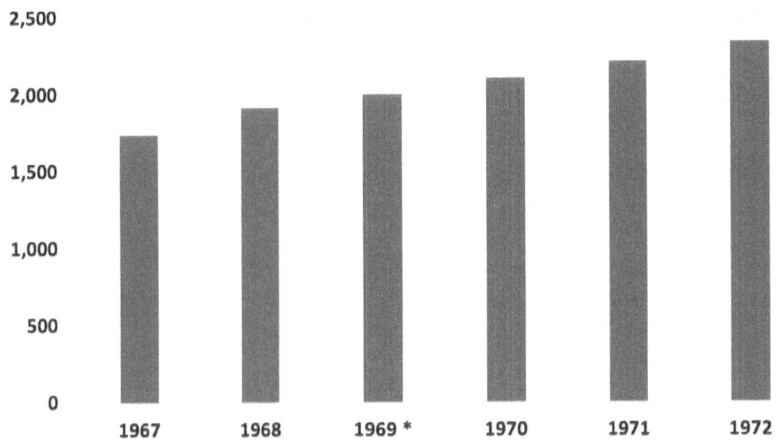

*Estimate
Source: Major League Baseball Players Association Benefit Plan, Annual Reports (1968, 1971, 1972)
Papers of Bowie K. Kuhn, National Baseball Hall of Fame Library

Table 1.2 MLBPA Payments

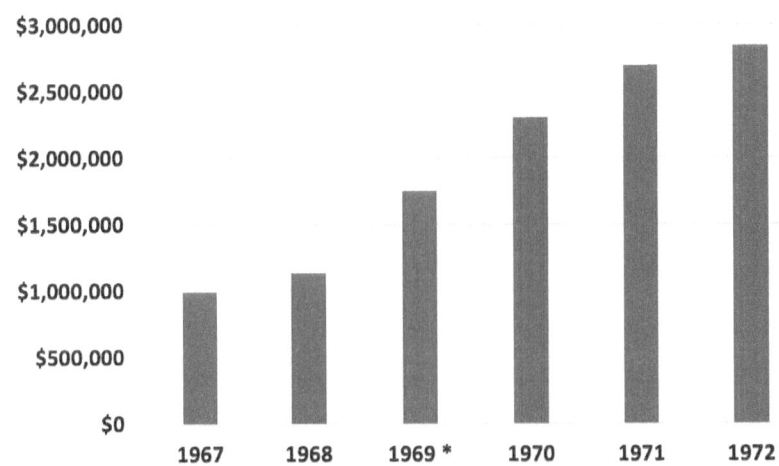

*Estimate
Source: Major League Baseball Players Association Benefit Plan, Annual Reports (1968, 1971, 1972)
Papers of Bowie K. Kuhn, National Baseball Hall of Fame Library

Table 1.3 Receipts
1970 World Series & League Championship Series
Receipts and Distribution

World Series Participants

	Baltimore Orioles Players (36%)	$617,150
	Cincinnati Reds Players (27%)	462,862

Championship Series Losers (25%)

	Minnesota Twins Players	214,288
	Pittsburgh Pirates Players	214,288

Second-Place Team in Each Division (9½%)

	New York Yankees Players	40,715
	Oakland Athletics Players	40,715
	Chicago Cubs Players	40,715
	Los Angeles Dodgers Players	40,715

Third-Place Team in Each Division (2½%)

	Boston Red Sox Players	10,715
	California Angels Players	10,715
	New York Mets Players	10,714
	San Francisco Giants Players	10,714

Clubs' Share

	Baltimore Orioles	363,887
	Cincinnati Reds	396,712
	Minnesota Twins	86,199
	Pittsburgh Pirates	119,025

Leagues' Share

	National League Office	277,687
	American League Office	277,686

Commissioner's Office   389,890

TOTAL $3,625,392

Source: Office of the Budget of the Commissioner
Papers of Bowie K. Kuhn, National Baseball Hall of Fame Library

This revenue total, also humorously small in the modern day, gave a handsome payout to Commissioner Bowie Kuhn's office but even the third-place finishers in each of the four divisions were able to parcel out a bit of pocket change to the players once individual shares were determined. For the record, the commissioner's assets and liabilities were in trim, balancing out at $1.2 million each.[3]

By 1970, while Curt Flood's resistance against the reserve clause took form and garnered much attention on baseball's labor front, Miller succeeded in scoring another victory for the players' union. As the 1969 basic agreement was extended beyond its expiration date in order for the players and owners to at least prevent a cessation of business as the new season commenced, finally on May 25 an accord was reached. The new deal, which would last through the 1972 season, made adjustments in the payout for playoff and World Series money, the former a result of the newly introduced league championship series stemming from the split of the AL and NL into East and West divisions.

Besides adjustments in expenses for relocation and those incurred during spring training, hotel and meal money, severance compensation for players who were released, minimum salary as well as maximum pay cuts—20 percent for one year, but no more than a total of 30 percent over two consecutive seasons—players were now officially allowed to be represented by an agent or other person of their choosing during contract negotiations with the club. However, the linchpin secured by Miller was the creation of a three-person panel that would settle disputes between the player and his team, provided that the point of contention did not involve "the integrity of the game," whereby the commissioner still maintained final authority.[4]

However, player grievances would now bypass the channel solely

Marvin Miller's diligent work on behalf of the Major League Baseball Players Association made it the most powerful union in professional sports.

occupied by Kuhn, whose role was functionally replaced by a representative of management. The other members of the panel would be one to represent the interest of the player and the third to act as an impartial jurist. The true significance of this grievance process would become clear several years hence when the basic agreement of 1973 allowed for salary arbitration. In the pact of 1970, however, Miller had shrewdly taken an incremental step in the quest for better pay and benefits for the players.

While the MLBPA and the owners wrestled, another imbroglio over the umpires emerged in the wake of the dismissals of American League arbiters Al Salerno and Bill Valentine, who were conducting unionization efforts in 1968. Umpires in the National League had been organized since 1963 when they reached an accord with then league president Warren Giles, who was receptive to "an effort to bring about greater uniformity and cooperation among the umpires and the league office."[5] This spirit of relative amity enabled the umpires to receive better pay and benefits, but their partners in the AL, who performed the same services, had no comparable union and drew less compensation. As Salerno and Valentine strove to bring fellow AL arbiters into the union fold, they were fired in mid-September 1968, with AL president Joe Cronin, who was averse to such an amalgamation, defending the dismissals on the grounds that the pair were incompetent performers while at once fatuously claiming to know nothing about their union activities.

Senior circuit umpires did allow their American League counterparts to join them—a mere two weeks after the firings by Cronin—in forming the Major League Umpires Association in early 1969. The new union opened a complaint with the National Labor Relations Board (NLRB) and, leaving no stone unturned, Salerno and Valentine, aggrieved at not having been reinstated, filed suit against the AL, Major League Baseball, Cronin, and Bowie Kuhn. By mid-1970, the outcast umpires had lost in the courts as they awaited a ruling by the Board, and there too they lost as the trial examiner of the NLRB recommended in November that the complaint be dismissed because not enough evidence had been submitted to support the claim that Cronin and AL umpire supervisor Cal Hubbard were aware of Salerno and Valentine's unionizing activities and had fired them on that basis rather than "incompetence."[6]

Valentine expressed a willingness to settle in a deal that would permit him to be reinstated—dropping the complaint as well as serving a probationary stint in the minor leagues to demonstrate his umpiring competence were the stipulations—but Salerno desired to continue litigation in the hope of receiving a significant financial payout. Whereas Valentine was open to the $20,000 offered by Major League Baseball, Salerno's pursuit of $100,000 forced the issue to move forward: Since their cases were being handled in tandem, they could not go separate ways.[7] Having exhausted their attempts at redress, including an ultimate appeal to the United States Supreme Court, which declined to get involved, and not willing to jointly comply with the terms offered for reinstatement, they permanently became former Major League umpires.

The Salerno–Valentine affair was not the only umpire-related controversy of 1970. Although arbiters earned regular-season increases in salary, along with better pension benefits and insurance coverage, the 12 umpires assigned to the pair of league championship series went on strike October 3. At issue was pay for arbiters working postseason contests, and this action just as the postseason was about to commence did not sit well with Kuhn, National League president Chub Feeney, nor the AL's Cronin. Several umpires indicated that negotiations had been ongoing since the All-Star break but produced no results, and a vote by the umpires was 37–12 in favor of a strike come playoff time.[8]

The league offices thought that they held the upper hand over an umpires' union that numbered but 52 members, and when the regular arbiters made good on their threat to strike, the opening games in Pittsburgh and Minnesota were played using a quartet of minor league umpires instead of the full complement of six Major League arbiters. But prior to the second game, the unionized umpires were now joined by "staunch allies in the Teamsters and Building Services unions, whose members staff Pittsburgh's Three Rivers Stadium." Suddenly the umpires had the support, both unexpected and sympathetic, that they needed to leverage a favorable deal as the stadium became inoperable because "[t]he local unions respected the picket lines the umps had thrown up around the stadium."[9]

When a hasty "retroactive agreement" was reached, the second games were played with the full, regular crews in place.[10] The umpires had forced a temporary increase for the current championship series assignments to $3,000 per man and $7,000 for the World Series, up from $2,500 and $6,500 respectively. While this stop-gap measure solved the immediate problem and allowed the league pennant contests to proceed with the normal arbiters, NL president Feeney explained that upon reaching a firmer accord, the umpires would retroactively receive any difference in pay. (Just days later, the final negotiations yielded the following: pay for league championship series topped out at $3,000, but that for the World Series went to $7,500 in 1971, then to $8,000 for the next two years.[11])

The one-day walkout, radical in its day and limited to a very small group of participants, seems quotidian compared to other strikes, notably by the players, that would take place over the next quarter century at the cost of many regular-season games and postseason contests that were cancelled. But as baseball's revenue stream continued to grow with succeeding television and radio contracts, it became obvious that there was more money to be shared by all parties. While the power of the umpires' union would never approach that of the MLBPA, the arbiters were entitled to reap what they could for the services they provided.

Spring training of 1970 was about to begin, and there was wonderment and speculation as to the chances of the miraculous New York Mets being able to repeat as World Series champions. Yet as players and coaches packed up to head to camps in Florida and Arizona, and long before Pete Rose would meet his gambling doom, Kuhn was alerted by the front office of the Detroit Tigers that their ace and co-winner of the 1969 Cy Young Award, Denny McLain, was "developing financial problems and getting behind on paying his bills."[12]

The sordid tale cast an especially unwelcome light on McLain when a cover story in *Sports Illustrated* drew a straight line from the hurler to the underworld connections of a bookmaking operation. Although Kuhn admitted that he initially was not completely sold on all aspects of the exposé, especially since McLain had confessed to the commissioner that his involvement "had not touched baseball," closer scrutiny by baseball's security director would very soon reveal damning evidence.[13]

Brushing aside the controversy at least for the time being, the commissioner penned a love letter to the game in anticipation of an exciting, new season. Effusive in optimism, he predicted, "our four new clubs in Kansas City, *Milwaukee*, Montreal and San Diego will show in 1970 that they will soon be championship factors," and he foretold stardom for "a startling array of new talent" that consisted of a "Major League *mod squad* of.... Bill Buckner, of the Dodgers; Thurman Munson, of the Yankees; Larry Bowa, of the Phillies; Luis Alvarado, of the Red Sox; and John Mayberry, of the Astros."[14] No record exists indicating for whom these remarks were intended, yet by cleverly co-opting the name of a popular television program—*The Mod Squad* was completing its second season on the ABC network—this sanguine paean reached out not only to a younger audience but also took delight in baseball's leaving the previous decade behind while anticipating a shifting balance among "a whirlpool of 24-club competition."

Yet, to address McLain directly and stifle the damage to baseball's image, a new Security Department was created under the auspices of the commissioner. At a joint meeting of the Major Leagues in mid–May,

The Commissioner stated that he was much concerned about the large sums of money which are being wagered on sports events, including baseball, throughout the country and asked the clubs to be alert to any association of their personnel with gamblers or any involvement of the personnel with gambling or betting, whether on baseball or other activities. He stressed that any such association or involvement must be immediately reported to the Commissioner's office, either to [security director Henry] Fitzgibbon or [administrative secretary Charles] Segar. He said that he also expected the clubs to report to the Commissioner's office any known investigation of their personnel by enforcement authorities, regardless of whether such authorities might have requested the club to keep the matter in confidence. The Commissioner advised them that Messrs. Fitzgibbon and [assistant security director Frank] Gallant will be visiting each club and the security officers of each club, as well as the local police department and other law enforcement agencies in the city.[15]

The message was unequivocal: It was imperative that all teams communicate with the commissioner's office regarding possible offenses, even to the point of breaching the confidence of local law enforcement. This approach, spelled out at the meeting in the presence of legal counsel for both leagues and Kuhn's own office, indicated the degree to which the commissioner wanted to gain control over unsavory episodes that had even the faintest tinge related to gambling. Also that same month, as the nationwide drug problem continued to hold sway, the commissioner implored all teams to actively promote "Drug Abuse Prevention Week" in conjunction with the effort sponsored by the Nixon White House. Public service messages, recorded by active players for airing on television and radio, were recommended as important contributions to discourage those tempted by the vice of drugs.

Part of the commissioner's reorganization efforts included amendments to the constitution of both leagues with regard to the duties of their circuits' presidents. During Kuhn's tenure, one of his favorite catchphrases became "in the best interests of baseball," and by the summer of 1970 when *Ball Four* author and former American League pitcher Jim Bouton along with current (but suspended) AL hurler Denny McLain were making news for reasons seen by the national pastime's hierarchy as unflattering or contrary to a sound public perception of the game, the commissioner determined that some moral belt-tightening was in order.

For a president of the American or National League already vested with "the power to impose fines and penalties ... upon any manager, coach, scout, trainer, player or other employee who, in his opinion, has been guilty of conduct which is not in the best interest of baseball," the passage related to "guilty of conduct" was expanded to qualify conduct "in public ... gross misbehavior, including intoxication, fighting, quarreling, indecency or other scandalous conduct, *whether on or off the playing field*, when such conduct is, in the President's opinion, calculated to bring disrepute upon the League or the game of professional baseball."[16] The emphasized text attempted to cover situations in which those who make a living in the world of baseball also make a poor choice to become involved in, say, gambling, publishing compromising narratives, or otherwise engaging in some other untoward action.

Awareness of baseball's image and any forces that might negatively affect the revenue stream to the sport's coffers held high priority in the minds of Major League executives. At the conclusion of the league championship series in early October 1970, which was only the second time these playoffs had been held, the drop in LCS attendance compared to the previous year was of concern to the Major League Executive Council.

To be fair, it must be noted that in the first two years during which the initial series were held, those in the American League were contested between the same pair of small-market teams in both seasons, and only one of the four National League playoff participants was from a large market. However, when the data is reviewed from the perspective of the percent of stadium capacity filled, *i.e.*, the number of seats for which tickets were sold, the decrease in the American League was sharper than that in the National League.

With the Baltimore juggernaut in full stride, perhaps there was less reason for fans to get excited about a rematch with the Orioles' opponent of the prior season. The NLCS of 1969 was certain to be a hit because of the phenomenal run by the Mets, yet the following year, the series between Pittsburgh and Cincinnati, already 13 games better than the Pirates at the close of the regular season, was simply less attractive perhaps because the Reds took eight of 12 regular-season games from the Bucs. (Although the Reds swept the NLCS in three games, no contest was a runaway, the scores being 3–0, 3–1, and 3–2.)

In an age before marquee games were staged in prime time, the desire of the Council to ward off more deficits could be achieved by lowering prices to stimulate ticket sales or "avoid[ing] home territory telecasts of the games, including, perhaps, telecasts of League Championship games being played in other cities." But a fresh idea that became an industry standard in the not-too-distant future was also proposed: "Playing the games at night."[17]

Table 1.4 LCS Attendance
League Championship Attendance, 1969 and 1970

American League—1969

	Attendance	Stadium Capacity	% of Capacity
Game 1 at Baltimore	39,324	52,137	75%
Game 2 at Baltimore	41,704	52,137	80%
Game 3 at Minnesota	32,735	45,921	71%
Total	113,763		

American League—1970

	Attendance	Stadium Capacity	% of Capacity
Game 1 at Minnesota	26,847	45,921	58%
Game 2 at Minnesota	27,490	45,921	60%
Game 3 at Baltimore	27,608	52,137	53%
Total	81,945		
Decrease	31,818		

National League—1969

	Attendance	Stadium Capacity	% of Capacity
Game 1 at Atlanta	50,122	51,383	98%
Game 2 at Atlanta	50,270	51,383	98%
Game 3 at New York	54,195	55,300	98%
Total	154,587		

National League—1970

	Attendance	Stadium Capacity	% of Capacity
Game 1 at Pittsburgh	33,088	50,235	66%
Game 2 at Pittsburgh	39,317	50,235	78%
Game 3 at Cincinnati	40,538	51,726	78%
Total	112,943		
Decrease	41,644		

Sources: Sporting News Official Guide—1971; baseball-reference.com

As was the case with all playoff action to this point in time, the contests were held during the afternoon, thereby depriving fans whose daytime occupations prevented them from going to the ballpark. Not only were daytime games rooted in tradition, but the major television networks were reluctant to upset their prime-time schedules as fall programming was underway.

The movement of the starting time to the early evening finally took place in 1971, and credit can be given to a pair of disparate personalities: commissioner Bowie Kuhn and Oakland Athletics owner Charlie Finley. The oft-times irksome Finley "had been advocating for night World Series games as far back as the early 1960s," early in his tenure as a club magnate. "We play night baseball all season and then don't even give the loyal fans of our country one night game during the Series," he argued.[18] For his part, Kuhn defended a change in broadcasting policy by pointing out the advantage of a larger television viewing audience that would give the games better exposure.

When Kuhn's office brokered a deal with the World Series telecaster, NBC, the experimental evening airing was to have been the second game, set for Sunday October 10 between the visiting Pittsburgh Pirates and the Baltimore Orioles. But when rain forced postponement of the contest to the next day at 7:00 p.m., the network was reluctant to give up timeslots for its *NBC Nightly News*, which featured David Brinkley, John Chancellor, and Frank McGee as anchors; the popular comedy show *Rowan & Martin's Laugh-In*, which aired at 8:00; and, beginning at 9:00, the *NBC Monday Movie*, also known as *Monday Night at the Movies*. "If baseball could move these giants," mused media columnist Jack Craig, "it must still have plenty of punch."[19]

In the event, however, the network held firm: Game 2 proceeded in the usual daytime manner, and with the Series shifting to Pittsburgh for the next three meetings, the fourth contest, slated for Wednesday October 13, was chosen to be the first played under the lights. Despite the delay, the results were revealing to all parties because before the month of October was concluded, an editorial in *The Sporting News* could find no fault with an occasion that seemingly everyone enjoyed. "Baseball's brass had reason to be pleased with the nighttime World Series experiment from an artistic viewpoint. The ratings for the prime-time TV showing also should make for good reading. Millions of fans whose jobs had prevented them from seeing midweek Series day games must have savored the October 13 contest."[20]

The lauding in the press was fully warranted: "The official Nielsen ratings ... show 21,610,000 homes were tuned in for the Orioles–Pirates game at Pittsburgh, the highest ever for a prime time sports event. An idea of the magnitude can be gained by noting that the Monday night NFL games reach around 12,000,000 homes."[21] At the joint meeting of the American and National Leagues held in December 1971, officials decided against immediate adjustments to when the best-of-five League Championship Series would begin, but "[i]t was agreed ... that the two League Presidents and the Commissioner should study the subject on a continuing basis in the expectation that schedule changes might become desirable if and when a larger number of post-season games were scheduled at night."[22]

Wasting little time, baseball took full advantage of this nocturnal epiphany and acted to schedule World Series Games 3, 4, and 5—these were all to be played Tuesday through Thursday—in the evening during prime time beginning in 1972. This measure served as a counterpunch of sorts to the National Football League's emergence as the pacesetter for television viewership—and revenue earnings—when the NFL's newest venture, *Monday Night Football* on ABC, debuted in prime time on September 21, 1970, and quickly gained a foothold with the American sporting public that endures to the present day.

Capitalizing on the national pastime's glamour events was one matter, but less profitable were the more mundane aspects of the enterprise. Baseball's partnership with NBC was showing signs of stress due to financial losses of nearly $3 million incurred by its Saturday afternoon *Game of the Week* broadcasts in the 1970 season and suffered another $2.6 million shortfall when the Baltimore–Cincinnati World Series lasted only five games.[23] (One year later, the network exacted a small measure of revenge when it withheld $288,000 from its last *Game of the Week* payment. NBC had pre-empted the baseball broadcast of Saturday July 30 to show the "moon-walk" by *Apollo 15* astronauts as "an event of outstanding importance" that allowed the network to avoid paying for a game that it contractually reserved a right to *not* broadcast.[24])

Shortly after Brooks Robinson and the Baltimore Orioles dispatched the Cincinnati Reds in the World Series and the labor dispute with the umpires was put to rest, a proposal was made by Bowie Kuhn to merge the umpiring staffs of the two leagues into a single entity. That new group was to be overseen by a supervisor who would be in charge of most day-to-day umpiring matters such as the selection of umpires and creation of crews, determining game coverage, and negotiating the contracts of individual arbiters. This was a part of the commissioner's overall goal to streamline the game and its highest offices, an effort that would take time and had been born of the recommendations by a study conducted by the Wharton School of Business and presented to the club owners in early January 1970.[25]

The Wharton plan would have given Kuhn much broader power than the commissioner already enjoyed. As envisioned, the new organization chart showed the commissioner occupying a heliocentric place in the Major League universe, with all other councils, officers, and executives reporting to him; even the icon for "Commissioner" was round, as if to replicate the shape of the sun, while all others were denoted by rectangles. By Kuhn's own admission, the presentation drew a stunned reaction from the owners, not least that by Pittsburgh magnate John Galbreath, who interpreted the new scheme as stripping ownership of authority over their teams. "If this gets adopted, it would eliminate control by the owner over his own franchise. I might as well sell the club," complained the Pirate mogul to Kuhn.[26]

Only incrementally over the ensuing years were various portions of the Wharton report implemented, such as increasing the number of members on the Executive Council from five to 11.[27] The practicality of having the offices of the two league presidents relocated to New York meant having to uproot Joe Cronin and his AL staff in Boston, plus Chub Feeney's NL group in San Francisco. Not until the middle of the decade would the commissioner's office, already headquartered in Midtown Manhattan, be joined by both leagues' headquarters only a few blocks away from each other. Along with the Player Relations Committee and Major League Baseball's Promotion Corporation, all parties were finally "under one roof" by 1983.[28]

Along with money matters, public relations held a prominent place in management's mind, and in the run-up to the 1970 season, executives were "encouraged to permit autographing by their players for *youngsters* interested in such autographs." The topic received scant attention in American League front offices, but those in the National League "felt that an area in the ball park should be set aside where players could be regularly assigned on a daily basis where the *youngsters* could obtain the autographs."[29]

Not all teams were transitioning from the cramped quarters of older stadiums that were handicapped by a lack of broad concourses or other open public spaces—think Fenway Park or Wrigley Field—that would come to define newer ballparks and provide for a more comfortable experience for game attendees. Having a player stationed in a common area had the advantage of allowing anyone to potentially obtain his signature rather than limiting this opportunity only to those fans holding tickets to field-level seats, especially those near the dugouts.

Even during the pre-game period, ushers could chase away those not possessing up-close ducats, so the idea of more egalitarian access away from the field had its merits. Fans with seats close to the field at National League stadiums were in luck because NL president Chub Feeney announced in late 1970 that "all players, managers and coaches on the field in uniform shall be permitted to briefly converse with spectators and sign autographs up to the scheduled end of batting practice," while the AL had already adopted a similar arrangement to officially sanction interaction between fans and uniformed personnel on the field.[30]

Also, in an era before the financial value of an autograph gained overriding consideration—to say nothing of the fact that the signatures were still fairly legible—the obvious appeal to fans in their teens or younger was a nod to cultivating a connection that youth would appreciate. Even a fleeting moment during an encounter between a bench player and a child could leave the latter star-struck, and it would be important for baseball to not let this chance slip away.

Another public relations effort to bring followers of baseball together with Major League figures came late in 1971 from a non–Major-League-affiliated, Ohio-based entity called the National Hot Stove Baseball League. The business purpose was to establish "hot stove clubs"—the name drew inspiration from "the old timers set around a pot belly stove talking baseball"—that would hold meetings at almost any time of the year "with planned programs, discussions, question and answer periods, clinics and guest speakers from Major League ball clubs."[31] The Hot Stove officials also proposed to act as a clearing house of sorts for all of its subsidiary chapters who wanted to engage a player or other team official for a meeting.

Although the organization's mission broadly had good intentions, its attempt to partner with Kuhn's office fell flat because Major League Baseball "[has] no right to tell a private organization what it can or cannot do," nor did baseball have a national bureau that could accommodate requests for speakers.[32] James Gallagher, an aide to Kuhn, investigated Hot Stove and found it to be a very parochial operation in northern Ohio that "make[s] grandiose claims" and "[has] been asking [Major League Baseball] for money for several years." It would remain for the Hot Stove League, or any fan club for that matter, to contact an individual team to satisfy its need for a player-speaker.

A few months before the Hot Stove inquiry and just weeks before his departure from the Baltimore Orioles, Harry Dalton offered the suggestion of creating a "National High School Baseball Tournament" that would be modeled after the American Legion World Series. The Orioles vice president recognized the logistical difficulty of "varying scholastic schedules throughout the country" and opined, "I have long felt that professional baseball misses the boat greatly in selling the attractiveness of a baseball career to high school students. There is little glamour in high school baseball. One way to counteract this would be to have a regional high school baseball tournament...."³³

Whether Dalton was aware or not, a scholastic team from Naugatuck, Connecticut, had completed its most recent season with its 44th consecutive victory and generated no small amount of interest in the Nutmeg State. Ultimately, in 1972 the Greyhounds of Naugatuck High School would fall one game short of tying the then-known record of 65 straight wins set by Waxahachie, Texas, but capitalizing on any spurt of enthusiasm for baseball, especially involving younger participants, would always be viewed in a favorable light.

One week after New Year's Day 1971, the baseball commissioner's secretary/treasurer, Sandy Hadden, sent a memo to Bowie Kuhn outlining his views of what made the national pastime so attractive and set it apart from other athletic endeavors. Dripping in sentimentality, the missive could have served as a beginning point for the comedian George Carlin's famous comparison of baseball versus football.

> Baseball is a complex game which appeals to many different levels of consciousness....
> Baseball is played outdoors, in good weather and in modern, comfortable, well-located stadiums. The game is bright, colorful, and cheerful.
> Baseball is a spectacle combining fast action, a great deal of strategy and tactics (much of which can be clearly seen and readily understood by the fan), the highest degree of athletic skill (e.g., Ted Williams' comment about the batter's art), and opportunity for reflection and relaxation (as opposed to the sometimes hypertense and even bloodthirsty emotions evoked by other sports).
> Increasingly, baseball's appeal is in tune with the temper of the times: the Country is evincing a desire to turn its back on many forms of aggression and violence.... The appeal is both to the intellectual and to the sports zealot.
> Baseball is good for American life. It is a model of integrity. It enthuses, provides recreation for, and serves as a role model for youth....³⁴

At once heartfelt and mawkish, the note nevertheless symbolizes the prevailing attitude that continued to reinforce baseball's stereotypical self-assessment, indicating that the status quo would always carry the day for the national pastime.

Others, however, were more forward-thinking—or radical, as some opinions might have it—in at least proposing ways to revamp the game in order to bring more participants to the field of play. A few weeks after the Hadden memo reached Kuhn's desk, another note offered commentary on the adoption of a wide-scale platooning system that appeared to mimic the two-way arrangement used in football.

But the negatives were found by Cal Gauss, the commissioner's assistant, to outstrip the benefits: "Detrimental in player development if only offensive or defensive skills are developed. Confusing to the fans. Would require fairly complex rules for substitution. Awkward for selecting All Stars. Would add to competitive imbalance by placing greater premium on depth. Likely to require expansion of 25 man roster limit."[35]

Allowing this type of laissez-faire lineup manipulation would have indeed radicalized baseball to the point of making it unrecognizable, but at least Kuhn's office was trying to stimulate some creative thinking that would shake the game from its complacency. And such thought processes would receive a bigger shock with the appearance of an article in a well-respected publication.

It was hardly an April Fool's joke, but the April 1, 1971, issue of *Forbes* magazine presented a cover story that portrayed baseball as "the beat-up national sport" and further criticized its ownership as being unwilling or unable to "pressure their baseball lieutenants to adapt the product to market."[36] *The Sporting News* took note of this unflattering critique as the new baseball season commenced and observed in an editorial that fans' increasing "demand for speed and violence" was leading many of them to turn their attention to football. Baseball could be rightly blamed for the sclerotic pace at which it enacted measures to lift itself from the lethargy it seemed mired in.

As the decades passed to reach the twenty-first century, the time of the average game grew from roughly two and one-half hours in the first two seasons of the 1970s to three hours and eleven minutes by 2021. Yet even in those comparatively quicker-paced contests of the 70s, at least one executive attending the Joint Meeting of the Major Leagues in the summer of 1970 made "[s]uggestions concerning the installation of a 20 second clock...."[37]

Perhaps embarrassed into deeper introspection by the *Forbes* critique, Kuhn charged Gauss with closely examining the "designated pinch hitter" being employed at various levels of the minor leagues, and as the calendar approached Memorial Day weekend, Gauss produced a detailed analysis of what the addition of a "DPH" would do for the Major League game. In his report, Kuhn's aide concluded that instituting a "DPH ... would increase the overall major league batting average at least 5–6 points a season ... would have a greater effect on Home Runs and RBI's (therefore runs scored) than on batting average," and he further speculated that "a DPH, undoubtedly one of the best non-starters, who hits 3–4 times a game is likely to produce more offensively than the regular pinch hitter who appears 'cold' once a game."[38]

Gauss was diligent in his research, having canvassed the five minor leagues using the early version of the designated hitter for their opinions in addition to reviewing the data he himself was gathering. At these lower levels, the position "was far more productive offensively than pitchers had been," and four out of five minor league presidents claimed that removal of the traditional weak spot in the batting order led to "increased drama and excitement" and sped up the game by as many as ten minutes.[39]

Transposing the minor league experience to the majors "would do much to demonstrate Baseball's responsiveness to 'need' for more excitement and speeding the pace of the game ... [and its] willingness to make significant changes where merited."[40] Gauss also recognized the advantages inherent in the DPH: Prolonged careers of good hitters suffering from physical limitations, quicker development of young hitters no longer consigned to sitting idle on the bench, and while finances were not mentioned specifically, teams could save money with a potential reduction in the size of the roster if clubs chose to carry at least one less pitcher.

Not turning a blind eye to the downsides of the DPH, Gauss believed that the new position only "would benefit those clubs with the stronger bench, especially the number 1 and 2 substitutes," presumably because those better players would see increased time at bat; the traditional strategy of pinch-hitting for the pitcher would be rendered obsolete; certain pitchers, presumably those who were capable hitters, would object to surrendering their offensive duties; and something he labeled the "Yastrzemski Theory" would tempt some pitchers to "more freely throw at hitters knowing that they would not be made vulnerable by having to bat themselves."[41]

The DPH affair followed baseball's slow, cautious course of taking time before being implemented, and even then only in stilted fashion. At the 1972 annual Winter Meetings in Honolulu, Hawaii, the Playing Rules Committee initially declined the American League's request to add the designated pinch hitter, this denial coming despite unanimity among the 12 AL clubs in their desire to do so. Permission was granted, however, for usage in the upcoming spring training games and for the three Triple-A leagues.

Only upon convening a special joint meeting of the American and National Leagues in January of 1973 was the junior circuit allowed to move forward. With the AL in favor and the NL strictly opposed, Kuhn served to break the tie and permit the DPH to become a reality, even if it was only for the Major League teams under the auspices of Joe Cronin.

The *For*bes-inspired wake-up call spurred Kuhn to ask teams in both leagues what they believed was good and bad about the game. Baseball was now on the defensive, and at a series of executive meetings in May 1971, Kuhn listened to the brainstorms of a host of club owners and officials to discern any improvements that could bolster the national pastime and its flagging image. In one of the early sessions, Oakland owner Charlie Finley, never a bashful man and already fully supportive of a DH, decried baseball's "continuously permitting defense to overcome offense," and proposed further enhancements such as waving a batter to first base on an intentional walk, use of a designated pinch runner, and allowance of free substitution, or "players in and out of the lineup."[42] (Note:—At this same gathering, Finley was kind to praise Kuhn before their relationship later curdled, stating, "This is my 11th year as an owner but this is the first time a Commissioner has gone around to the clubs to hear what they've got to say. It's gratifying to know that the Commissioner is interested.")

Contrary to some of Sandy Hadden's idyllic opinions, Finley from his youth said that he "looked forward to seeing some rhubarbs.... I think we need more nose-to-nose arguments" with umpires, though he added a confounding opinion on the topic of spitballs: "The spitter is okay, but no foreign substances should be used."[43] Just moments later, player personnel director Phil Seghi of the Cleveland Indians wondered why the bases were square "and home plate hexagon?" and for good measure, the irascible Finley plugged his orange-colored baseball as a way to help batters see pitches better.

In a session with the New York Yankees, president Michael Burke and general manager Lee MacPhail gave Kuhn a balanced account on some of the issues in question. Burke enjoyed the game's "leisurely pace" but believed "the present rule should be enforced" regarding the delivery of a pitch within twenty seconds, and he also favored letting the batter simply take first base on an intentional walk.[44] For his part, MacPhail confessed, "I like an occasional fight. Rhubarbs are good for the game," yet he preferred the status quo of the pitcher needing to deliver four pitches to intentionally walk the batter.[45] Burke may have given the most erudite opinion on the game's pastoral ambience: baseball, he said, "has become a Lord Fauntleroy game because we don't have flamboyant players. Life has taken on an air of violence everywhere. One of baseball's essentials is the non-violent aspect. I think the public is beginning to be saturated with violence. Baseball gives people a respite."[46]

When Kuhn met with personnel of the crosstown Mets front office, the team's business manager, Jim Thomson, stated, "We do a great deal of promoting, perhaps more than any other club. We cater a lot to the kids ... banner day, camera day, autograph day, etc. We have a special department that only handles kids mail. We purchase thousands of pictures that we have autographed for the kids."[47] Mets board chairman M. Donald Grant observed, "For the first time, baseball has some real competition.... Baseball is the most scientific game and it is much more difficult to understand—and play.... Right now football and basketball are riding high, [but] the people will realize that football and basketball are becoming freak sports. I think baseball has done a magnificent job to hang on despite adversities."[48]

The main adversity of the national pastime was professional football, which broke new ground as the NFL opened its 1970 season in its newly merged form. The NFL was divided into a pair of 13-team conferences split further into three divisions (the five-team East Division was accompanied by Central and West Divisions containing four teams apiece); this format created, by necessity, the need to introduce the concept of a wild-card entrant to ensure a minimum of four teams that would qualify for the postseason playoffs: three division titlists and the team with the best record among second-place finishers. Major League Baseball, itself having created two six-team divisions a year earlier, quickly entertained several proposals to emulate what Pete Rozelle had already accomplished with the National Football League.

Not to be outdone—but still in reactive mode—the baseball commissioner's office began 1971 by mulling over a reconfiguration of the existing 24 teams. Public relations director Joe Reichler informed Kuhn that Rozelle envisioned the NFL adding six teams by the end of the 1970s to bring his league to a total of 32, and Reichler "believe[d] the time will come when major league baseball will also have 32 teams."[49] At a time when the Washington Senators still called the nation's capital home, he speculated that Dallas–Fort Worth, Toronto, Buffalo, and New Orleans were possible candidates for expansion clubs along with the far-distant site of Honolulu: "It would be nice if we could beat football to that [Hawaiian] city, which has great potential." Reichler also threw in Puerto Rico, Mexico City, Miami, and Denver as places worthy of consideration.

Beyond the guesswork of venues for future expansion, Reichler took the current 12-team Major Leagues and re-aligned them within their extant circuits but with a firm nod to sensible geographic assignment.

Table 1.5 New Divisions Plan for Three Divisions in Each League (Proposed in 1971)

American League

Division A	Division B	Division C
Baltimore	Chicago	California
Boston	Cleveland	Kansas City
New York	Detroit	Minnesota
Washington	Milwaukee	Oakland

National League

Division A	Division B	Division C
Montreal	Atlanta	Houston
New York	Chicago	Los Angeles
Philadelphia	Cincinnati	San Diego
Pittsburgh	St. Louis	San Francisco

Source: Papers of Bowie K. Kuhn, National Baseball Hall of Fame Library

And with only some minor adjustments to scheduling, he proposed a slate of 158 games that would compare most favorably with the current 162-game setup: Teams would play 18 games against each of its three in-division rivals, 14 against all teams in one of the other divisions, and 12 games against all teams in the third division. Clubs would alternate the inter-division matchups each year, and there was no provision for inter-league play at this time.

The introduction of a lone wild-card entrant for the playoffs would be based on the second-place team with the best record, and the wild-card team would face a division winner—Reichler did not indicate whether it was the team with the best record—who would be given the option of playing the first game on the road and the last two at home, or vice versa, in the best two-of-three series. First-round winners would advance to the second round, best-of-five series to determine the league champions, who would in turn move on to the World Series and the traditional best-of-seven match.

Once more, if imitation is the sincerest form of flattery, proof could be found in the conclusion of Reichler's memo:

> The addition of a second place team may have the aspects of a "gimmick" to many but we can't escape the fact that this formula adopted by [pro] football has added tremendous interest to football's championship races and has been wonderfully received by the news media—both press and radio-TV—as well as the fans. Thanks to this formula, 13 of the 26 teams were in contention at the start of the final week of the football season.[50]

Falling back on the bromide of "great minds think alike," no less a figure than Los Angeles Dodgers chairman Walter O'Malley fired off a letter to NL president Chub Feeney—with copies to Kuhn and Joe Cronin—proposing the same league and division arrangements but with a variation in scheduling. Coming barely one month after Reichler's proposal, O'Malley's version had teams facing their divisional opponents 22 times—"going back to the old 8-club set-up," when a team's schedule totaled 154 games—and then played all the clubs in the other two divisions 12 times each.[51] This formulation came to the convenient total matching the current 162 games.

O'Malley liked the strengthening geographic rivalries within each division and the potential of reduced travel expenses, but the playoffs in his scheme would involve only the trio of division winners. "The play-offs for league championships would be conducted on a round-robin A-B-C basis in which two defeats eliminates a team until one stands either undefeated or beaten only once. A plays B, B plays C, C plays A, each on the home field of the first. Each will have played two games at the end of the first round of games; each will have enjoyed an off-day and each will have had a home game. If no team is eliminated at this point, the succession can resume."[52]

In theory, this appeared to be a fair plan, but O'Malley failed to account for the logistics of how this was to be easily accomplished given the necessity of travel by the three division winners among their respective cities. "The play-offs can begin on Saturday and conclude, at the latest, by Thursday and the World Series can then get under way on the succeeding Saturday," he claimed, yet had this plan been in effect for the upcoming season, the AL's three presumed division winners—Baltimore (East), Oakland (West), and Detroit (Central)—and those in the NL—Pittsburgh (East), San Francisco (West) and St. Louis (Central)—would have been bearing the burden of cross-country jaunts under less than optimal time constraints.[53]

Another missive dealing with three-club championships was sent to Kuhn and offered "a partial interleague best 2 of 3 set-up, followed by a three-club World Series" in which "one league would have two representatives, other league one representative."[54] The Fall Classic in this scenario could be staged as a baffling triple-elimination round-robin or an even more bewildering quadruple elimination structure. Meanwhile, Reichler pointed out an inherent flaw using a three-team round-robin, whereby "[u]nder this system, the only way to arrive at a true winner in this type of playoff is for one of the three clubs to either sweep every game from its rivals or win three out of four."[55]

In mid–April 1971, a plan for a three-way World Series that allowed for a maximum of four losses before a team was eliminated was directed to Kuhn, and it became clear that baseball's policy was being desperately driven by its fixation on the NFL three-division standard. In football's case, where playoffs consist of single elimination that excludes multiple-game series, there were no worries about how to accommodate contests mere days apart held at sites that could be separated by a great distance.

By that summer, it appeared, at least for the time being, that baseball's brain trust realized that fitting their three divisional playoff scheme into an NFL-style mold was not practical, and as is customary when intractable problems arise, the issue was tabled. "Members of the American League unanimously submit that a complete study of the championship series program should be undertaken; and that included in the study should be possible realignment of Major League Baseball and the possibility of inter-league play by the 1973 season."[56]

As 1971 drew to a close, one last bit of postulation surfaced, and it foreshadowed what eventually transpired in the AL. Harry Simmons, a jack-of-all-trades in the commissioner's office, drew up a three-division plan under the assumption that the junior circuit would be expanded to 14 teams, with an East division that included new entries in Toronto and Washington (the expansion Senators, born in 1961, were presumed to be in Texas at this point). Regular-season schedules were comprised of between 154 and 164 games depending on the split of inter-divisional and intra-divisional contests.

While Simmons was still beholden to a round-robin, three-way playoff, he did propose a new AL with a simple pair of seven-team divisions that followed the contemporaneous playoff format.[57] The ballclubs listed by Simmons in his theoretical divisions were not a perfect match, but upon expansion in the American League in 1977 and that league's 1994 realignment, he came as close to predicting the future as anyone with a learned opinion.

Table 1.6 AL Division Comparisons

Proposed 1977 AL Division Setup		Actual 1977 AL Division Setup	
AL East	AL West	AL East	AL West
Baltimore	California	Baltimore	California
Boston	Chicago	Boston	Chicago
Cleveland	Kansas City	Cleveland	Kansas City
Detroit	Milwaukee	Detroit	Minnesota
New York	Minnesota	Milwaukee	Oakland
Toronto	Oakland	New York	Seattle
Washington	Texas	Toronto	Texas

Proposed 1977 AL Division Setup			Actual 1994 AL Division Setup		
AL East	AL Central	AL West	AL East	AL Central	AL West
Baltimore	Chicago	California	Baltimore	Chicago	California
Boston	Cleveland	Kansas City	Boston	Cleveland	Oakland
New York	Detroit	Oakland	Detroit	Kansas City	Seattle
Toronto	Milwaukee	Texas	New York	Milwaukee	Texas
Washington	Minnesota		Toronto	Minnesota	

Sources:
Papers of Bowie K. Kuhn, National Baseball Hall of Fame Library; baseball-reference.com

Subsequent research was commissioned by the American and National Leagues to investigate other configurations of the 24 teams. "The conclusions reached from the study," according to a schedule consultant for Major League Baseball, "are that either three-league play with 150 games or four-league play with 154 is feasible. Either alternative would save roughly half a million dollars in travel costs over the present two-league arrangement."[58]

One last bit of futuristic dreaming attended the end of the year when Bowie Kuhn's office looked into the possibility of staging an international World Series but was confronted by a host of issues that thwarted hopes for such an event in the short term. Series of exhibition games had been played occasionally between the Major League World Series champions and teams in Japan at the conclusion of the Fall Classic, but the concept of clubs representing their nation to participate in a tournament to determine a true *world* champion went well beyond the scope of playing a relatively meaningless exhibition contest only for bragging rights if not a little national pride.

Joe Reichler's initial list of concerns—worries about long-distance travel, the "disparity in ability" between Major League players and their foreign competitors, and whether this new tourney would "[m]inimize importance and impact of our own World Series" were chief among them—was augmented by contributions from John Johnson, the commissioner's administrative officer.[59] Johnson questioned whether the American World Series winner would be the default choice to enter this new competition, how compensation of players and umpires would be handled, and, perhaps with an eye to this event's being held in a land less friendly to the United States than Japan—Cuba comes to mind, if that nation was even thought to be included—what were the views of the State Department in Washington, D.C.?

This proposed series followed the path set for many years by various international amateur tournaments and foreshadowed the World Baseball Classic that would be first held in 2013, far later than Reichler's predicted timeline of the late 1970s or early in the next decade. "When it comes, hopefully in eight or ten years," Reichler wrote, "it will be a milestone in baseball history, making our game a truly international sport and placing it head and shoulders above football and basketball."[60] His timing was inaccurate, but the spirit reflected in his words later put baseball in a firmer place on the international stage.

Shortly after the 1970 campaign got underway, the game's image was still chastely intact, yet there was some irony and poignant timing to comments made by the commissioner to the mid–May gathering of the Major League magnates. According to the meeting minutes, Kuhn "discussed the subject of public criticism of baseball and baseball personnel by others in baseball. In general, he stressed the necessity of avoiding public statements which adversely affect the best interests of baseball."[61] The commissioner likely may have been addressing the release of a book by Detroit Tiger catcher Bill Freehan, whose *Behind the Mask: An Inside Baseball Diary* was a close look at his team that included personal criticism of club management for letting pitcher Denny McLain seemingly establish his own rules of conduct.

But at nearly the same time, Kuhn implored all parties connected with the game to keep their interpersonal grievances to themselves, the reason being that *Look* magazine had published the first set of excerpts of Jim Bouton's *Ball Four* that set a new standard for revelatory sports literature and was quickly causing no small amount of angst in baseball's highest office.

Ball Four's burgeoning popularity following its June release delighted or offended readers depending on one's point of view regarding the sanctity of the clubhouse. Feeling the pain of others who took umbrage and failing to force Bouton to retract what the commissioner deemed unflattering passages, Kuhn requested his director of security, Henry Fitzgibbon, to create a list of talking points for him to address during his tour of training camps in the spring of 1971. Benign items such as the autograph policy, drug abuse program, availability of the latest film of World Series highlights, and "the Negro Hall of Fame Program" would be spoken to, but the top three items left no doubt as to the need to uphold the national pastime's image[62]:

1. Importance of Honesty & Integrity for All Connected with Baseball
2. Urge All to Promote the Game of Baseball
3. Be Alert to Speak Out & Defend Baseball Against Its Detractors

Further down the list were a reminder about the ills of associating with gamblers and criminals as well as a nebulous "Plea for Cooperation & Assistance," in which Kuhn was to "acknowledge there are some areas for disagreement but you are open to negotiation on all these and will act on what you perceive to be in the best interests of all of Baseball, owners, & the fans." No specific examples of supposed points of contention were offered, nor what exactly was to be negotiated.

This open-ended olive branch being waved at the players was accompanied by an invitation for them to feel free to contact him with "any suggestions or comments critical or otherwise concerning any matter they consider important to Baseball as a sport or to them as an individual player.... [and that] all such matters ... will be treated as furnished in confidence...." With a fair amount of resentment directed by some players at Bouton for his violation of the implicit sanctity of the clubhouse, Kuhn was obliquely leaving the door open as a way for potential informants to alert him to other episodes that could be a source of embarrassment.

At the onset of the 1970s, there were other matters on the business front that continued to hang over baseball's head like the sword of Damocles. Curt Flood's

Author of the controversial book *Ball Four*, Jim Bouton gained notoriety for calling out past Yankee teammates and, in the eyes of the baseball establishment, revealing a less flattering side of the national pastime.

challenge to the reserve clause rankled ownership and management because this crucial passage in every player's contract for nearly a century was seen as the element that ensured the clubs' control over their respective players. An open labor market in which a player could offer his services to the highest bidder, or at least to a team of his own choosing, would be, according to the management traditionalists, the ruination of baseball as everyone knew it. Arguments were advanced about the destruction of competitive balance, and the best way to thwart that was to continue to allow a club to determine which of its players it chose to reserve year after year, or until such time that it decided to trade or release them.

Flood's temerity to refuse his trade from the St. Louis Cardinals to the Philadelphia Phillies in late 1969 prompted his filing of a lawsuit against Major League Baseball in an attempt to win his freedom. In 1970, Flood's case wended its way through the court system, while the high offices of baseball maintained that the outfielder was his own worst enemy. "Plaintiff is not wholly excluded from baseball," argued Kuhn's legal team. "He has been offered a contract by the Philadelphia Club for the 1970 season at the same $90,000 salary he earned at St. Louis. It is *his* choice not to play baseball. He has a duty to mitigate his damages" rather than hold out his services to seek redress through the courts.[63] For his part, Flood and his attorneys continued to protest the player's "being sold to Philadelphia like so many pounds of beef, or worse" as "[h]is baseball life is daily trickling away."[64]

Sitting out the 1970 season, Flood was still the property of the Phillies and in early November—almost a year to the day of his trade from St. Louis—he was dealt to the Washington Senators, whose owner, Robert Short, was trying to bolster the sagging fortunes of his team by importing not only Flood but also another pariah, pitcher Denny McLain. A preliminary injunction in that year as well as two other filings in 1971 argued that the reserve clause violated the Sherman Antitrust Act and allowed baseball owners to act in concert to prevent the movement of players on the latter's terms.

Ultimately reaching its conclusion in the United States Supreme Court, unhappily so for the now former Solon outfielder, Flood's case was poorly argued before Warren Burger's bench by Arthur Goldberg, himself a one-time associate justice of the Supreme Court who served from late 1962 until the summer of 1965. Having known Goldberg through their work together with the Steelworkers Union in the late 1950s and early 1960s, Marvin Miller was confident of Goldberg's ability: "It would have been impossible to imagine anyone better suited to lead the fight against the reserve clause," wrote the MLPBA's director in his memoir.[65]

Goldberg, however, grew distracted in 1970 when he became enamored with seeking public office and ran as the Democratic candidate for governor of New York, facing off against—and losing to—the incumbent,

Nelson Rockefeller. By the time the nation's highest court agreed to hear Flood's suit in the spring of 1972, Goldberg "argued the case like a man preoccupied," and already feeling "betrayed" by Goldberg's political diversion, Miller rued not selecting another barrister to go before the Supreme Court when he learned of the woeful quality of Goldberg's oral argument.[66] Flood's biographer, Brad Snyder, likened Goldberg to the great Willie Mays, who was "stumbling around in the New York Mets outfield" in the final year of his otherwise stellar career, and the former justice found himself an object of "disgust" by the current panel of jurists.[67]

Whether it was his poor preparation or an assumption that he would be given a high amount of deference by the court that he once served, Goldberg and his client wound up on the losing end of a 5–3 verdict when the Supreme Court decided the case in June. It can only be left to speculation how the justices would have voted had Goldberg demonstrated the same talent that had won him over in the eyes of Marvin Miller.

If the team owners breathed a sigh of relief, they were far less comfortable with a second issue running concurrent with the Flood case. Baseball's exemption from federal antitrust legislation had become a time-honored mainstay that ownership held sacred if not took for granted. Surviving numerous legal challenges over the last half century since the Supreme Court's 1922 ruling in *Federal Baseball Club of Baltimore, Inc. v. National League of Professional Baseball Clubs, Inc.* that baseball did not engage in interstate commerce, baseball's status had been tested most recently in the fall of 1967 when American League approval of Charlie Finley's transfer of the Kansas City Athletics to Oakland created a firestorm of protest led by U.S. Senator Stuart Symington, whose home state of Missouri had now been fleeced of a Major League club.

The movement of the team that had relocated from Philadelphia only in 1955 stirred the politician's furor after the A's spent barely over a decade in the Midwest, this coming on the heels of the shifting of the Milwaukee Braves to Atlanta in 1966 after calling Wisconsin home for just 13 seasons. Symington's demand for an immediate replacement franchise was not completely irrational: the American League in 1960 announced an expansion campaign in which a new team would be located in Los Angeles and another to be placed in Washington to give the nation's capital baseball continuity since the original Senators had been moved to Minneapolis. Both new franchises had mere months to organize their teams for the 1961 season.

The danger of courting Congressional outrage by Calvin Griffith's vacating Washington in favor of the Twin Cities was quickly stifled when the second version of the Senators was seamlessly installed in 1961, yet this strategy came with a price. Had Griffith's club remained in the nation's capital and baseball installed an expansion franchise in Minnesota instead, fans of the original Senators would have witnessed the blossoming of the roster of players who would capture the American League pennant in 1965. In the event, the club that became the Twins did so to the delight of fans in the Upper Midwest while the re-created expansion Senators offered little inspiration to its Washington followers. As baseball historian Andy McCue observed, "The [AL] owners' go-along-to-get-along practices also ensured that fans in Congress would continue to see a bad team."[68]

But as pro football's increasing popularity brought new pressure to bear on baseball—NFL Films, founded in 1962, began delivering artistically developed highlight and feature reels that burnished the luster of action on the gridiron—the national pastime found itself not only wanting to expand to establish new markets, it also was in the curious position of having to backfill cities recently abandoned: Washington's instant renaissance in 1961 allay any hurt feelings, yet even that franchise was soon imperiled; the National League's creation of the New York Mets the following year was a salve for the loss of the Giants and the Dodgers; lastly, the sudden collapse of the Seattle Pilots and their subsequent move to Milwaukee in 1970 raised the hackles of politicians in the Pacific Northwest while at once calming the hurt feelings in Wisconsin over the move of the Braves in 1966.[69]

Thankfully, the birth of the Kansas City Royals under the aegis of Ewing Kauffman provided a welcome degree of stability when they began play in 1969, and the new NL entry in Montreal won over those who were skeptical of Major League success north of the border. Yet, all this business was being conducted while somehow avoiding being categorized as interstate commerce. Even the U.S. Supreme Court's ruling in late 1953 that upheld *Toolson v. New York Yankees* had two justices who recognized the reality of how the baseball enterprise was functioning when they wrote in dissent, "[I]t is a contradiction in terms to say that the defendants ... are *not* now engaged in interstate trade or commerce...."[70]

In the case of the Expos, the *international* commerce in which they were involved caused no small amount of angst among Major League executives because while they enjoyed a degree of latitude with the American system of government, the same could not be said about their relationship with politics as administered in Ottawa. "Should the Canadian government decide, after examining all of the arguments for and against the Reserve Clause in its present form as it applies to baseball, to either eliminate the Reserve Clause altogether, or modify it by making portions of it illegal in Canada," wrote team chairman Charles Bronfman and president John McHale, "the Montreal Expos would be faced with an intolerable situation."[71]

If the Canadian legislature were to strike down the reserve clause, the Expos executives contended, "any player who normally would have been reserved by the Montreal Expos, could leave the team if he could negotiate a higher salary with some other Major League team, or if, for other personal reasons, did not wish to play baseball in Montreal." Further, the franchise itself would be faced with a mutually exclusive predicament: the Expos were bound by terms of the National League Constitution of Rules and associated agreements with other parties related to Major League Baseball that were germane to their admittance to the league, but as an entity operating in Canada, the club was obligated to follow the laws of that country, "and the consequence of either of these actions would be that the Expos could not operate a franchise in Canada."

A ray of hope existed in the fact that teams were forbidden from tampering with players of another organization, and the baseball magnates expressed a willingness to negotiate with both the American and Canadian governments to institute "such modifications to the reserve system as are mutually satisfactory...."

The fear of an international dispute would soon become a moot point when the Seitz decision in the Messersmith–McNally case invalidated the reserve clause in late 1975, yet baseball's highest offices enumerated the primary reasons for justifying antitrust exemption: the need to maintain competitive balance; preservation of integrity and public confidence; high costs of player development; and benefits of economic stability.[72] The defense of competitive balance impresses as quite stilted given the game's recent history, especially that of the American League. While the NL could make a bit of an argument that competition existed among a cohort of pennant winners since World War II, the same could hardly be said of the AL.

Table 1.7 Pennant Winners
Pennants Won, 1941–1970

National League		American League	
Dodgers	11	Yankees	18
Cardinals	7	Orioles	3
Braves	3	Indians	2
Giants	3	Red Sox	2
Reds	2	Tigers	2
Cubs	1	Browns	1
Mets	1	Twins	1
Phillies	1	White Sox	1
Pirates	1		

Source: *baseball-reference.com*

One cannot fault the Yankees for their success, but winning the league championship 60 percent of the time over these decades far diminished the ability of its rivals to stake their own claim. At least it took two clubs in the National League, the Cardinals and Dodgers, to equal the same number of titles as the Bronx Bombers, thus offering a glimmer of hope for teams striving to legitimately contend.

"The record shows that, without the balance provided by the reserve system, the clubs with greater financial resources would attract the most outstanding players," claimed the owners, hoping that few would bother to look at the contradictory track record.[73] "Without the stability afforded by the reserve system, successful and balanced league play [would be] impossible to maintain," they continued, and, citing differences among revenue streams taken in by the teams—which was to say that those in large markets held an inherent advantage over small-market clubs—Cincinnati Reds president Francis Dale lamented that without the reserve system to prevent the flow of players to richer teams, "the poorer or weaker franchises would not be able to compete for the better players and therefore baseball would be destroyed."[74]

Of course, putting all Major League clubs under a revenue-sharing system, similar to that instituted by the National Football League, would have alleviated the financial distress suffered by 13 of the 24 Major League teams that "suffered losses, some of them very substantial," in 1969. Yet, the owners preferred to maintain the status quo of the reserve clause and the financial philosophy of "every man for himself" rather than be subjected to the taint of socialism via sharing the pot of revenue more equitably, to say nothing of the peril of allowing players access to an open labor market.

The privilege of antitrust exemption meshed well with the sanctity of the reserve clause, the previous challenges to which had always been successfully thwarted by baseball, leaving Dave Oliphant, George Toolson, and Danny Gardella on the outside looking in due to their quixotic efforts. In late 1969, "the federal district court in New York City held that *Toolson* is a bar against actions charging antitrust violations in the structure of Organized Baseball," and early the following year, Kuhn's counsel, Paul Porter, noted, "It is still quite clearly the law that if the antitrust laws, in whole or in part, should be applied to Organized Baseball, that decision is to be made by Congress, not by the courts."[75] Porter's interpretation would buy plenty of time for baseball to react to any potential legislation and lobby against it given the literal act of Congress he envisioned necessary to strike down or otherwise alter a long-established system.

It is important to bear in mind that Bowie Kuhn was just over two years into his tenure as baseball commissioner, and as a former attorney in his mid-forties with well over a decade's worth of experience working with legal aspects of the sport—he was a lawyer for the National League from the early 1950s until his appointment as temporary commissioner in February 1969—he was more sensitive to how the affairs of the game were being handled, certainly far ahead of his clueless predecessor, William Eckert. Taking the pulse of the teams' front offices positioned the commissioner to let the owners provide input that could be considered as future action items for modernizing the game and bringing it to a wider audience. To this point in time, Kuhn had yet to become embroiled in the tussles with both labor and fractious ownership groups that eventually made him a marked man and led to his undoing.

Although 1970 and 1971 constituted but a brief interlude in baseball's already lengthy history, the events of this period draw notice for being part of what may be described as a swinging pendulum approaching the apex of its arc in favor of team ownership. Gains made by the Major League Baseball Players Association to this point—collective bargaining agreements, improved benefits for its members, and, especially, arbitration of grievances—became the assets that Marvin Miller accumulated to give his charges the confidence they needed to demand their fair portion of the proceeds from a group of magnates whose reluctance to share was endemic and an ingrained business practice.

Several more years would be required before that pendulum not only stopped but reversed fully in the direction of the MLBPA. However, in the nascent years of the 1970s, the shifting of momentum was slow yet discernible, and Miller, gifted with business smarts and patience, understood ownership to be reactive rather than proactive. He also knew that time and circumstances were on his—and the players'—side.

2

Notable Exits

The ebb and flow of Major League seasons is always attended by the changes in the composition of every team's roster. These changings of the guard, as it were, never wait until the end of a spring training camp or the conclusion of the regular season, although there is a pause for the solidification of postseason playoff rosters. Yet, in the wake of the final World Series out being recorded, little time passes before general managers begin their search for new blood to bolster their teams' fortunes. In an era when the reserve clause was ironclad, the trade market that was such an integral feature of the annual Winter Meetings almost always guaranteed an abundance of topics and speculation for the offseason Hot Stove leagues. The phrase "on paper" served as a frequently used qualifier for fans to evaluate the latest version of a team's makeup and its chances for success, but there would be no proof in the pudding until all of the uniformed personnel stepped onto the field and put their talent to use.

However, not all currently active players who were expected to be in uniform in 1970 were available for duty. Three in particular became pariahs and were smitten by circumstances that were at once out of their control yet overlaid by no small degree of self-infliction. The first of these, after receiving his second consecutive Cy Young Award, was an ace pitcher pained by the toll of a heavy workload on his arm, and he compounded his misery through a series of personal associations with questionable characters that cast serious doubt on his judgment regarding the company he kept. Secondly, a stellar defensive outfielder was traded following the 1969 season, and not wishing to be uprooted from the city in which he had made his mark, he took the bold step to sue the game for the freedom of movement that he believed he had earned.

Finally, a former All-Star pitcher whose own ailments had forced his decision to recast himself as a knuckleballer, assumed the role of author to reveal the hidden game of baseball as it existed not only on the diamond but also off the field and away from the ballpark. His book drew laughs, gasps, dismay, and criticism from all corners of the bleachers and the world of the national pastime because the narrative exploded the sanctity of the clubhouse and pierced the sacred veil cloaking some of the game's luminaries. The common thread among this trio is that, in their own way, each of them ruffled the feathers of the staid baseball establishment and became outcasts for differing reasons.

For players choosing not to buck management or succumbing to the shortfalls of misfortune, their careers moved apace as some burst onto the scene like a nova, younger veterans continued to make their mark for profit, and as age caught up with those more elderly, the greybeards prepared to segue into retirement. A chosen few of this latest group would receive a telephone call informing them of their election to the Hall of Fame, the capstone of any career.

Of course, the players passing through Major League Baseball in 1970 and 1971 were part of the continuum of those who imprinted the game with the stamp of their era. The game, always in transition, was still inflected with traits of the 1960s, yet it was headed toward making its mark in a new decade with an evolution of faces old and new.

"You gotta do what you gotta do when you gotta do it." So said Denny McLain as a senior citizen in his mid-seventies reflecting on the method he found necessary—an estimated 230 to 240 shots of cortisone—to be able to answer the call for his pitching assignments, a fair number of which led to victories that earned him two Cy Young Awards.[1] Those honors, coming as they did in 1968 and 1969, only make McLain's disastrous year of 1970 all the worse, in part because the deterioration of his ailing right shoulder finally caught up with him, but also due in part to his freewheeling attitude toward life, how he carried himself, and the people with whom he chose to associate. Collectively, these traits played a huge role in the suddenness of his fall from grace.

McLain entered that fateful campaign having just turned 26 years old, yet he seemed to have already lived well beyond those years. In 1965 the hurler found his footing in the rotation of the Detroit Tigers, posting a sharp 16–6 record with an efficient 2.61 ERA, and the following season he logged his first 20-win campaign. In 1967, McLain totaled 17 victories, but this seemed an underachieving number due in part to time missed in the heat of that season's frantic pennant race. The cause of his absence was a foot injury of dubious origin, but he endeavored to make amends in 1968 by winning 31 games en route to capturing the American League Cy Young and Most Valuable Player Awards. Dropping a bit to "only" 24 victories in 1969, McLain tied Mike Cuellar of Baltimore for top pitching honors, all the while exuding the devil-may-care swagger that helped him accrue the special attention to which he had grown accustomed.

2. Notable Exits

Mayo Smith, the Detroit manager, nonetheless stood by McLain, willing to tolerate the pitcher's overarching braggadocio because his top righthander, along with southpaw Mickey Lolich, formed the bedrock of the Tiger rotation. Being named the best pitcher in the AL, as McLain had been, brought with it the privilege of skirting the team rules that applied to his teammates, a policy that irked more than a few of them. Arriving 20 minutes before game time (on non-pitching days) as well as dressing and leaving the ballpark once he had been removed from a contest were among the freedoms accorded McLain, while his fellow Tigers were required to report at least two hours ahead of the first pitch or stick around after they had been taken out of a game.

A licensed pilot, "Sky King" McLain was never bashful to hop in his $80,000 airplane and fly wherever he felt the next adventure would lead him, especially jaunts that put him in the musical spotlight to perform on a state-of-the-art Hammond X-77 organ, and he played in the same milieux as some of the best nightclub entertainers.[2] Besides an endorsement deal with Hammond, McLain also slaked his thirst with a near-endless supply of Pepsi Cola, the soft-drink company paying him $15,000 to "mention my love for Pepsi, try to drink one during an interview, and make a few personal appearances."[3]

Smith defended his pandering to McLain's whimsical schedule with the claim that a happy pitcher was a winning pitcher, but the manager also feared that disciplining his star hurler might negatively impact his productivity. As long as the innings pitched and victories kept mounting, Smith felt

Denny McLain won 31 games in 1968 but just two years later had become a baseball pariah due to a series of personal problems that included run-ins with the law.

that the ends justified the means; thus, the righthander had earned his privileges even at the cost of "bother[ing] a lot of the younger players."[4] But McLain's life away from the clubhouse was breeding an ugly undercurrent of issues soon to capture national attention—and that of the commissioner's office.

On the recommendation of teammate Joe Sparma, McLain began using attorney Ed May to tend to his personal financial affairs in the summer of 1969, but soon both pitchers discovered that "May had stolen every dime from both of us."[5] By McLain's accounting, he was now over $400,000 in debt, and his life unraveled further in early 1970 when revelations emerged about his connection to a small nightclub in Flint, Michigan, whose owner was involved with sports bookmaking.[6] This relationship began in 1966, and having caught the betting bug, McLain became steeped deeper in his own participation—as a financier of an operation rather than a true bookmaker—over the ensuing years.

By February, as McLain faced eviction from the home he was renting in a Detroit suburb, *Sports Illustrated* had concluded an investigative report that was ready for release, much to the consternation of the baseball establishment. Bowie Kuhn summoned McLain to his office for an explanation about the pitcher's dealings and anything that might be linked to a national gambling investigation being conducted by the FBI. Connections to the Mafia raised red flags as the probe expanded and McLain's finances were investigated by a federal grand jury in Detroit. "McLain was contrite," the commissioner later wrote of his meeting with the pitcher. "He had no business being connected to any kind of gambling operation, whether baseball was involved or not."[7] For his part, the pitcher willingly put himself at the mercy of Kuhn, pleading his case that he had been led on by the figures who ran the Flint business and that baseball betting was not among the interests to which he had been a party.

The commissioner's security chief, Henry Fitzgibbon, launched his own inquiry as spring training was about to commence, and Kuhn was stuck between a rock and hard place: The grand jury's work proceeded slowly, and the tardiness—to say nothing of circumstantial evidence—led many to assume that McLain was guilty, so pending the outcome of the ongoing probe, Kuhn suspended the pitcher for three months beginning April 1. There was proof of "associations with the operation's criminal element, [but] the evidence strongly suggested he was more a dupe than anything else," according to Kuhn.[8] McLain confessed to the unsound connections he had fostered but claimed that many of *Sports Illustrated*'s allegations were false, including how he had sustained the foot injury in 1967 that the magazine attributed to a roughing-up by some gamblers with a vested interest in the outcome of that season's pennant race.[9]

Still—and in the manner of former commissioner Kenesaw Mountain Landis, who made a name for himself in the wake of the Black Sox scandal—Kuhn was unforgiving of the untoward publicity visited on the game by McLain's poor judgment. The current commissioner believed that banishing McLain for, in essence, half the regular season was sufficient to the purpose, although Landis may have thought this penalty too lenient. The press was split between members who had already determined that McLain was guilty and deserved a longer suspension, and others who thought the penalty too stiff since betting on baseball was lacking in the case. "[I]t would appear that in fact he was the victim of a confidence scheme," Kuhn informed a press conference.[10]

So, was McLain guilty or not? His batterymate, Bill Freehan, who was critical of the pitcher's divisive behavior, wondered, "Half a season? Funny. It's like saying he almost did something wrong," while Tiger infielder Dick McAuliffe mused, "If Denny's innocent, it should be nothing. If he's guilty, then this is not enough."[11] McLain paid the immediate price of enduring his three-month exile, during which time he used his brother as a catcher for trying to keep his arm in shape as the end of his suspension drew near. Jim Campbell, the general manager of the Tigers, "stepped to my defense and helped me out with money from time to time ... to cover my legal expenses and basic expenses," a welcome reprieve for McLain since he knew "I'd made the club a ton of money at home and on the road in '68 and '69" as fans flocked to stadiums to watch one of the best pitchers in the game.[12]

Upon completion of his suspension, McLain again proved his power as a drawing card by enticing a crowd of over 53,000 to Tiger Stadium to watch his 1970 debut on July 1. He pitched into the sixth inning, not getting the decision in Detroit's 6–5 victory over New York in 11 innings, yet the hero's welcome he received from the stands hinted at a fair degree of forgiveness. But the once-dominant hurler was, to all intents and purposes, missing in action: McLain finished his abbreviated season with a record of 3–5 with an ERA of 4.63 over 91.1 innings pitched, and after his losing effort on August 26 at home against the California Angels, his career in a Detroit uniform came to a crashing conclusion. As the home town cheers turned to boos, McLain was clearly at a crossroads, and not even his supposed cumulative income of roughly $200,000—this total was from his baseball contract, nightclub gigs, and endorsement deals—seemed capable of rescuing him.[13]

Two days after his latest failed outing, McLain doused two Detroit beat writers with buckets of water in what he claimed was a clubhouse prank that was abetted by some of his teammates. McLain took exception to aspects of the scribes' stories of his last appearance and "decided to have some fun with the writers" when he poured water on reporter Jim Hawkins, and then after gaining the confidence of Watson Spoelstra, the pitcher let him have it with another bucket.[14] Spoelstra frankly related details of the entire episode in *The Sporting News* and was hardly amused: "The inside hurt was much deeper than the penetration of ice water in a man's jacket."[15]

As soon as Spoelstra found a telephone after McLain's hijinks, he called Tiger general manager Jim Campbell to tell him what had just occurred; the outraged executive immediately apologized and quickly suspended McLain, initially for 30 days but then reduced the period to seven days. The season was winding down, and though the Tigers had little chance of overtaking the powerful Baltimore Orioles, McLain was assuming that he would be back on the mound in roughly one week.

However, Bowie Kuhn requested an audience with him in New York, and at this meeting on September 9, the commissioner advised McLain that he was under investigation for allegedly carrying a gun during a trip to Anaheim and Oakland a few weeks earlier. McLain stated that he legally owned a gun but did not carry it—he also fingered backup catcher Jim Price as the snitch who unmasked him—yet this latest incident gave Kuhn reason to impose another suspension, this time for the remainder of the season. (From the day of this three-hour meeting until the schedule ran its course, the Tigers won only a handful of games, imploding with a record of 5–16 down the stretch. Mayo Smith was fired, and the combustible Billy Martin was brought in as his replacement.)

Another Detroit baseball writer, Joe Falls—he managed to avoid McLain's water-bucket shenanigans—noted that the pitcher "keeps saying he's sorry and this always wins a lot of sympathy for him, but when does he start backing up his words with deeds?" Falls also cut to the chase by pointing out a simple problem related to McLain and his gun: "So, once and for all, let's get it straight—it's against the law to *carry* a concealed weapon without a permit."[16] McLain was not licensed in either of the states, Michigan and Florida, he claimed as residences.

In mid-September, McLain agreed to undergo a psychiatric evaluation, his three-day stint at Henry Ford Hospital in Detroit showing "that I wasn't nuts," but his seemingly uncompromised mental status did not earn him a reinstatement from Kuhn.[17] However, it gave a degree of confidence to a certain baseball team owner who was willing to take a chance on adding McLain to his roster. So it was on October 9, 1970, that a trade between the Tigers and Robert Short's Washington Senators was completed, Detroit packaging the former 31-game winner along with Elliott Maddox, Norm McRae, and Don Wert in exchange for Eddie Brinkman, Joe Coleman, Jim Hannan, and Aurelio Rodríguez.

2. Notable Exits

Robert Short was never bashful about making a publicity grab, and this trade was a perfect example. The transaction had to be facilitated through the commissioner's office because players on the suspended list were ineligible to be traded, but Kuhn terminated McLain's suspension on October 1, which was the end of the regular season, knowing that the Senators and Tigers had been in negotiations over a deal. Short's impulse was purely driven by the dollars he envisioned flowing into the Senators' coffers every time McLain took the mound before a presumably packed stadium.

However, the owner was living in the past, believing that McLain would somehow find his footing and contend for another Cy Young Award; saner minds understood that the pitcher, now damaged goods, was likely to have little positive impact with a new team. Meanwhile in the Motor City, the Tigers improved markedly through the addition of "the two best [infield] arms [Rodríguez and Brinkman] side-by-side in the league, and two starting pitchers."[18] Indeed, the trade turned Detroit into a contender, helping them to a second-place finish in 1971 and an AL East pennant in the stilted, strike-riddled 1972 season when the Tigers edged out the Boston Red Sox by one-half game.

For his part, the trade's center of attention was lukewarm about plying his skills in the nation's capital. McLain knew that the Senators were a perennial loser even though Short had coaxed Hall-of-Famer Ted Williams out of retirement to be the club's manager. The Splendid Splinter's dugout debut in 1969 resulted in the pleasant surprise of 86 wins, but Washington found its accustomed place in the basement the very next season, logging a 70–92 record as Williams's honeymoon period was clearly at an end and the turnstiles at RFK Stadium clicked in just under 825,000 fans, eighth out of 12 American League teams. McLain was later critical of Senator pitcher Dick Bosman for being "Ted's boy" as well as for blaming his teammates for the club's shortcomings when many believed that the fault for Washington's poor record lie with Williams rather than the players.[19]

Assuaging some of McLain's angst was the reported $100,000 salary that the foolhardy Short lavished on him, and the pitcher spent the first month of 1971 behind the keyboard of a Hammond organ at a Washington-area nightclub. With outfielder Curt Flood in attendance one evening, McLain and the Ron Kramer Trio gave the audience a set of pop tunes including "More," "Going Out of My Head Over You," and "Watermelon Man" before he segued into bantering with the crowd. "I'm a little nervous. Bowie's not here yet, is he?" he quipped, but the scribe reporting on the show for Associated Press yearned to see less of McLain as entertainer and more of him in a baseball uniform: "[O]ne gets the feeling that the month until the opening of spring training is too long to wait."[20]

Upon their initial meeting, McLain tried to cultivate a relationship with his new manager, not least because of the common ground of their both being aviators, Williams having served as a fighter pilot in World War II and the Korean War. But the pitcher took exception to Williams's demeanor, the skipper already possessed of a general distain for pitchers and now displeased by Short's having traded away the team's two best infielders for several players that included a free-spirited former ace who was carrying a lot of unbecoming baggage. This situation was exacerbated when McLain formed what came to be known as the Underminers' Club, whose mission "was simply to sabotage Ted's tenure as manager."[21] Bernie Allen, Dick Billings, Tim Cullen, and Tom McCraw were fellow members of the group who instigated derelictions of duty such as breakage of curfew by many teammates, encouraging them to take taxis from the hotel to the ballpark instead of the team bus, and, not least, playing golf, which Williams had declared verboten because he believed it to have an ill effect on one's baseball swing.

In between all of the scheming, McLain nonetheless took his regular turn in the rotation but with uninspiring results as he availed himself of cortisone injections for his ailing right shoulder. Struggling to a 5–15 record by early July, he landed on the disabled list and returned to win in four of his next five appearances in August before losing his remaining six starts.

By closing his 1971 campaign with 10 wins and 22 losses and an ERA of 4.28, McLain had turned the Baltimore Orioles' star third baseman into a prophet, of sorts. When the Tiger–Senator trade was announced, Brooks Robinson had voiced his opinion of the deal by stating, "[Joe] Coleman might win as many games for Detroit as McLain wins for Washington," and with 20 wins to his credit, Coleman quickly established himself as an integral member of the Tiger rotation.[22]

The end of that season also saw the transfer of the Senators to the Lone Star State where they were rechristened the Texas Rangers. McLain was still the property of the club, and he did promotional work to help give the franchise some brand recognition in its new market. His 31 victories of 1968 still had some cachet and enabled him to make public appearances on behalf of the Rangers and spin yarns about that great achievement even though he would never again reach those heights. McLain's star had faded to barely a flicker, but Robert Short was still willing to use him to tap into the fan base of the greater Dallas area.

Yet, as McLain tried to make his mark during spring training in 1972, he was traded in early March to the Oakland Athletics, for whom he pitched but five games and served a stint in the A's farm system at Birmingham. Traded once more in late June, this time to Atlanta, he lost five of eight decisions with an ERA over six; for the entire year, he went 4–7, logged a composite ERA of 6.37, and admitted, "The cold truth was that I just couldn't pitch anymore."[23] Despite knocking around Triple-A and Double-A the following year, McLain had become another player whose statistics could be finalized in the next edition of *The Baseball Encyclopedia*, never in need of updating. His life and business ventures would collapse under the weight of a series of misfortunes, some his own fault, others the result of fate.

"After retiring from baseball, I played golf every day for money for about 20 years," McLain said in an interview nearly a half-century after his 31-win season. "It was in my DNA." Momentarily speaking of himself in the third person, he also put his two subsequent prison terms—he was convicted for racketeering, extortion, and drug trafficking in 1984, and then embezzlement, money laundering, mail fraud, and conspiracy nine years later—in perspective: "Denny McLain has had two tragedies in his life: Our daughter was killed by a drunk driver [in 1992], and my wife, Sharon, getting Parkinson's disease. Otherwise, I've had a great life."[24] Considering all of his trials and tribulations, this interpretation of "a great life" impresses as confounding.

By the time the former Cy Young winner reached his mid-seventies, he continued to hold dear the singular piece of glory that came his way when he was in his prime in the late 1960s. "Denny McLain, 31–6, 1968" was the signature and brief curriculum vitae he scratched out when signing autographs. The argument can be made that Dennis Dale McLain lived several lifetimes in his outsized years as a dominant Major League pitcher, hustler, and post-playing-days convict who never knew a dull moment.

That Curt Flood was partaking of Denny McLain's musical performance in January 1971 provides an intriguing intersection of baseball personalities. While the latter was hell-bent on enjoying himself, the former, who also knew a good time, was in the midst of a struggle intended not just for personal benefit but for the good of all baseball players. The common ground of McLain and Flood was that they both fought the baseball establishment, albeit in different ways.

Born in Houston, Texas, Flood grew up in Oakland, California, from the age of two when his family moved to the Bay Area. After playing high school baseball under legendary coach George Powles—Frank Robinson and Vada Pinson also enjoyed the same experience—he was signed by the Cincinnati Redlegs in 1956, registered two solid seasons in their farm system, and earned very brief appearances with the Major League club each of those years.

Traded from Cincinnati in December 1957 because of "the unspoken quota system employed by most major league teams of the late 1950s and early 1960s" that limited opportunities for Black players, Flood blossomed as a bona fide ballplayer for his new team, the St. Louis Cardinals.[25] He served an apprenticeship as a pinch runner and spare outfielder early in his tenure, but when Johnny Keane took over as the Cards' skipper in July 1961, Flood soon emerged as the regular centerfielder. Keane was open to allowing the other Black St. Louis players, Bob Gibson and Bill White, to come into their own, all the better for the Cardinals as they became two-time World Series champions—they also captured another National League pennant—before the decade was out.

Through the end of the 1960s, Flood won seven Gold Gloves as the preeminent defensive centerfielder in the NL, and this ability as well as his skill as a batter who would end his career with a lifetime .293 average led him to command one of the best salaries in baseball at $90,000 in 1969.[26] But the sting of his trade from St. Louis to Philadelphia following that season quickly grated on Flood, and his reaction must be viewed in the context of the era. In the 22 years since Jackie Robinson integrated Major League Baseball, notable instances of civil rights initiatives developed: the 1954 *Brown v. Board of Education* decision, Rosa Parks and the Montgomery bus boycott of the following two years, the 1961 Freedom Rides, 1964's Civil Rights Act, and the 1965 Voting Rights Act all proved to be impactful toward equal rights for Black Americans.

After sitting out the 1970 season to fight the reserve clause, Curt Flood returned to the game briefly in 1971, but the erosion of his skills and physical condition hastened his departure from baseball.

The brutality of rioting in the Watts section of Los Angeles (1965), in Newark and Detroit (1967), and in many urban areas across the U.S. after the assassination of Martin Luther King, Jr. (1968), also became emblematic of the African-American struggle during the nation's most volatile decade.

Flood was only 31 years of age when the Cardinals sent him East, the multi-player trade with the Phillies including another major star, Dick Allen. Although Flood's batting average had dipped over the last few seasons—he reached his career high of .335 in 1967, hit .301 in 1968's so-called "Year of the Pitcher," and most recently batted .285 over 153 games in 1969—he was hardly over the hill. Still, there were issues that gave Cardinal management reason for pause, namely Flood's consumption of alcoholic beverages, his misjudging of a flyball in the final game of the 1968 World Series that cost St. Louis the championship, and his quest for a salary of $100,000. These demerits left a bad taste in team owner August Busch's mouth and gave encouragement to general manager Bing Devine to find a new address for Flood.

Besides being a ballplayer, however, he was clearly a man of his times. "[Jackie] Robinson inspired Flood to get involved in the civil rights movement," noted Brad Snyder, Flood's biographer. "In 1961, Flood spoke out against segregated spring training camps in Florida. The next year he spoke with Robinson at an NAACP rally in Mississippi. Flood integrated a white Bay Area neighborhood after the 1964 season with a court order and armed police protection. In 1969, he served as the president of Aunts and Uncles, a St. Louis organization that provided shoes and clothing to underprivileged children."[27]

Refusing to play for the Phillies, a franchise Flood believed was "rivaled only by the Pirates as the least cheerful in the [National League]," he at first indicated a preference for retirement from baseball in favor of devoting more time to his photography and portrait-painting businesses.[28] In an effort to entice Flood to accept the trade, the Phillies offered him a $100,000 salary, but Flood ignored the phone calls of Philadelphia GM Bob Quinn as the outfielder was about to depart for a vacation in Denmark mere days after the trade. Flood's business associate, Marian Jorgensen, hearing him complain about the reserve system that bound a player to his team, suggested that he sue Major League Baseball to overturn the manner in which baseball had contracted its players for nearly a century.

Impervious to Quinn's sales pitch of coming to play for the Phillies, Flood complained to his attorney, Allan Zerman, about the unfair nature of the reserve clause. As Jorgensen had just done weeks earlier, Zerman also floated the idea of taking legal action against the baseball establishment. With "[t]wo of the people Flood trusted most" sharing the same opinion, Flood moved forward to initiate what, prima facie, appeared to be a quixotic joust. Marvin Miller, the MLBPA director, listened to Flood's desire to sue but had little faith in a successful outcome for the plaintiff. Marshalling the support of the members of the players' union would be paramount to Flood's mission, but this would be no easy task.

Baseball's legal track record was already decidedly in favor of ownership. The sport had been found exempt from the Sherman Antitrust Act in the 1922 case of *Federal Baseball Club of Baltimore, Inc. v. National League of Professional Baseball Clubs*, again in the 1947 suit of Danny Gardella—at least initially in this complex legal action—and in the 1953 case *Toolson v. New York Yankees*, the Supreme Court upheld an earlier ruling against the complainant. Despite the fact that baseball was indeed engaged in interstate commerce and therefore subject to the Sherman Act, Miller was painfully aware that the existing precedents were likely to retain their unwavering status, and he dutifully explained these circumstances to Flood.

By stepping away from the game to pursue his legal fight, Flood would be forfeiting his substantial salary, and in Miller's eyes, a victory in court seemed impossible despite Flood's promise "to fight the reserve clause to the finish."[29] Miller advised him of the vast expenses that would certainly be incurred during this battle, prompting Flood to seek the assistance of the players' union. At this same time—late November 1969—Flood met with Phils GM Quinn as well as with an executive in Philadelphia associated with a chain of art galleries interested in doing business with Flood. The financial package Flood sought was within his grasp, and the lure of an artistic enterprise sweetened the pot, but by early December, Flood and attorney Zerman resolved to press forward in court.

Through the nascent steps of Flood's action, Miller was impressed by his determination, and he understood that the outfielder had no way to bring his case before a baseball-related arbitrator because the sport had no such procedure in place at that time. In a meeting with Flood, Miller further "realized that once we started down this road, we couldn't abandon the case.... We'd have to follow it through to the end, no matter how long, expensive, or bitter the struggle."[30] Most of the expenses would have to be borne by the Players Association, and it was up to Flood to convince that group's board, which was comprised of current player representatives from various teams, that his venture was worth pursuing and, not least, receiving financial backing.

When Flood presented his case, Tom Haller, a catcher with the Dodgers, asked him if the lawsuit stemmed from any racial resentment Flood, as an African American, may have harbored against the game. Flood admitted to being "more sensitive" about issues related to race while at once declaring that he was acting as "a ballplayer, a major league ballplayer," with no hint of a racial agenda.[31]

Yet despite this virtue, "Flood sought to take what his hero, Jackie Robinson, had accomplished a step further" because he "recognized that racial equality could not be achieved without the freedom to sell one's talent to the highest bidder."[32] The reserve clause itself was conflated with the institution of slavery by a pair of prominent sportswriters, Red Smith and Jim Murray, who supported the idea of freedom for players to seek employment at their preferred locale. However, a win in court by Flood would open the door for *all* players, not just minorities, and the board expressed its faith in him through its unanimous support for the case.

So emboldened, Flood took his stand, first by petitioning commissioner Bowie Kuhn as 1969 drew to a close. Conveying his wish not to be treated like "a piece of property to be bought and sold irrespective of my wishes," Flood signaled his desire and ability to play the next season but also wanted to reserve his "right to reconsider offers from other clubs," especially those in locations he would have deemed preferable to Philadelphia or Pittsburgh.[33] The commissioner replied, pretending to be sympathetic—"I certainly agree that you, as a human being, are not a piece of property to be bought and sold"—while remaining steadfastly in the corner of ownership and the game's business tradition as upheld in previous court cases: "The provisions of the playing contract have been negotiated over the years between the clubs and the players," and Kuhn closed with a denial to "comply with the request" to inform all Major League clubs of Flood's availability for the upcoming season.[34]

Officially rebuffed in his attempt to gain contractual access to all 24 teams, Flood sat out the 1970 season, as Miller and the legal team, led by the well-connected Arthur Goldberg, pressed on, full in the knowledge of a likely defeat in the quest for $4.1 million in damages from Major League Baseball. (Note—The Phillies remained optimistic that their new centerfielder would be on hand, giving Flood the full treatment in their 1970 media guide.) Goldberg drew notice because of his impressive résumé, which included a Cabinet post in the recent Kennedy Administration as well as his past roles as U.S. ambassador to the United Nations and, not least, a justice of the Supreme Court.

Flood was physically removed from the fray in the courtroom: His businesses in St. Louis had collapsed, the Internal Revenue Service was after him for nearly $7,000 in back taxes, and he sought refuge in Denmark as a place where he could "clear his head."[35] Meanwhile, the initial round of action in New York's U.S. District Court before Judge Irving Ben Cooper produced the first setback in August when he upheld baseball's exemption from federal antitrust laws but noted that a change to the reserve system could be brokered between owners and players.

As an appeal was filed in early November, Flood learned that Washington Senator owner Robert Short was interested in acquiring him for the 1971 season. This information provided much good news for the cash-strapped player-in-exile, who stood to receive a windfall of a $110,000 salary courtesy of the flamboyant Short.[36] A trade between the Phillies, to whom Flood belonged, and the Senators put him in a Washington uniform, forming a peculiar union with Ted Williams and Denny McLain. Flood, still smarting from monetary shortfalls, was in the odd position of abiding by the reserve clause of his new contract while at the same time fighting it via his ongoing legal battle.

When the Senators assembled for 1971 spring training in Pompano Beach, Florida, Flood had reneged on his pledge to report two weeks early to get himself in shape after his extended absence from the field. Coming in only a day ahead of schedule, Flood continued to be burdened by excessive use of alcohol, and though he defended his physical condition, the team physician said, "Flood has to have the oldest 33-year-old body I've ever examined."[37] The litigant trying to keep his footing on the comeback trail fooled nobody, as his poor performance in exhibition games—both in the field and at the plate—raised eyebrows and drew pity from those who knew how great he had been. The fact that his return drew hordes of media, some asking pesky questions, made Flood want to retreat into himself.

Almost as if the schedules of the Senators and the courts were in sync, Washington opened the season by defeating Oakland—the young phenom Vida Blue was the losing pitcher—on April 5 and two days later the Court of Appeals for the Second Circuit upheld Judge Cooper's original ruling. This latest verdict set the stage for one final legal thrust to occur before the U.S. Supreme Court, but along with Flood's unimpressive renaissance in Florida, it foretold how the rest of the month would transpire for him.

Flood played in just 13 games, recording seven base hits (all singles) in 35 at-bats for a weak .200 average. His manager, Ted Williams, quickly reduced him to platooning against lefthanders, and Short's investment was proving to be a flop. Confessing to Frank Howard that he was incapable of playing like his former self, Flood was consoled by his teammate, who advised him to be patient in getting reacclimated, yet it was too much to bear. Having collected half of his salary upfront but distraught about his situation—two losses in court, a media corps asking endless questions concerning his battle with the baseball hierarchy, and now his poor performance back on the field that coupled with the stress of his aforementioned personal problems—Flood left the club on April 27.

Finding his way to New York's JFK International Airport, Flood paid cash for a first-class ticket on Pan Am World Airways to Barcelona, Spain.

His escape was not as stealthy as he would have liked, and he threatened a press photographer who tried to record his exiting. Joe Reichler, the baseball commissioner's head of public relations, was dispatched by Short to the airport in a last-ditch effort to intercept Flood, but as Red Foley explained in the *New York Daily News*, "Flood couldn't pick up the pieces in Florida and when his once superb game continued to shatter, he finally rejected baseball for Barcelona."[38]

About three hours before boarding his flight, Flood sent a telegram to Short, thanking him for "your confidence and understanding" but also citing his absence from the game in 1970 and the "serious personal problems mounting everyday" that informed his decision to quit.[39] Flood did keep his word regarding another pressing matter: His finances were in such poor condition that there was an easier route he could have taken to start life over, but "Flood refused to declare bankruptcy because he wanted his shot before the Supreme Court of the United States. He sacrificed everything to get it."[40] Despite the immense havoc in his life, he was unwilling to break his promise to the MLBPA to see his fight through to its conclusion.

When the nation's highest court finally heard oral arguments in March 1972, National League chief counsel Lou Hoynes, Jr., "charged the Players Association ... was trying to subvert the bargaining process through litigation and 'seize clout at the bargaining table,'" as if the owners had not already been holding the upper hand over the players for the last century.[41] But Flood and, by extension, the MLBPA, were handicapped by the inferior work of Arthur Goldberg, in whom so much trust was placed for conducting a competent argument. To all appearances, Goldberg was eminently qualified since he had once served as an associate justice on the very court before which he would represent Flood. Not only did Goldberg misstate some basic facts about Flood but he also prompted the ire of the current justices for the manner in which he was handling his presentation. The verdict came in June 1972, 5–3 in favor of upholding the reserve clause, sending Flood down to defeat for the third and final time.

It can be easy to view Curt Flood's journey as simply self-inflicted harm because he had been advised of the major pitfalls prior to his taking the decision to act against baseball's well-entrenched norms. Troubled by demons that affected his physical and mental states, Flood indeed sacrificed what was left of his baseball career, but if not for his driving a stake in the ground against the reserve clause, what other player would have made a similar stand? As Bowie Kuhn wrote fifteen years after the Supreme Court's decision, "Basically, the trial pitted me against Marvin Miller," and while there is a degree of truth to this, it can only be left to speculation as to how much longer the reserve clause would have lasted had Flood not taken umbrage at his October 1969 trade.[42] In the event,

Marvin Miller continued to press for better bargaining agreements for the players, and where the previous lawsuits of Federal Baseball, Toolson, and Gardella failed to gain traction, Flood's case was overseen by an MLBPA director with a keen eye for finding a way forward in the face of opposition by the club owners.

Writing in *The Sporting News*, Leonard Koppett reminded readers of "exactly what the Supreme Court did and did not rule," not least of his points being, "It did NOT say, 'The reserve clause is okay.' It did NOT say 'Baseball alone should be exempt from antitrust law.'"[43] Flood's battering ram was too weak to breach the fortress of the reserve clause, yet Miller confessed in his memoir that at the time of the verdict, "I hadn't realized ... how close we came to winning at the Supreme Court."[44] Thus, the importance of giving Flood credit for at least cracking the protective shell of the reserve clause that just a few years hence would crumble under the weight of the arbitrator's decision in the Messersmith–McNally case.

Flood's attitude was consistent with minority views in striving for racial equality, and his comparison of the reserve system's bondage to slavery was compelling. The reserve clause held sway over *every* player, and he must be commended for his desire help them all at the cost of forfeiting what remained of his playing career.

Whereas Curt Flood's focus was his challenge to the reserve clause, a former All-Star pitcher contravened, in book form, the national pastime's tradition and veneer of wholesomeness. Jim Bouton's release of *Ball Four* in the spring of 1970 created a tempest of great controversy, and if any of the narrative can be linked to Flood's battle, the former Yankee hurler revealed his experiences of dealing with front-office management, mostly of the expansion Seattle Pilots, with regard to his own labor-relation issues such as salary negotiations, management's responsibilities to him, and the like.

Instead of simply informing fans of the mundane aspects related to the business side of the enterprise and furnishing an otherwise blasé view of life as a Major Leaguer, Bouton delighted in spicing his diary-style account with clubhouse antics, sexual escapades of fellow players, criticism of his field manager and general manager, and calling out the tics, foibles and eccentricities of teammates past and present.

Another recent diary of a major sports team, Jerry Kramer's *Instant Replay* published in 1968, told the story of what turned out to be the final season of the National Football League legend Vince Lombardi's tenure as coach of the Green Bay Packers. The Packers were dynastic in their own way as had been Bouton's original team, the New York Yankees, and

Kramer informs of his own physical trials, the tough conditions of practices, and what life was like training and playing to become a champion. Readers gain a full appreciation, sans the ribaldry inherent in a male jock milieu, of how football crowns were forged in a small city that took on the quaint appellation of "Titletown" due to the Packers' overwhelming success under Lombardi's rule.

By stark contrast, Bouton went out of his way to ensure that confidentiality and the sanctity of the locker room—to say nothing of his teammates' bedrooms, for that matter—were least among his worries while at the same time shielding his own backside. "Although Bouton later admitted he was unfaithful to his wife during his playing career, he portrayed himself in *Ball Four* as the faithful husband and regaled his readers with stories of others' infidelities," as historian Bill Ryczek has critiqued the book. Denouncing others is one matter, and "[h]arsh words are justifiable when used to tear down powerful, evil, public menaces. But Joe Schultz, Elston Howard, and Steve Barber were neither evil men nor a danger to society."[45] Just the same, in Bouton's view, they rubbed him the wrong way for having handled him poorly, behaving disingenuously toward the press, cheating on behalf of a teammate, or trying to hang on to a Major League job (ironically, as Bouton himself was doing).

The clamor over *Ball Four* took little time to be scrutinized not only by parties specifically named or otherwise offended but also, and predictably, baseball's highest office. Called on the carpet to explain himself, Bouton reveled in the attention as sales of the book exceeded all expectations, and he was thrilled to "acknowledge a deep debt to Bowie Kuhn, our Commissioner. There are some who say it's a quarter million [copies sold]."[46] In a June 1 meeting between Kuhn, Bouton, and Marvin Miller (as well as Dick Moss, also of the MLBPA), the commissioner, who thought the salacious parts of the book "struck me as not very credible stuff," harrumphed about what the conservative baseball establishment objected to.[47] "On an intellectual level, [Kuhn] knew he should hold his tongue," noted Mitchell Nathanson, Bouton's biographer, "but on a visceral level it bothered him and he was determined to speak his mind."[48]

And speak it, he did—"I advised Mr. Bouton of my displeasure with these writings and have warned him against future writings of this character," Kuhn announced to the press after the meeting—but the commissioner realized that he was only adding fuel to the fire that translated to further sales of the book.[49] Through his work, Bouton exercised his right to free speech and "did it not to please the baseball people but I did it for the fans ... and to let them know what baseball was really like, both the good and the bad."[50]

In a follow-up book to explain the fallout of *Ball Four*, Bouton continued to tweak the commissioner by observing that readers should be able to understand the actual intent of some jokes made between teammates. A concerned Kuhn had told Bouton, "You have Gary Bell telling Ray Oyler to bring home his socks because he left them under Oyler's bed. People are going to think that ballplayers are sleeping with each other's wives," yet the author could not believe that the commissioner failed to understand that this was simply verbal banter absent any real action.[51] (The Oyler–Bell episode occurred in 1969, but in March 1973 Yankee pitchers Fritz Peterson and Mike Kekich stunned the baseball world, or at least the portion of it with a conservative bent, by announcing that they were swapping wives and their respective families. "Hell, players aren't screwing around with each other's wives," Bouton had written in 1971. "At least not as far as I know."[52])

Bouton basked in what turned out to be more than fifteen minutes of fame, whereas Detroit catcher Bill Freehan, following in Bouton's footsteps coincidentally yet independently, found a swift, unfortunate end to his literary aspirations. Freehan chronicled the Tigers' 1969 season in his own book, *Behind the Mask: An Inside Baseball Diary*, but almost immediately rued its March 1970 release. An "artistic and financial flop," according to baseball writer Jerome Holtzman, Freehan's work took Denny McLain to task and "pictured Mayo Smith as a nice guy but ineffective manager" for facilitating McLain's preferential treatment.[53] When the catcher took much blame from the press for his harsh treatment of the 31-game winner, Freehan greatly regretted what he had written, apologizing to his teammate and manager as well as third base coach Grover Resinger, who felt betrayed that any player would take to becoming an author with revelatory and potentially embarrassing intent.

Joining this literary parade was none other than Curt Flood, whose 1971 exposé, *The Way It Is*, told the story of baseball's inside game from his perspective. An excerpt of the book that ran in the February 1 issue of *Sports Illustrated* focused only on his trade from St. Louis and the subsequent legal wrangling. But as if to imitate Bouton, Flood's full narrative related episodes in which he and some of his Cardinal teammates "swapped booze and chicks" on road trips.[54] By the time of the book's release, however, Flood was very soon to abandon the Senators and make a permanent exit from the game, and his publication had little impact.

If nothing else, Bouton had paid attention when his mother advised early in his career that he should write a book to chronicle his observations and experience as a player because "[t]hey were not the sorts of stories that could be found in the sports section."[55] And when those tales did make it into print, they formed the text of what became one of the most important and recognizable sports books ever published.

◆ ◆ ◆

The three main personalities covered in this chapter were clearly rebels in the view of baseball's highest offices. By stepping outside the bounds of ethically sound personal associations and challenging baseball's written rule—in the form of the reserve clause—or unwritten rules governing clubhouse privacy, they found different drummers to lead their respective marches and soon were effectively out of Major League Baseball. Denny McLain's swan song was in the role of a hanger-on for 20 forgettable games in 1972; Curt Flood fled Washington—and the country—in the spring of 1971, never to return to the game; and although Jim Bouton would stage a contrived comeback with the Atlanta Braves in 1978, his Major League career to all intents and purposes ended in August 1970 when he was released by the Houston Astros. Gone but not entirely forgotten, these unique characters bowed out in the earliest years of the decade, yet they were accompanied by some prominent brethren.

Other notable exits occurring in 1970 include Bob Allison of the Minnesota Twins, the lanky three-time All-Star who won American League Rookie-of-the-Year honors in 1957 when the club was still in Washington; Allison's former teammate, John Roseboro, who was a winner of two Gold Gloves as a catcher; and Bo Belinsky, who got more mileage out of his brief Major League career than any other player through embodying the life of the ultimate playboy. In 1971, the game bid farewell to Yankee alumnus and third base stalwart Clete Boyer; yet another former Twin, standout hurler Camilo Pascual; and longtime infielder Dick Schofield, who wore the uniform of eight different teams.

Among the stars-of-stars who called it quits in 1971 were two future Hall-of-Famers. Jim Bunning was a 20-game winner only once but won 19 on four other occasions and was a mainstay of both the Detroit Tigers' and Philadelphia Phillies' rotations beginning in the late 1950s. Chicago's "Mr. Cub," Ernie Banks, retired with 512 lifetime home runs, a pair of NL MVP awards, and a legendary enthusiasm for the game of baseball that was surpassed by no one.

Bunning's passage to Cooperstown came via the Veterans' Committee in 1996, while Banks's arrival to the Hall was secured in 1977, his first time on the voters' ballot.

Remarkably, the crowd at Wrigley Field in Mr. Cub's final game was only 18,505, this coming in an age where not as much emphasis was placed by fans on being present for a pre-determined farewell. Although everyone in attendance had the privilege of witnessing the end of a truly remarkable career, Banks remained dedicated to the mission of the day: "There'll be no nostalgia. Let's just play this one to win. Let's have everyone go home happy, except the Phillies," he said before taking the field.[56] Like Bunning in his heyday with Detroit and Philadelphia, Banks wore uniform number

14, which was retired by the Phillies and the Cubs, respectively, for these star players.

One final departure—through the inevitability of death—occurred in the spring of 1971 upon the passing of former commissioner William Eckert, Bowie Kuhn's predecessor. The former Air Force general, possessed of virtually no knowledge about the national pastime, was miscast as a baseball executive, and his time in office was a short, regrettable endeavor, especially coming in the mid–1960s as professional football began its surge in popularity. Kuhn was asked to give a brief graveside testimony for Eckert's interment at Arlington National Cemetery, and he delivered remarks that were compassionate but necessarily omitted any reference to the obvious shortcomings of the deceased as pertained to his time as the sport's leading figurehead. "He came to us from a long and distinguished military career," Kuhn said of Eckert, continuing:

> He had little experience in Baseball but at our request he came to our game as Commissioner. I think he took this difficult assignment because he felt that service to our National Pastime was in a meaningful way a continued service to his country. Over the three years of his time with us he encountered perplexing problems, some beyond any near-term solution. These were critical years for baseball. In these years when the Commissioner's role demanded dedication almost beyond human power, he gave us his total devotion.... Yet however much he gave these years to Baseball, I think he would most like to be remembered here today as a man who loved his country and served it well. Now Spike is gone. He was our friend and we loved him. There is no way to measure how much we will miss him.[57]

Whereas Eckert was overmatched for the commissioner's seat, Kuhn brought baseball smarts with him but would be confronted and at times overwhelmed by problems that developed on baseball's evolving landscape, especially in the struggle with the players' union over the ensuing years.

The names and faces of baseball, never remaining static, remind us of the melting pot of personalities that arrive at and eventually find their way out of the game. Colorful, impactful, or self-destructive, they are all subject to the forces of the human condition and represent the good, the bad, and the indifferent among the population of the national pastime.

3

Fresh Faces at the Helm

In one of the baseball community's most important books, historian Paul Dickson notes that the term "skipper" has Dutch etymology rooted in the word *schipper*, used "as a form of address for the captain or master of a ship."[1] Such a man in charge of a watercraft needs to be possessed of a temperament able to handle every situation encountered in both maritime conditions and the disposition of the crew under his command. There is no coincidence that his duties are also mirrored in those of the manager of a baseball team, who is tasked with guiding his team through the uncertain passages of its schedule while dealing with the various personalities on his roster.

The earlier history of the national pastime is populated with successful managers whose conduct and demeanor ranged from calmly stoic (Connie Mack) to confrontational (John McGraw), from affable (Wilbert Robinson) to pensive (Joe McCarthy). Whatever means this clutch employed to spur their charges, they nonetheless reached a common bond of winning pennants if not baseball's ultimate prize of a World Series championship, and as the 1970s began, a fresh group of managers was given the responsibility of molding their club's lineup in pursuit of a title.

Several managers in this select faction actually debuted on the cusp of the new decade and quickly produced victorious teams under the divisional arrangement created when the latest round of expansion was implemented in 1969. An even narrower subset of them established winning reputations that fostered continuing success on the field and subsequently led to enshrinement in the Baseball Hall of Fame. These skippers, to employ the above moniker, made their respective marks on the game and, for the most part, were able to take best advantage of the players they had at their disposal.

At midseason of the 1968 American League campaign, first-base coach Earl Weaver of the Baltimore Orioles was handed the club's managerial reins when Hank Bauer was dismissed during the All-Star break. The 37-year-old Weaver was no stranger to scrappiness, being born in St. Louis and having grown up admiring the Cardinals' famed Gas House Gang, to whom he delivered their uniforms from his father's dry cleaning business. As a young ballplayer, Weaver emulated the style of play he saw the Cards demonstrate at Sportsman's Park, and despite never growing beyond his frame of just over five and a half feet in height, his grit on local high school fields caught the attention of the St. Louis Browns director of minor league operations, Jim McLaughlin.

From his youth, "Earl was an intelligent player," observed McLaughlin years later, but Weaver's ability as an undersized infielder took him only so far in the Cardinal farm system after the team signed him.[2] The odds, already long, against Weaver joining the big club as a second baseman grew even more daunting when he estimated that there were more than 50 men competing for the same position at the franchise's spring camp in Albany, Georgia, in 1948. Yet, his perseverance shone through in decent fielding and adequate hitting that earned him four most valuable player awards in various minor league cities, and three years later he gained an invitation to spring training with the Cardinals. Weaver made the most of his opportunity, capably filling in for Red Schoendienst, the regular second baseman who was holding out in a salary tussle with club ownership, but when the issue was resolved, Weaver found himself back in the minors. The resentment he harbored about his demotion affected his performance, and Weaver's status as a hustling, Eddie Stanky–type of prospect eroded.

By the time his contract was sold to the Pittsburgh Pirates in 1955, Weaver had assumed the role of journeyman minor leaguer with little hope of reaching the majors. The following year, while still plying his trade as a second baseman, he accepted the chance to be player-manager of the Knoxville Smokies of the Class A South Atlantic League, described by Weaver's biographer as "the pits of the Sally League."[3] But this seemingly dead-end scenario quickly revealed a ray of hope when Baltimore Orioles assistant farm director Harry Dalton visited Knoxville and was impressed by Weaver's passion for his job. The Browns' recent relocation to Baltimore foretold of a reunion, of sorts, with Jim McLaughlin when he brought Weaver in to manage the Orioles' Class D club in Fitzgerald, Georgia, thereby commencing the manager's lengthy association with the Baltimore franchise. McLaughlin recognized his talent as "a natural manager," and the organization was in turn rewarded for having faith in Weaver despite the unwelcome reputation he was building as a thorn in the side of umpires.[4]

Working his way up Baltimore's minor league ladder over a total of 11 years, Weaver was also instrumental in the formation of what was

After becoming manager of the Baltimore Orioles midway through the 1968 season, Earl Weaver turned the club into an American League power that won three straight AL pennants.

termed the "Oriole way," a methodology of consistently instructing players throughout the farm system so that they would hone their skills without having to relearn them—or placate their current minor league manager—upon moving from one level to another. As Weaver himself progressed, he garnered three championships and five second-place finishes before his promotion to Baltimore, at general manager Harry Dalton's behest, as a coach in 1968. Although the Orioles had a respectable won-lost record of 43–37, they languished in third place in the American League and were ten and one-half games out of first. When Bauer was jettisoned as manager, he was of the opinion that coach Billy Hunter should have taken his place—"He knows the players better," claimed the now ex–Oriole—but Dalton wanted a fresh face "who would shake things up."[5]

Weaver's philosophy of picking his starting lineup tended to indulge a player's offensive ability over his defensive shortcomings, yet this was not necessarily applied in every case. Rather, his knack for "putting the right man in the right spot" was done with the purpose of "keeping the odds in favor of his team."[6] At the time of his naming as the Oriole manager, Weaver had inherited the framework of a sound ballclub, so a major rebuilding of the roster was hardly needed—Baltimore finished the 1968 season 48–34 under Weaver, good for second place but still 12 games behind Detroit. But the Major League landscape underwent a radical change in the runup to Opening Day in 1969.

Besides implementing rule changes that would put more run production back in the game, Major League Baseball expanded through the addition of two new clubs to both the American and National Leagues, prompting their split into East and West divisions containing six teams apiece. The Orioles were placed in the AL East along with the defending World Series champion Tigers, the Cleveland Indians, the New York Yankees, the Washington Senators, and the Boston Red Sox, who were only one year removed from their "Impossible Dream" season of 1967.

But a crucial trade executed by Dalton delivered Mike Cuellar to the Oriole pitching staff, and the southpaw won 23 games to become a co-recipient of the 1969 AL Cy Young Award. When solid offensive output from Frank Robinson, Brooks Robinson, Boog Powell, Don Buford, and Paul Blair combined with the strength of a rotation led by Cuellar, Dave McNally, Jim Palmer, and Tom Phoebus, Baltimore outpaced its divisional rivals with 109 victories, swept the Minnesota Twins in the inaugural American League Championship Series, and entered the World Series against the upstart New York Mets.

The Mets were not about to be intimidated by any foes that year, and dispatched the Orioles in five games. If any lessons were imparted to the Orioles, they only sharpened the team's focus for the following season. "We played equally tough baseball in 1970," wrote Weaver in his 1983 memoir, "winning 40 of the 55 games we engaged in that were decided by one run."[7] Purpose-driven and wanting to atone for the embarrassment of losing to the Mets, Baltimore seemed to coast to 108 wins, but Weaver's charges pressed on in September even though they had a double-digit lead in the AL East. Winning their final 11 regular-season contests provided momentum to again vanquish the Twins in the ALCS, but the Baltimore manager felt a palpable discomfort about facing the Cincinnati Reds in the World Series. "One thought kept reverberating through my mind: The Reds are going to win it. Somehow I couldn't shake my conviction that everything pointed to them," Weaver recalled.[8]

In the event, Brooks Robinson put on a command performance to take Series MVP laurels, and after winning two close games at brand-new Riverfront Stadium, the Orioles won two of three back home in Baltimore to capture their second World Series title. The postgame revelry following the clincher saw Dalton and Weaver deposited in the training room's ice water–laden whirlpool tub, and the manager minded not a bit—he was thrilled to have reached the apex of the baseball world. He also was quick to acknowledge the team concept that resulted in this success, saying, "Everything has been easy for me. Twenty-five ball players made it easy."[9] Indeed, Weaver was learning how to manipulate his lineup for profit, and he became supremely skilled at using his entire roster, an ability that firmly validated Jim McLaughlin's observation.

Weaver had taken umbrage at being labeled a "push-button manager" by some members of the media, and he countered the claim by pointing out that "I had gone through a stretch of more than 40 ball games in which I'd had a different lineup everyday."[10] It was exactly this skill that demonstrated his desire to prevent reserves from sitting on the bench too long as well as make minor adjustments to the batting order so that the offense could maximize its output based on advantageous matchups versus opposing pitchers.

A profitable defense of their title in 1971 seemed nearly a foregone conclusion for Baltimore. With little turnover on the roster, Weaver once more had his team running like a fine-tuned machine, yet he even admitted that his team "played good but not great ball in the first seven weeks of the season."[11] He pointed to the nightcap of a May 31 doubleheader as the turning point that began a nine-game winning streak and propelled the club into first place for the remainder of the year. Although the Orioles' regular-season win total slipped to 101 victories, they remained unbeaten in ALCS action by sweeping Oakland for their third straight American League title. "Next year we break the record. We'll make it four in a row," claimed the manager, referring to setting a new standard for consecutive 100-win seasons.[12] Of more immediate concern was the upcoming World Series against Pittsburgh, and in anticipation of another victory in the Fall Classic, Weaver mocked the push-button tag by claiming, "I've got *too* good a ball club. It just keeps on winning."[13]

History shows that Weaver had hoisted his own petard: The Orioles jumped to a two-game lead over the Pirates, but Baltimore ultimately lost in seven games of this thrilling World Series. The club that kept on winning fell one game short, although he was quick to give appropriate credit. "[Roberto] Clemente was great, [Bruce] Kison turned the Series around," acknowledged Weaver in citing two valuable members of the opposition, "but [Steve] Blass was Mr. World Series."[14] If the disappointment of missing a second successive world title left any kind of a lasting mark, it was not in evidence very long as the Orioles soon departed on a month-long tour of Japan that was thoroughly enjoyed by the Baltimore entourage.

Never losing his trademark feistiness—Weaver eventually totaled 96 ejections as well as several suspensions over his managerial career—he gave Oriole fans good reason for hope each season because of his ability to field a competitive team. For the remainder of his first tenure as Baltimore's manager, up to and including the 1982 campaign, the Orioles could be expected to be in the hunt for the AL East pennant, finishing as low as third or fourth place on just three occasions while coming in first or second all other years.[15] His diligence leading a small-market club was no mean feat: Once free agency became a reality in 1977, a season in which the Orioles lost some key personnel, Weaver's ability was tested especially against a resurgent New York Yankee team whose owner, George Steinbrenner, was willing to spend lavishly to assemble his own powerhouse roster. That Baltimore remained so competitive in the face of seemingly overwhelming odds sheds ample light on the qualifications that earned Earl Weaver his place in the Baseball Hall of Fame.

The Cincinnati Reds, Earl Weaver's opponents in the 1970 World Series, had not been to the postseason since 1961, when they were ousted by a New York Yankees team that many rank as among the greatest of all time. In the final season prior to National League expansion, the Reds outlasted the Los Angeles Dodgers to take the NL pennant by four games, but they lost all three of their home games to the Bronx Bombers in the Fall Classic. Cincinnati remained competitive under manager Fred Hutchinson in 1962 and again in the frantic NL pennant race of 1964, a season in which "Hutch" stepped away after 109 games in order to take treatment for lung cancer. Dick Sisler brought the club to within one game of taking the title, but thereafter the Reds seemed destined to be a team mediocre at best.

This mediocrity, mostly under the guidance of manager Dave Bristol, was nonetheless attended by a slow influx of newer players who gave hope for the future. As the names of Pete Rose, Tony Pérez, Tommy Helms, Lee May, and Johnny Bench gained traction in the Reds lineup and fueled expectations of a pennant in the first year of divisional play in 1969, misfortunes with the pitching staff wrought havoc, especially with Gary Nolan and Jim Maloney unable for many starting assignments. Finishing in third place just four games behind Atlanta was not enough to save Bristol's job at season's end, and the Reds moved swiftly to fill the vacancy.

At a press conference on October 9, Cincinnati general manager Bob Howsam introduced George Anderson as the new skipper, and unfairly or not, *The Sporting News* marked the occasion by observing, "The firing of Bristol wasn't a big surprise. He had been expected to guide the Reds to a flag just as Anderson is expected to do in 1970."[16] But "Sparky," as Anderson was better known, arrived in the Queen City well-credentialed.

Born in 1934 in Bridgewater, South Dakota, a town populated by fewer than 650 people, Sparky was the second of five children born to Lee Roy and Shirley Anderson, and when the clan moved away from the harsh winters of the upper Midwest to Los Angeles in 1942, the youngster quickly took a liking to baseball. Despite claiming to enjoy basketball as his favorite sport, Sparky found fast company with the head coach of the University of Southern California baseball team, Rod Dedeaux, who let Sparky serve as the Trojan batboy as long as he kept his grades in school up to standard. Anderson's time spent with Dedeaux, when conflated with the examples set by his father, shaped Sparky's personality.

"My daddy was ... lead-pipe tough," Anderson recalled, "he taught me never to run scared." Although his father "got into some of the nastiest fights you could ever imagine, [he] didn't want [his children] fighting," at the same time he imparted the important lesson of simply being nice to people to cultivate good relationships.[17]

Sparky Anderson delivered a National League pennant to Cincinnati in 1970, his first year at the helm of the Reds. Under his leadership, the team became one of the most dominant in baseball through the mid-1970s.

For Dedeaux's part, the legendary collegiate coach recognized Sparky's intensity but he "taught me another dimension. He taught me enthusiasm."[18]

As Sparky's baseball skills improved, he abandoned the basketball court to concentrate on the diamond, and his American Legion team won the 1951 national championship. Not least to further these formative aspects of Anderson's early life, he met Harold "Lefty" Phillips, a part-time scout for the Cincinnati Reds who would sign Sparky to his first contract in 1953 when Phillips moved to the Brooklyn Dodger organization.

An undersized prospect at just five-foot, nine inches in height, Sparky was a second baseman who carried his grit with him as he worked his way up the ladder of the Dodger farm system and made the Major League 40-man roster in 1958. Disappointed in being demoted to class Triple-A Montreal, he nonetheless kept to his work ethic and earned recognition as the Royals' most valuable player, a feat that drew the notice of the Philadelphia Phillies. When the Phils acquired him in a trade in 1959, Sparky became their regular second baseman, but having hit a meager .218 for a basement-dwelling team, his job security was short-lived. He was sold to Toronto of the International League (IL), for whom he played and also drew his first managerial assignment in 1964.

For the time that Anderson spent playing in the IL, "the *Toronto Globe & Mail* [annually] published a poll rating the league's top players in a variety of categories. For all seven years Sparky was voted 'smartest player in the league.'"[19] That level of intelligence continued to be honed when he moved to the St. Louis Cardinal organization and won the Western Carolinas League championship in 1965, took the St. Petersburg team to the Florida State League finals (but lost) in 1966, and after pairing up with future Cincinnati Reds general manager Bob Howsam, led the Modesto Reds to the 1967 California League finals and captured the Southern League crown in 1968 at Asheville. His journey through the minor leagues ended when he accepted a position as a coach with the new expansion San Diego Padres in 1969.

Las Vegas odds-makers installed Cincinnati as 8–1 favorites to win the 1970 NL pennant, fifth overall among senior circuit clubs, with St. Louis, the top favorite, and Atlanta chosen to win their respective divisions. Scribe Earl Lawson rated the Reds' offense as "pennant caliber" but recapped the team's chances with a cautionary note: "Same old story. Team will go as far as pitching carries it."[20] The overt challenge in *The Sporting News* statement upon Anderson's hiring, indicating pressure to produce for the Reds in 1970, was a gauntlet that the rookie manager picked up with gusto.

In a cultural sense, 1970 was simply an extension of the 1960s, a time when defiance of authority, especially as manifest in protests against the war in Vietnam, pervaded American society. From Sparky's perspective, he believed that it was his responsibility to set the tone for the manner in which he would discipline his players and how he expected them to comport themselves. "How a manager conducts his life goes a long way in determining how his players act. If a manager acts like a jerk, chances are his players will act like jerks. If a manager meets his responsibilities and conducts himself with dignity, chances are his players will do the same."[21] Anderson brooked none of the physical appearances that defined the younger, carefree generation: his men would not be adorned with facial hair—or any long hair, for that matter—and they wore proper attire on road trips.

"[S]ome players called his spring training a 'slave camp,'" but this was the manner in which Anderson believed the fundamentals of baseball were to be stressed, and the results he obtained at the minor league level soon followed him when he became a Major League manager.[22] Although Sparky was not bashful about dressing down the entire squad—he would do this in general terms without mentioning specific names—he was less interested in frequent team meetings than in dealing with players individually, favoring face-to-face sessions as his preferred means of communication to address issues. He held these conversations in private, and to gain the trust of his men, he promised to never reveal the content of the discussion.

Anderson's stroll to the NL West crown in 1970 appears to be a cakewalk. Other than a one-day slip to second place in the season's opening week, Cincinnati led its division wire-to-wire, and at the end of the regular campaign, the pitching staff's composite earned run average of 3.69 was second only to that of the New York Mets, a statistic that was nicely complemented by their league-leading 60 saves. The Reds indeed went as far as their pitchers carried them.

Yet, the final numbers mask the ordeal that Sparky endured in guiding the Reds to the NL's only 100-win record, 102 to be exact. He lost the services of five pitchers over the course of the year, not least among them top starter Jim Maloney, but the skipper was able to rely on fresh arms to fill the voids. When the Reds swept the Pittsburgh Pirates in the National League Championship Series, they appeared to be well-matched against Baltimore in the World Series, but Brooks Robinson stole the show in leading the Orioles to victory. Curiously, in a poll of Major League managers by *The Sporting News*, Pittsburgh's Danny Murtaugh was chosen by his peers as the Manager of the Year, garnering eight votes, while the New York Yankees' Ralph Houk (five votes) placed second, and Anderson, in spite of his rookie job status and a record superior to all other NL clubs, received only four.

Installed as favorites to repeat as NL West champs if not NL titlists in 1971, Cincinnati was hit very hard by injuries to a pair of starting pitchers as well as the loss of outfielder Bobby Tolan, who missed the entire year with a ruptured Achilles tendon. Dropping to fourth place, the Reds also suffered from a decline in offensive output from most of the regulars, and the resulting 79–83 won-lost record proved to be a humbling experience. Soul searching by general manager Bob Howsam would lead to one of baseball's greatest trades and invigorate the vaunted Big Red Machine for most of the coming five seasons.

That trade fortified the Reds' transformation into one of the signature teams of the 1970s, and Sparky Anderson would be on hand for the entire stretch. Following his controversial dismissal from Cincinnati near the close of the decade and his subsequent hiring by the Detroit Tigers, for whom he provided both leadership and a World Series championship, he, too, would be enshrined in Cooperstown.

Unlike his managerial peers mentioned above, Dick Williams had a lengthy Major League career as a player that lasted from 1951 to 1964. Like Earl Weaver, Williams was a native of St. Louis, born in 1929 on the cusp of the Great Depression. He admitted in his adult life that he suffered "child abuse" and "special beatings" at the hands of his father, Harvey, when discipline was lacking.[23] Williams's older brother Ellery was a member of the Sportsman's Park "Knothole Gang," and through him Dick was able to cultivate a youthful love of baseball, especially the rougher side of the game as demonstrated by the play of the Gas House Gang. The charitable side of Harvey also had a positive influence in helping his sons enjoy the game, sometimes taking them to watch neighboring amateur contests at which he occasionally served as an umpire.

Despite the harsh treatment of his father, Williams learned the value of authority and its application, assets that would serve him well later on. When Harvey relocated the family to Hollywood, California, Dick became completely immersed in high school athletics, taking a special interest in baseball. He drew the notice of a Brooklyn Dodger scout—this was in 1947, a decade before the team moved to the West Coast—and signed for a modest bonus of only $1,200 and began toiling in the low minor leagues. "I was a good ballplayer—I swung the bat well and hustled my ass off," Williams wrote years later, "but I always had to be something more. I had to be the intimidating ballplayer, the mean ballplayer, the guy who left no doubt about his intentions."[24]

Williams in these formative years developed a distaste for losing, further hardening his authoritarian views and honing a penchant for throwing tantrums while also learning the tricks of the managerial trade by paying close attention to Bobby Bragan, one of his managers in the Brooklyn farm system. From the Brooklyn dugout where he spent time as a bench jockey, Williams witnessed firsthand the Dodgers' infamous collapse during the 1951 NL pennant race. Yet he learned the valuable lesson of "need[ing] to radiate calm confidence more than the shared worry" of panicking when events take a turn for the worse.[25] This brave facade, however, belied the intensity that never deserted him.

His diligence and ability to play a variety of positions earned him several callups to the Dodgers from 1951 to 1956, but his playing time with the veteran-laden Brooklyn team was limited. A severe shoulder separation in an August 1952 game at St. Louis thwarted what could have been a noteworthy Major League career, and in 1956 he was waived by the Dodgers and claimed by the Baltimore Orioles. With the exception of catcher and shortstop, Williams played around the diamond and proved that he could hit big league pitching. Despite spending his remaining playing career mostly with second-division clubs—Kansas City, Cleveland, and Boston were his other stops—he could wield some power (11 home runs in 1956, 16 and 12 during 1959 and 1960, his two seasons with the Athletics), and finished with a .260 lifetime average.

By the time Williams donned a Red Sox uniform in 1963 with his hardened attitude still intact, he bristled at what he found at Fenway Park. "The place was a country club," he recalled of the lax atmosphere that prioritized having fun rather than winning: "[T]he best way to describe the entire Red Sox state of mind in the early sixties [was] ... Losers."[26] Having complained so much about the manner in which management handled its personnel, Williams was given a challenge by the franchise's minor league director, namely to manage for himself so that he could see how difficult a task it really was. Upon his release after the 1964 season, Williams was offered a position as player/coach for Boston's Triple-A affiliate in Seattle, but when that club was shifted to Toronto for the 1965 season, he was unexpectedly given the chance to manage the Maple Leafs despite having no previous managerial experience other than for a rookie team in a spring training intrasquad contest.

Williams quickly made an impression with the Red Sox front office when he led Toronto to a pair of International League pennants in 1965 and 1966. When the Major League club faltered in that latter year, winning only 72 games and finishing in ninth place 26 games behind American League and World Series champion Baltimore, Boston could only anticipate improvement by changing managers. Indeed, there was nowhere to go but up, which is exactly what happened when Williams was promoted and steered the Red Sox through 1967's frantic pennant race that came to be known in Boston as "The Impossible Dream," a co-opting of a song from the recently popular Broadway musical *Man of La Mancha*.

This magical journey was fully invested with the new manager's stern approach that was a complete turnaround from what some Sox veterans had become accustomed to. Just as Williams was offended by the laid-back approach he found at Fenway, so too were many players put off by the brusque, businesslike attitude now being foisted upon them. But he was determined to instill respect in his men and have them playing fundamentally sound baseball. Williams believed that he had been hired to win games, not make friends, and he seemed to accomplish both.

Although the Red Sox edged out three other contenders for the 1967 AL title then lost the World Series to the St. Louis Cardinals in seven games, they were still the toast of the baseball world for having overachieved. But this derring-do also created the expectation of a repeat performance, however unfairly such hopes may have been raised. Boston fell victim to several instances of misfortune in 1968, not least of which was the loss of the services of Cy Young Award–winning pitcher Jim Lonborg due to an offseason skiing injury. When the Red Sox dropped to a record of 86–76 and fell to fourth place 17 games behind Detroit, the novelty for Williams was wearing off, and he admitted to venting his anger—verbally, not physically—on his wife and children as well as trying to find solace in a bottle of Scotch.[27]

By 1969, Red Sox players grew increasingly disgruntled with their manager, and Williams's relationship with team owner Tom Yawkey was souring. Sox star Carl Yastrzemski, always a favorite of the Boston mogul, was fined and pulled from a game in early August for failing to employ his best effort, a disciplinary action that raised eyebrows. "Williams maybe wanted to light a fire under the team," observed Red Sox historian Bill Nowlin, but the move only put the manager in an even deeper hole.[28]

That former Red Sox legend Ted Williams was enjoying success in his first year as a Major League skipper with the Washington Senators perhaps gave Yawkey reason for pause, but as the campaign drew to a close, Dick Williams was fired even though Boston fared well by winning 87 games, still no match for the burgeoning powerhouse Orioles who were victorious 109 times. The now ex-manager blamed Yawkey more than the fallout from any curdled interaction with his players, but Williams put this chapter of his life behind him by returning north of the border.

Hired as the Montreal Expos third-base coach, Williams spent 1970 partnered with the team's manager, Gene Mauch, and he found the experience worthwhile. Renowned as one of the game's better tacticians, Mauch influenced his new coach by "advancing his knowledge of how to think ahead two or three innings, [and] how to balance work and rest for bullpen pitchers."²⁹ With the Expos in only their second year of play, there was little pressure for the club to contend, and Williams's stint in Montreal provided him with time to decompress by way of curtailing his drinking as well as stabilizing relations with his family.

For all the advantages that accrued to this lifestyle change and the detour in his career, Williams never lost the desire to run a ball club once more, and a job opening was created in the immediate aftermath of the 1970 season when Oakland manager John McNamara, a relatively mild-mannered sort, was ousted by the team's owner, Charlie Finley. Athletics catcher Dave Duncan sparked controversy with a remark that Finley, not only as an owner but also an incessant meddler in the daily functioning of all aspects of the club, was the de facto manager and that players were reluctant to voice any opinions for fear of losing their job.

Finley took umbrage at Duncan's comment but vented his wrath at McNamara for failing to control his player, and with the Athletics having barely closed out the season, McNamara was fired. The move bewildered McNamara, who claimed that it was not his place "to go around and censor ballplayers on what they say or check reporters' notes before they leave the clubhouse. Also, there's the First Amendment."³⁰ That wholesome segment of the Bill of Rights remains an important part of a citizen's entitlement, but its exercise can also prove to be detrimental to one's employment. In Finley's view, criticism of him from any source—Oakland's rising star, Reggie Jackson, also found himself being benched

Manager of the Boston Red Sox "Impossible Dream" team of 1967, Dick Williams turned the Oakland Athletics into an American League West pennant winner in 1971 and took the team to World Series titles in 1972 and 1973.

for unwanted comments—was unacceptable. The owner had considered bringing in the fiery Billy Martin halfway through the season to provide a spark that McNamara lacked, but for 1971 Finley turned to Dick Williams, already battle-tested during "The Impossible Dream" episode.

The Athletics had finished 1970 in second place in the AL West with 89 wins, just nine games behind the Minnesota Twins, and their roster was stocked with a bevy of young talent that, given the proper handling, might be capable of reaching the top of the division. As Dick Williams embarked on his second managerial job at the Major League level, he said, "I'm from the old school as far as fundamentals and execution are concerned, but I believe in letting them play their game on the field." Recounting his earlier run-in with Carl Yastrzemski, the new Oakland manager added, "If they hustle, we won't have any problems. The only thing I've ever asked is that they give 100 percent. If they didn't, then I had to take action."[31]

Handling his players was one thing, but dealing with an irascible owner was quite another. Williams and Finley had only briefly crossed paths back in the spring of 1961 when the former was still wearing an Athletics uniform and getting in shape for the coming season, while the latter had recently purchased the team, which was based in Kansas City at the time, and was getting his first taste of club ownership. Williams was traded to the Orioles in April and had no further contact with his former team, but less than a decade later, the circumstances surrounding the owner, one-time player, and the relocated ballclub were vastly different.

Finley's choice for his new manager returned a prompt dividend when the 1971 Athletics improved by 12 victories over the previous season, ending with a 101–60 record and winning the AL West by a resounding 16-game margin over the runner-up Kansas City Royals. By tying powerful Baltimore for the most victories in the American League, Oakland served notice that its own youthful roster was ready to make its mark as a contender. Exposed to an ownership milieu that was the polar opposite of his experience with Tom Yawkey in Boston, Williams's tenure in Oakland would last three seasons before he stepped away following the Athletics' uproarious 1973 World Series win over the New York Mets. Unable to tolerate Finley's interference with the roster in the wake of the infamous Mike Andrews incident, Williams had announced in private to his team that he was resigning at the conclusion of the Series, and he expressed amazement of having lasted as long as he did without being fired by the cantankerous Finley.

Although Dick Williams failed to work his winning magic with the same frequency of the first six years in which he served as a Major League manager—his later seasons with the California Angels and the Seattle Mariners were particularly fraught—he led the San Diego Padres to their first National League pennant in 1984. As described by one of his biographers, Williams excelled because of his "skill to use what resources were on hand.... He could adapt his tactics to the roster he had, something few managers beyond baseball could do."[32] This talent, in addition to the pennants his teams captured, earned him his induction into the Baseball Hall of Fame in 2008.

The anodyne entry for "MARTIN, Alfred Manuel" in the 1971 Detroit Tigers media guide shows much information about Billy Martin's days playing across several minor and Major Leagues, yet those who look closely will see his eye-popping .392 batting average and 174 RBIs with Phoenix of the Class C Arizona-Texas League in 1947. "The name 'Billy' had come from 'Belliz,' an Italian diminutive meaning 'most beautiful' which was the nickname he had been given by a relative when he was young."[33] That glowing appellation, however, contradicted the outward manifestation of Martin's often pugnacious demeanor that he developed from an early age growing up in the hardened section of West Berkeley, California. Fighting was a lifestyle if not a means of survival, and Martin learned how to stand his ground lest he succumb to the unsavory aspects of the street. He augmented this by becoming an amateur boxer while also gaining experience as a sandlot baseball player.

Born in 1928, Martin seems to have remained in high school only for the sake of playing sports as well as suiting up for an amateur team associated with the Oakland Oaks of the Pacific Coast League (PCL). After his graduation in 1946, Martin signed with a Class D team in Idaho Falls and later caught the attention of the Oaks, who saw enough promise in Martin to buy his contract. Martin's new club was managed by Casey Stengel, and it was the "Old Perfesser" who took a most active interest in developing the youngster's skills. After two years of seasoning with the Oaks, Martin was sold to the New York Yankees, who sent him to Kansas City of the American Association in 1950 before recalling him to the Bronx, where he was reunited with Stengel.

Not a player to hit for a high average, Martin's "forte was his consistent defense and his ability to come up with big hits in crucial situations."[34] For a Yankee lineup featuring the likes of Yogi Berra, Mickey Mantle, and other big run producers, Martin's relative lack of punch was a luxury that Stengel could afford. But despite the assets he brought to the club, Martin never gained a level of maturity that allowed him to step away from potential trouble. "Off the field he ran with Mickey Mantle and Whitey Ford. Their often alcohol-fueled antics were not viewed favorably by the Yankee management, which saw Martin as a bad influence on their star players."[35]

When Martin became a central figure in a donnybrook at New York's Copacabana nightclub, the front office traded him to the Kansas City Athletics, thereby initiating a desultory journey with six different teams in as many years until he was released by the Minnesota Twins in the spring of 1962.

Martin's post-playing career included his work with the Twins as a scout and a return to the Twin Cities in 1965 as a coach under manager Sam Mele. Martin coached third base and was instrumental in raising the degree of aggressiveness the Twins showed on the base paths, a trait that help Minnesota to its first pennant since the team's relocation from Washington in 1961. Three years after his initial coaching success, Martin was handed the reins of the Denver Bears, the Twins' Triple-A club in the PCL, partway through the 1968 season, and his success in the Mile High City encouraged the Twins to hire Martin for his first managerial job at the Major League level.

At the age of 41, Martin turned around a Minnesota team that had grown limpid after almost winning the AL pennant in 1967. Dropping to seventh place with a losing record of 79–83 in 1968 under Cal Ermer, the Twins hired Martin, who "forged the team into his own image: aggressive on the bases and well versed in the subtleties of base stealing, the hit and run, and the suicide squeeze."[36] Rebounding in 1969 when the American League split into two divisions, Minnesota won the AL West, its 97 wins second only to the Baltimore Orioles across all American League teams. But when the Twins were swept by the Orioles in the first League Championship Series, club owner Calvin Griffith, who had sparred frequently with Martin, dismissed his manager in order to restore a sense of calm. That Martin had previously engaged one of his starting pitchers, Dave Boswell, in a fight in August, served as an updated version of the Copacabana affair, demonstrating that Martin's combativeness was ever-present.

Work for Grain Belt Brewery and a Minneapolis radio station filled a void in Martin's life, but he was impatient to get back to where he felt he belonged. He told a reporter in the spring of 1970 that nobody would hire him, yet finding comfort with his current employment, he said, "I don't need baseball anymore."[37] That little bit of venting may have been good for his soul, but it would be hard to believe that he could remain away from the dugout for very long. As mentioned above, Charlie Finley discussed bringing Martin in as the new Athletics manager and they had an agreement in principle, at least according to the Oakland owner. But after Calvin Griffith informed Finley of some of the unsavory aspects of dealing with Martin, Finley scuttled his plans for hiring him.

When the Detroit Tigers fell below .500 that year, their front office believed that a firebrand to replace manager Mayo Smith would put the club back on a winning path and "change the chemistry of the team."[38] General manager Jim Campbell confessed to Martin that there were a few uncomfortable factors he would need to confront as manager: several cliques in the clubhouse, a degree of complacency that lingered from the team's triumph in the 1968 World Series, and a roster comprised of mostly veterans who were growing old together and reluctant to modify the style of play to which they had grown accustomed under Smith. Further, there were issues with the left side of the infield, where inconsistencies among several shortstops and third basemen were a problem.

In early October 1970, Martin was introduced as the new Tiger manager, and at his first press conference in Detroit he stated, "Defense makes pitching and we'll do something about the defense." With a dash of swagger, he added, "If I didn't think we had a chance to win next year, I wouldn't be here."[39] Barely one week later, Campbell announced the trade that at once shored up the major infield weaknesses and removed the nettlesome Denny McLain from Detroit before he had a chance to engage Martin. But the manager was intent on fulfilling a commitment he made at the media gathering, namely to personally visit each of his new players.

Quickly wearing out his welcome in 1969 as manager of the Minnesota Twins, Billy Martin brought his fiery style to the Detroit Tigers in 1971.

Paying a call to Tiger left fielder Willie Horton, Martin "laid it on the line for me. He believed that I could be a better player than I had shown the previous two seasons." Horton accepted Martin's evaluation that he would find time on the bench unless he put more energy into his performance on a full-time basis. This was a wake-up call that Horton appreciated because if Martin "had to offend some people along the way or hurt his own reputation to [succeed], he was willing to pay the price.... He wanted his players to believe they had to re-earn their starting positions every day."⁴⁰

"Billy Martin—Born a Battler," was the heading of feature in a 1971 Tiger publication that stressed this characteristic of his personality. "Once it was said of him, 'He's a manager's type of player, a leader, a scrapper.' Now, they say the same—in reverse." Martin was quoted as indicating that loyalty between him and his players was expected to be shown both ways, and he refused to tolerate "alibiers, con men, complainers and liars."⁴¹

The Tigers finally began to evince the traits of their manager's toughness, and after playing just over .500 ball through late July, they stirred and made a gainful run at the ever-powerful Baltimore Orioles, ultimately finishing in second place with a 91–71 record, twelve games off the pace but still the third-best win total in the American League. "I enjoyed this year," said future Hall-of-Famer Al Kaline. "The way we finished leaves a good taste in your mouth."⁴² Martin employed innovation at times, such as when he batted Kaline second in the order, and he was not afraid to put a player in an uncomfortable spot in an effort to make him adjust in facing his fears and hopefully be successful. Psychology was certainly part of Martin's repertoire.

Detroit bought into their manager's philosophy and went one step farther in 1972, unseating Baltimore for the AL East pennant, although that season was marred by the stilted schedule resulting from the early April games that were cancelled due to the strike by Major League players. Not every team played an equal number of contests, and the Tigers outlasted the Boston Red Sox by defeating them in a season-ending, head-to-head matchup at Tiger Stadium, finishing one-half game ahead of the Sox.

Unfortunately for Martin, his tour of duty in the Motor City was the second time in which he wore out his welcome, and he was fired with one month of the 1973 regular season remaining. The pattern of turning a team's fortunes around to be followed shortly by one controversy or another—and a requisite dismissal—was established. "All the Way with Billy the Kid," was the title of an upbeat cartoon by Bill Gallo that depicts the Tiger manager exhorting his team by demanding, "I said WIN... I don't care HOW... but WIN!"⁴³ Winning was Martin's hallmark, and there have been calls over the years to have him added to the Hall of Fame, but the less than wholesome baggage of his pugnacity has always thwarted these attempts.

Polar-opposite in his demeanor from Billy Martin was another product of the Brooklyn Dodger system whose managerial skills were not evident at the onset of his post-playing career but whose place in baseball history would be fated in the most positive manner and, sadly, a most tragic way. The record of Gil Hodges while leading the Washington Senators did not necessarily portend how events would develop during his second managerial job, this being most famously with the New York Mets. Neither could anyone possibly know that 1971 would be his final season nor that just days short of his 48th birthday in the spring of the following year he would be fatally struck down by a heart attack. The truncated managerial endeavor of Hodges will remain a subject for debate as to how many more championships the Mets might have garnered had he lived.

In a playing career that spanned the middle of World War II—as a teenager he appeared in a single game for Brooklyn in 1943 before spending the next two seasons in the Marines—until his retirement in 1963, Hodges belted 370 home runs, the most at the time by a National League righthanded batter. This slugging prowess was further enhanced by his eight All-Star selections and the three Gold Gloves he earned as the cornerstone at first base for the great Dodger teams of the 1950s, and finally in 2022 the Golden Days Era Committee saw fit to vote him into the Hall of Fame as a player.

As a 39-year-old trying to hang on with the expansion Mets and recuperating from knee surgery in May 1963, Hodges was contemplating what the future held for him. Pee Wee Reese, his Dodger teammate for so many years, had indicated that Hodges would be ill-suited for leading a team because he was "the nicest guy in the world and is so good-natured, so kind and gentle that he doesn't fit the managerial description."[44] George Selkirk, the Washington Senators general manager, traded Jimmy Piersall to New York in exchange for Hodges, who was installed as the new Solon skipper despite having no prior experience. Casey Stengel, Hodges's Met manager, directed praise toward his former player, citing his desire "to work with young players and he has the ability to teach them the things that made him a great hitter and a great defensive player."[45]

Selkirk seemed to make an incongruous choice for his new manager, and while Hodges's easy manner may have been an asset while serving as an instructor, running a club under Selkirk's edict "for a tough attitude toward careless ball players" was another matter.[46] At least Hodges's apprenticeship would be with a third-year expansion team, so there was little expectation to bring home a pennant-winner. Washington finished in the basement in 1963 with a dreadful 56–106 record—Hodges logged a 42–79 mark since taking the reins—but over the ensuing four seasons the Senators showed gradual improvement. The following year they won six more games and escaped the AL basement by finishing ninth; in 1965 Hodges moved the team to eighth place on a 70–92 record; there was a repeat eighth-place finish in 1966, winning 71 games in the process; and in 1967 Washington tied with Baltimore for sixth on the strength of 76 wins against 85 losses.

The learning experience for Hodges was complicated by the culture of the mid-1960s as shown by his run-in with Ken "Hawk" Harrelson, whose mod looks and free-spirited demeanor conflicted with his manager's conservative tastes and comportment. Yet, Hawk later paid tribute to Hodges by acknowledging the manager's instruction in the techniques of how to play first base, and the steady rise in Washington's win total, stemming from their manager's ability to coax increasing production from his men, was earning him credibility. Developing a methodology for handling the pitching staff, in which he was aided by coach Rube Walker, became a hallmark of Hodges's assets.

No doubt observing this progression was the front office of the New York Mets, and their chairman, M. Donald Grant, saw the struggles of the club as it briefly shed its "lovable loser" reputation in 1966 by finishing in ninth place and *not* losing 100 games for the first time in franchise history. But after winning 66 games and taking the defeat 95 times that year, the Mets backslid in 1967 to tenth place (61–101 record, 40½ games behind St. Louis), and it was time to take corrective action.

Through another trade consummated between the Mets and Senators during the 1967 Winter Meetings, Hodges returned to New York in a deal that sent pitcher Bill Denehy and a reported $150,000 to Washington. The manager wasted little time in molding his new club according to his needs. "From the time he arrived in 1968, Gil Hodges methodically, studiously began creating a positive clubhouse culture that allowed every individual piece of the Mets' whole to feel important.... [he] understood the importance of making every player feel involved, keeping every player fresh, giving everyone on his roster a slice of ownership in what the collective team was doing."[47]

That first edition of the Mets under Hodges failed to raise the temperature very much at Shea Stadium if only viewed from the standpoint of the club's ninth-place finish. However, the gain of 12 additional victories over their 1967 win total that set a new club record of 73 was admirable, although it came at a steep price for Hodges when he suffered a mild heart attack—his three-pack-a-day cigarette habit was wreaking havoc on his health—as the 1968 season drew to a close. This pivotal year was fueled by the performance of several young pitchers, including Tom Seaver, Jerry Koosman, and Nolan Ryan, and if New York could improve its weak offense, which ranked last in team batting average and ninth in runs scored, perhaps pennant contention was in the Mets' future.

As storied as the Boston Red Sox "Impossible Dream" run had been, the attainment of the World Championship by the Mets in 1969 obviously went one better, and Hodges's steady hand was instrumental in making that run by the "Miracle Mets" a reality. Counseled by doctors to remain as calm as possible following his coronary of the previous year, "[o]nly twice during the unbelievable season did Hodges lose his cool. Once behind closed doors, another time in front of several thousand Shea Stadium fans."[48] His dressing-down of the team and his pulling of left fielder Cleon Jones from a game—Hodges was dissatisfied with Jones's effort in chasing down a double and calmly walked out to remove him in the middle of the inning—left no doubt as to who was in charge of the team.

Jones was easily the Mets' best hitter, but this prowess was no excuse for his slipshod play. After walking out to confront Jones, "Hodges did an about-face and plodded to the dugout, followed a dozen paces behind him by the only .346 hitter he had."[49] This public embarrassment showed that no player was above the standard demanded by Hodges.

Over the course of a momentous season, the Mets overcame the challenge from their biggest divisional rival, the Chicago Cubs, to win the National League East pennant, then swept the NL West titlist Atlanta Braves in the first NL Championship Series, and achieved everlasting glory by defeating the powerful Baltimore Orioles in the World Series. Long after the tickertape parade in Manhattan honored the diamond heroes from Flushing, the Mets publicity department waxed eloquently about Hodges in the team's 1970 media guide, citing the previous year

Quiet but stern, Gil Hodges turned the baseball world on its head when his New York Mets captured the 1969 World Series. It is left to speculation as to what else he might have accomplished had he not died unexpectedly just prior to the opening of the 1972 season.

as "represent[ing] eloquent testimony to the spiritual strength, determination and ability of the soft-spoken, if firm, man who transformed the Mets from Pagliaccis to Paganinis. Suddenly the clowns were capable of beautiful music—led by a conductor who didn't miss a beat."[50]

A champion is always tasked with the difficulty of defending its crown, and this was surely the case for the Mets in 1970. No small amount of pressure was exerted by *Sports Illustrated*, which on the cover of its April 13 issue featured a photo of Koosman, who was twice victorious in the Fall Classic, surrounded by the caps of the other 23 Major League teams under a banner reading, THE METS AGAINST THE WORLD.

This first season of the new decade brought a hard reckoning when they dropped to third place, winning only 83 games and losing 79, although the Mets contended all year and on September 14 were tied for first in the NL East before fading to finish six games behind Pittsburgh. Unlike the *SI* cover, it was not only the Mets against the world, but at times it was the Mets against themselves as "discontent among players was pretty much out in the open, and winning another title wasn't what a lot players were focused on."[51] Pitchers Nolan Ryan and Gary Gentry complained about the manner in which they were being used—or *not* used—while several players groused that Hodges was a poor or ineffective communicator. The promotion of prospect Ken Singleton from the Triple-A Tidewater club caused an uncomfortable ripple effect in the lineup that was exacerbated, according to Ron Swoboda, when the young outfielder "failed to produce in a big way."[52]

The postseason trade of Swoboda eliminated one thorn from Hodges's side for 1971, and the team contended early that season. However, Koosman suffered a back injury at the end of May and wound up winning but six games all year, and by dropping 11 of their first 12 games in July, the Mets fell by the wayside as Hodges, quiet and aloof, inspired muted confidence. Benefiting from great overall pitching but hobbled by weak run production, New York, at 83–79, again placed third in the NL East.

Through a trade that seemed to offer a solution to their persistent problem at third base, the Mets acquired Jim Fregosi from the California Angels in exchange for Nolan Ryan—a handful of lesser players were also involved—and the Mets believed that they were dealing from a position of strength given the surplus of quality pitching they had. The team also added a quality bat in the form of Rusty Staub in an exchange with the Montreal Expos, and the rumor mill had it that Willie Mays, despite his advanced age, was headed to Shea Stadium in yet another trade. Optimism ran high that in 1972 the Mets could break out of their 83-win rut.

But the ultimate tragedy struck Hodges when he succumbed to a heart attack on the brink of his 48th birthday as the conclusion of Spring

Training coincided with the players' union beginning their first strike. The death of the Mets manager at such a young age was a body-blow to the entire organization, its fans, and the baseball world at large. "He was a strong man," remembered Hodges's manager of a decade earlier, Casey Stengel. "He had a strong character underneath a soft exterior. He had a terrific respect for standing up for the rights of others."[53] The bugbear of cigarettes nagged Hodges to the end, and this habit coupled with the stress of managing to detract from the salubrious conditions necessary for sound physical and mental health.

Suddenly and unexpectedly thrust into the role of manager of the Mets, Yogi Berra took up the cause for his late friend and brought the team to the World Series again in 1973 as more promising players emerged from the farm system (Jon Matlack and John Milner) or were acquired via trade (Félix Millán and George Stone from Atlanta). It can only be left to speculation how Hodges, had he lived and been able to continue his duties, would have fared with these personnel and under the same circumstances. The name of Gil Hodges will live on through his election to the Baseball Hall of Fame, but in the broader scope of the game's history, his legacy as manager of the 1969 World Series champions remains as important if not more so than his deeds as a player.

Several other managers active in the 1970–1971 timeframe are also worthy of attention, not least being one who retired twice in the 1960s and two more times in the following decade. Success is nearly always fleeting, and each of these last three subjects, at one time or another in their career, enjoyed the spray and taste of champagne after a World Series triumph.

First employed as the manager of the Pittsburgh Pirates beginning in 1957, Danny Murtaugh took a moribund team—the Bucs had a woeful 36–67 record at the time Bobby Bragan was fired—and got them to play .500 ball (26–25) for the remainder of the season. The 40-year-old Murtaugh led the Pirates to a surprising second-place finish in 1958 on the strength of an 84–70 record, only eight games behind NL-pennant-winning Milwaukee, this achievement coming exactly a decade after Pittsburgh's last visit to the first division. Slipping to fourth place in 1959, the Bucs rebounded with gusto in 1960 as they won 95 contests and then bested the New York Yankees in a dramatic World Series.

Pittsburgh suffered a letdown for most of the next four seasons and failed to contend. It was during this time that Murtaugh discovered that he was afflicted with a heart ailment, and he retired at the conclusion of the 1964 campaign but returned three years later to manage for the latter half of the 1967 schedule when Harry Walker was dismissed. Murtaugh stepped away at season's end but returned in 1970 to guide the Bucs to the NL East pennant, and although they were swept by Cincinnati in the NLCS, the front office proudly noted their manager's accomplishments: "The 1970 Pirates were a loose ballclub, thanks to Murtaugh's low-key approach.... Win or lose, he never lost his sense of humor. When injury after injury crippled his ballclub, especially his pitching staff, Danny utilized his full bench to maximum advantage; and young pitchers saw action in clutch situations."[54]

Murtaugh secured Manager of the Year honors from *The Sporting News* and the Associated Press, which encouraged his continuance as the Bucs' leader, but on May 20, 1971, he was felled by chest pains while the team was in Cincinnati. His precarious health again interrupted his tour of duty—coach Bill Virdon stepped in during Murtaugh's absence—and after a tentative recovery he was back on June 6. Murtaugh blamed stress, a manager's constant companion, for the negative impact it had on his condition, and the daily anxiety of running a contending team would not abate in what was shaping up as a championship season.

If Murtaugh could find any comfort through the Pirates' performance, his team finished seven games ahead of St. Louis to win the divisional pennant with a 97–65 record, the best in the National League. After losing to San Francisco in the opening game of the NLCS, the Bucs swept the next three contests to earn the right to face the Baltimore Orioles in the World Series. Just as the 1960 matchup with the Yankees had been memorable, so too was the 1971 version of the Fall Classic. In another nip-and-tuck tilt, Pittsburgh outlasted their opponent in seven games, almost letting a three-games-to-two advantage get away. The acclaim of a second championship was not lost on Murtaugh, but health being of primary importance, he decided to retire while on top.

Having worked off the field with General Manager Joe Brown to make various personnel decisions, Murtaugh told catcher Manny Sanguillen upon his latest retirement—this was actually a move to become Pittsburgh's farm system director—"I built this team. I built the foundation for you guys to keep it up. I want you to keep playing the same way."[55] This was part of the heritage that Murtaugh had worked so diligently to achieve, and he implored his player to carry on with those good deeds. Taking it to heart, the Pirates repeated as NL East champs in 1972 under Bill Virdon, who managed the team into 1973 when he was replaced by none other than Danny Murtaugh for that season's final 26 games. Murtaugh remained for three more seasons, bringing home one last divisional pennant in 1975 and then retiring for the last time in 1976. The Pirates mourned his passing when he died of a stroke two months after that season concluded, and he was memorialized the following year when his uniform number 40 was retired.

One of the longest-tenured managers in Major League history, Walter Alston of the Los Angeles Dodgers had the benefit of ushering several prospects to his roster from their minor league apprenticeships. Bill Buckner, Steve Garvey, and Bill Russell were leading a movement of the organization's top talent to Chavez Ravine beginning in 1969. Alston was relying on veteran position players to shoulder most of the regular lineup's burden, and after a very distant second-place finish to Cincinnati in 1970, the following season the Dodgers went 18–9 in September to nearly overtake the San Francisco Giants, falling one game short. "Alston often expressed delight in the Dodgers' system. It seemed to link quite nicely in his mind with the faith he always held in the family and small-town Ohio solidity," yet he was also willing to gamble on a player like Dick Allen, whom Los Angeles acquired in a 1971 trade.[56] More minor leaguers would emerge in the very near future and solidify the Los Angeles roster for the years beyond Alston's retirement at the end of the 1976 season.

Lastly, Bob Lemon, a workhorse of the Cleveland Indians' pitching staff from 1946 to 1958, segued into the role of minor league pitching coach after his arm gave out and soon after became a manager with the California Angels' Pacific Coast League club in Seattle, where he won Manager of the Year honors in 1966. After a coaching stint for the Angels in Anaheim in 1968 and managing at Triple-A Vancouver the following year, Lemon coached the pitching staff of the expansion Kansas City Royals in 1970 and was named the team's manager when Charlie Metro was fired in early June.

The following year, he shepherded the club to a second-place finish, well behind American League West champion Oakland at 16 games out but with a surprising 85–76 record, an encouraging mark for a club in only its third year of existence. "His managerial career followed a similar pattern everywhere he went—take on an underachieving team, lead it to success, and then get fired the next year."[57] Lemon survived the 1972 season, but true to form, Lemon was axed when Kansas City came in fourth with a 76–78 record. A few seasons later, Lemon worked his magic with Bill Veeck's Chicago White Sox in 1977 and after the maverick owner let him go in late June of 1978, Lemon stepped into even greater tumult by becoming the third New York Yankee manager that season and delivered a World Series title for the Bronx Bombers.

While an association with the Brooklyn or Los Angeles Dodgers was not universal among this chapter's managers, there is little doubt of that franchise's influence on enough of them to conclude that the skills and discipline underpinning the organization also carried over as these former players, regardless of the highest level they achieved, transitioned to their roles as managers. Nevertheless, absent a Dodger connection, the practice and observance of baseball's fundamentals, adhering to a code of conduct—that is, at least on the playing field—and attention to detail combined to enable these managers to move a team in a positive direction.

Gil Hodges and Earl Weaver were opposing managers in a World Series confrontation for the ages, and their personalities could not have been more divergent. Yet, in their brightest moments, each commanded the respect necessary for his team to get the job done when it counted most, and the same was true for their successful contemporaries. Focusing here on the more successful managers of this period affords a segue to the teams that they guided for profit.

4

Teams in Transition, Mostly for the Better

There are a multitude of ways in which teams can be viewed as being in a state of transition. Since the goal of each club is—or should be—to win baseball's ultimate championship, it can be assumed that every team is in the process of trying to improve their roster by addressing weaknesses that will enable it to move up in the standings. This is the state that most teams find themselves in, while the true contenders may need fewer adjustments to reach the top, and the defending champions perhaps requiring only some finetuning to remain on top. Suffice it to say, every team roster is literally a living, breathing entity always in flux.

In the earliest years of the 1970s, several teams were on the verge of bringing or holding together the right blend of players that would serve them well in the immediate years ahead, thanks in part to the work of the managers described in the previous chapter. Some emerged as champions and realized their dynastic aspirations, while others strove to establish—or re-establish—themselves in the nascent age of leagues now split into two divisions, meaning that even a cellar-dwelling club only had to pass five rivals to win a share of supremacy in its circuit. By simple numbers, this reduction offered a specious ray of hope and the chance to participate in the postseason.

Of course, the imposing work of winning still lie ahead.

Without question, the most dominant team of this brief era was the Baltimore Orioles, who had laid waste to its American League opponents from 1969 to 1971. Despite having lost the World Series in 1969 and 1971, Earl Weaver's club was vivid proof that it had matured and segued over the last ten years from its famed "Kiddie Corp" of pitching prospects and bonus babies beginning in the late 1950s to a lineup replete with veterans, the most noteworthy of whom were Brooks Robinson and Frank Robinson, the latter acquired in a trade of late 1965 with Cincinnati.

The Orioles seemed to have no weaknesses: a solid starting rotation, strong defense, and a potent offense combined to huge benefit, and the team not only excelled because of the leadership of its manager but also because of a change in pitching coaches. When he assumed control of the staff in 1968, George Bamberger set a tone different from his predecessor, Harry Brecheen, by having pitchers throw more frequently to keep their arms better toned, while Ralph Salvon, the team's new head trainer, was on hand to tend to ailments and keep an eye on other health issues. When former Rookie of the Year Curt Blefary was traded to Houston for southpaw Mike Cuellar—a few lesser players were also exchanged—the addition of a second lefty to the rotation in 1969 to complement Dave McNally made general manager Harry Dalton look like a genius when Cuellar tied Detroit's Denny McLain for American League Cy Young Award honors. Despite the shock of losing to the New York Mets in the World Series, there was little cause for panic at Memorial Stadium entering 1970 since few roster changes were expected to be made.

"The blueprint was the same as '69," wrote John Eisenberg of Baltimore's approach to the new year, and the Orioles were determined to use "an intimidating sense of purpose" to show that they would not let another chance for a world title slip away.[1] That Baltimore won one fewer regular-season game in 1970 than the year before mattered little: the Orioles' 108 victories again far outpaced the rest of the American League, they swept Minnesota in an ALCS rematch, and then anticipated meeting Cincinnati in the Fall Classic.

Chan Keith of the *Baltimore News American* wrote an essay for the 1970 World Series game program that summarized Baltimore's deeds and described some of the fluctuations occurring during a season that had one final round to go for the Orioles. "Like all campaigns before, it was a collection of memories ... of the young turks pressing the veterans and the regulars responding to the challenge with just that much more. Of a bull pen [sic] that either worked overtime, or during some stretches, did not work at all. Of a manager, enjoying a 10 run lead, but coaxing all the while for more and more yet."[2] As the Orioles later put it—in mocking tones *and* speaking of themselves in the third person—this refusal to ease up ultimately resulted in "a confrontation for the biggest prize of all, [when] they junked the Big Red Machine from Cincinnati."[3]

During that season, the Orioles saw the Robinsons continue to age—Frank was 34, Brooks 33, as was Don Buford—but they glimpsed the future as prospects were emerging from the farm system. Outfielder Merv Rettenmund performed solidly (.322, 18 home runs, 58 RBIs, 13 stolen bases) as he gained more playing time, while another outfielder, Don Baylor, and infielder Bobby Grich both were showing that they needed no further seasoning at the Triple-A level. The pleasant problem for Weaver and the front office was trying to find spaces on the roster for the young bona fide talent ready to settle into Major League employment.

After hitting his stride in 1969 by winning 16 of his 20 decisions, pitcher Jim Palmer, only 24 years old, won 20 games for the first time. Meantime, veteran first baseman Boog Powell, who had placed second in Most Valuable Player voting in 1969 and arguably could have been first, was named the AL MVP despite a slight reduction in output (.297, 35 HRs, 114 RBIs) compared to his runner-up season. Gold Glove Awards for fielding prowess were garnered by Brooks Robinson (third base), Davey Johnson (second base), and Paul Blair (center field).

Expectations ran high in 1971 for a third pennant in Baltimore, and both fans and prognosticators would not be disappointed with the end result. But the journey to the flag was less certain, at least in the early going when the Orioles spent the entire month of May in second place. A victory at Milwaukee on June 5 put them on top of the AL East, where they remained for the rest of the year despite some injuries that would have stymied a lesser club, especially when McNally was sidelined for over five weeks due to problems with his left elbow. But Weaver was fortunate to have Pat Dobson, new to the Orioles' pitching staff thanks to a December 1970 trade, and the former San Diego Padre won eight decisions in July alone during the course of a personal 12-game winning skein. When Powell broke his wrist early that month, forcing Weaver to shift Frank Robinson from right field to first base, this move enabled Rettenmund to get more playing time. The fill-in first baseman also blasted his 500th career home run in mid–September.

The final accounting showed the Orioles logging 101 victories and 57 losses, 12 games ahead of Detroit, and putting an exclamation point on their season with an 11-game winning streak as the schedule came to an end. Even as Baltimore was coming down the stretch in early September, Ray Scarborough, who formerly served the organization as a scout, minor league manager, and coach, forwarded his thoughts to Dalton, strongly recommending that the scouting department budget not fall victim to "a tightening of the purse strings" that would disrupt finding the quality talent necessary to replenish the minor league rosters, while at the same time warning against "[t]rying to be too selective in drafting and signing fringe prospects." Scarborough cautioned Dalton of any "complacency" that might infect the mindset of the organization "just because we are winning," and he suggested that "trades that would deplete our supply of young players" should be avoided.[4]

The statistical gem that endures to this day are the four pitchers who each won at least 20 games: McNally, elbow misery notwithstanding, was 21–5, Dobson finished at 20–8, while Cuellar and Palmer, who suffered shoulder discomfort, both went 20–9. This quartet is likely to remain the last such group to accomplish this feat for one team in the same year. While McNally was the only pitcher to receive any votes for the AL Cy Young Award, Weaver was again left by the wayside for the league's Manager of the Year honors.

Come playoff time, Baltimore was nothing if not consistent, registering their third sweep in as many appearances in the ALCS, this time over the Oakland Athletics. The Orioles scored five runs in each of the three games, which were played on consecutive days despite the necessity of cross-country travel from Charm City to the Bay Area for the third contest. When they squared off against the Pittsburgh Pirates in the World Series, the Orioles took the first two games at home but lost all three on the road, including the first night contest in Series history. Returning to Memorial Stadium along with the apparent home-team advantage intact, Baltimore edged the Bucs in Game 6, yet their luck ran out in the finale when Steve Blass hurled a four-hit, one-run masterpiece to give Pittsburgh the win.

Changes were in the offing for the defending AL champs, and they commenced in the immediate aftermath of the conclusion of the World Series. When the Orioles departed in late October for a tour of Japan and a series of exhibition games in the Land of the Rising Sun, not among the club's contingent was their general manager. Harry Dalton was looking for a new challenge and found it in Anaheim, California, where he staked out his next place of employment with Gene Autry's Angels, and Frank Cashen succeeded Dalton as the Baltimore GM.

Dalton left Cashen with suggestions on areas where the Orioles could use some improvement, important among these being a way for younger farmhands like Baylor and Grich to finally leave their minor league days behind them. Wanting also to head West in order to maintain his ties with Dalton was minor league skipper Cal Ripken, who was managing in Puerto Rico when Dalton announced his departure. "I sincerely hope you will consider me for the managers [sic] post with your new club," Ripken wrote in a note to the new Angel executive. "You know me quite well and I know I can do a good job for you."[5]

The Orioles also had to deal with Father Time as Buford and the aging "Robinson brothers," as they were sometimes jokingly called, were not getting any younger. Brooks, the local legend, continued to anchor the hot corner, but Frank would be one of the principals of an upcoming trade that signaled the early stage of a youth movement. As usual, it was up to Earl Weaver to craft his lineup to extract the maximum performance from the collective roster, an endeavor that solidified his reputation as one of the best managers in the game and brought more pennant-contending teams to Baltimore over the following decade.

Stinging as the Orioles' loss to Pittsburgh was, it is difficult to deny them their rightful place as a dynasty by selectively reserving that distinction only for World Series champions. Their resounding regular-season record and ensuing ALCS playoff sweeps from 1969 to 1971 firmly place them among the elite teams of any era. Yet, in a bit of ironic timing, Baltimore's opponent in the 1971 American League Championship Series was on the cusp of forging not only an imposing club but also one that did reach the lofty standard of a true dynasty.

"Oakland was real good, but they were young," recalled Frank Robinson of that playoff encounter. "We left them crying on the dugout steps. They just got wiped out. They were shocked. They were upset. They were out there crying."[6]

Robinson's view of the Athletics' reaction to those three straight losses might have been a bit overblown, although Reggie Jackson did indulge a lengthy period of solitary quiet time on those steps as the field was cleaned and his teammates showered and vacated the clubhouse after Game 3. But it speaks well of the level of competitiveness Oakland expected to maintain after they had far outdistanced their rivals in the American League West and coasted to a 16-game margin over their closest divisional rival, Kansas City, while equaling the Orioles' total of 101 victories for most in the league.

Tears and disappointment aside, the Athletics could look with pride on their 12-win improvement over 1970, and new manager Dick Williams had an unexpectedly potent weapon at his disposal in the person of Vida Blue. The lefthanded pitcher from Mansfield, Louisiana, took the baseball world by storm, securing Cy Young and MVP laurels on the strength of 24 wins against eight losses, a league-best 1.82 ERA, and eight shutouts to lead the Major Leagues. A foretaste of this greatness came the previous year when Blue, just 20 years old, threw a one-hitter and a no-hitter among his six starts at the end of that season.

Blue's stunning success carried into 1971: After losing the season opener to the Washington Senators, in which he was chased in the second inning, he reeled off 10 wins in as many decisions, and his dominance continued throughout the year. Oakland owner Charlie Finley, never one to let an opportunity for publicity go ignored, "wanted to call his prize pitcher True Blue," reported Wells Twombly in *The Sporting News*. "That didn't work because the kid rebelled."[7] Also among the proposed aliases were "The Blue Streak," "Little Boy Blue," and "The Vidamin Kid," but the pitcher was content with his status quo.

Other forces were at work in the Athletics' brimming success story. The coalescing of their youthful talent had Jackson, Catfish Hunter, Sal Bando, Rollie Fingers, Dave Duncan, Joe Rudi, Bert Campaneris, and another Blue—John "Blue Moon" Odom—hitting their stride with Oakland as the late 1960s moved into the next decade. Vida Blue showed such dominance in 1971 that it prompted his manager to comment, "I think two things have made him special. One, his natural ability. And, two, his poise. I guess he was born with poise and I think he got it polished in his upbringing."[8] Blue seemed to be the next superstar in the making.

Coincidentally or not, Blue's breakout year was the pitching bedrock that the Athletics could rely on, but Williams's influence played a key role when he assured Bando that he would retain his role as team captain, and when Jackson butted heads with Finley by holding out in 1970 after he showed his star potential the previous season by hitting 47 home runs and driving in 118 runs. When Jackson finally returned, the running feud between the owner and the outfielder, who was in a lengthy slump, came to a head in early September after "Reggie hit his first major league grand slam home run and told Finley to go f--- himself."[9] Finley tried to suspend Jackson, but under duress Reggie signed an apology for his action. This was but one instance of many that caused an untold amount of friction and angst between Finley and his manager as well as the owner and his players in the ensuing years.

The no-hitter that Vida Blue pitched during a late-season call-up in 1970 was a precursor to the astounding season he forged in 1971, when he took honors as the American League MVP and Cy Young Award winner.

4. Teams in Transition, Mostly for the Better 91

Entering 1971, Williams gave his outfielder a vote of confidence by announcing, "I expect Reggie Jackson to play everyday. I have no thoughts of benching him against left-handers."[10] Jackson responded, increasing his 1970 output of .237 / 23 HRs / 66 RBIs to .277 / 32 HRs / 80 RBIs in Williams's first year at Oakland, with an AL MVP award shortly to follow. Six other Oakland regulars—Duncan, Rudi, Bando, Mike Epstein, Rick Monday, and even the light-hitting Dick Green—reached double-digits in homers that season, and the pitching staff fell only a bit short of Baltimore's standard, the Athletics team ERA of 3.05 just 0.06 behind that of the league-leading Orioles. Catfish Hunter (21 wins), Chuck Dobson (15–5 record), Blue Moon Odom, and Diego Segui, the latter two with 10 victories each, more than held their places on the mound, and all the while the entire operation was lorded over by a man who simply could not keep to himself.

Charles Oscar Finley had purchased a large share of the Kansas City Athletics in late 1960 and shortly thereafter assumed full ownership of the club. By the end of the 1967 season when the Athletics were destined to move west to Oakland, Ed Lopat decided he had had enough in his role as the fourth general manager under Finley and announced his resignation, at which point Finley added GM to his own responsibilities. However, the move was not as if Finley had not already been serving in that capacity. "Finley ran the entire operation to an extent that was startling. He not only made all the baseball decisions in Oakland—deciding whom to draft or sign, making trades, suggesting the lineup, advising in-game strategy—he often wrote the copy for the yearbook, made out the song lists for the organist, decided the menu for the press room during the World Series, and designed the uniforms."[11]

Always an entrepreneur in spirit and in action, Finley had grown accustomed to success in running his insurance business during the 1950s, and he expected the same from his investment in the world of baseball and from those who were in his employ. Petulant, demanding, quick to reward, and equally quick to berate, Finley used his boundless enthusiasm to cajole, meddle, and otherwise influence all aspects of the Oakland organization, especially regarding his players while the reserve clause was intact. For all the fame and attention that Vida Blue earned during his burst onto the Major League stage in 1971, Finley's skinflint tendencies regarding player salaries were in conflict with what the pitcher expected in his next contract, and there followed a lengthy and controversial holdout that kept Blue off the pitching mound until the end of May 1972.

Although the demise of the reserve clause through the Seitz ruling of late 1975 would drastically change a team's grasp over its players, Finley did what was in his power to maximize the club's winning potential.

The downside of his overbearing personality, however, rankled many at all levels of his franchise, among baseball's other ownerships, and eventually the commissioner's office. Fans also expressed their displeasure with their feet: From 1971 to 1975, during which time the Athletics won the AL West each year as well as three World Series, attendance at Oakland–Alameda County Coliseum ranged from a low of 845,693 in 1974 (11th of 12 AL clubs) to 1,075,518 the following year (seventh of 12), hardly awe-inspiring figures given the accomplishments of the hometown team.

In the wake of Oakland's defeat in the 1971 American League Championship Series, tears were indeed shed by some Athletics who thought that the brass ring of an AL pennant was within their reach. Fate was not on their side, but a trade the following season to add Ken Holtzman to the rotation—"a thinking man's pitcher, not a flame thrower," in one writer's evaluation—became the answer to the missing ingredient as Oakland scrapped its way to the first of three consecutive titles in the Fall Classic.[12]

Yet, the Athletics benefited from playing in a weak division. The Minnesota Twins, two-time defending AL West champions, were entering a period of extended mediocrity, joining the Chicago White Sox and California Angels in that category, while the two latest expansion teams in Kansas City and Seattle had ups and downs, the Royals actually faring well in 1971, while the Pilots shifted to Milwaukee after a single, dismal season in the Pacific Northwest. As was befitting of the uniforms they wore, the Oakland Athletics were certainly colorful, not simply in the visual sense, but also through the interaction the players had with Charlie Finley, possibly the most irascible of any maverick to ever occupy the owner's box.

If the Athletics could be labeled a dynasty, the same term was being bandied about, even tentatively, with regard to the Cincinnati Reds before they had captured a single World Series in the 1970s. One look at first-year manager Sparky Anderson's roster gave rise to a surge of optimism when his club captured the 1970 National League pennant with a nucleus of 20-somethings. Among the regulars, Pete Rose and Tommy Helms were the elder statesmen at the age of 29; Tony Pérez was one year younger, and Lee May just 27; Bobby Tolan, in his second season as a Red, was 24; and Johnny Bench, Dave Concepción, and Bernie Carbo, at 22, were barely eligible to vote. Not quite an afterthought was outfielder Hal McRae (24), who shared playing time in left field with Carbo.

On the mound were starters Jim Merritt and Jim McGlothlin, both 26, Tony Cloninger (29), Wayne Simpson (21), Gary Nolan (22), and a 19-year-old kid named Don Gullett. Milt Wilcox (20) and Pedro Borbón (23) were trying to make their respective marks, and the bullpen was anchored by 29-year-old Clay Carroll and closer Wayne Granger, just 26. Expected to be promoted from Triple-A Indianapolis was Ross Grimsley (21). Gordy Coleman, the first baseman on the last Cincinnati pennant-winners of 1961, noted that his teammates were more advanced in age—to say nothing of less talented overall—than the current crop of Reds, saying, "The team this year, because of its youth, can do nothing but improve."[13] Already a winner of two Gold Gloves, Bench, in a bit of self-deprecation, confessed, "I'm not knocking myself.... I'm not saying I'm a terrible catcher. I'm just saying there's room for improvement in handling pitchers, preventing wild pitches and pass [sic] balls, things like that."[14]

A youth movement having already arrived, it was now up to the manager to orchestrate what needed to be done, and Anderson was candid in admitting, "If we win [in 1970], this team and the players on it will establish my reputation."[15] The era of the "Big Red Machine," credited by authors Gregory L. Rhodes and John G. Erardi as starting with the opening of Cincinnati's spring training camp on February 20, 1970, can actually be dated to the previous summer when the Reds mounted a comeback in early August to beat the Phillies, 19–17, and a reporter for the *Los Angeles Times* used the "seemingly innocuous phrase" to describe the Reds' power.[16]

Rose, remarking about his team's home run barrage and high-energy offense in 1969, told *The Sporting News*, "I'm telling you, 'The Big Red Machine' has all the rival pitchers talking."[17] Helms joked that the machine actually was comprised of the "Nasty Six and Two Judies," the latter pair being himself and shortstop Woody Woodward, who were the lightest of the hitters in the regular lineup, or, in a manner of speaking, the back half of the Punch and Judy tandem.[18]

Beside the players assembled by Sparky Anderson, his coaching staff was integral to making the machine run well. A former slugger who could also hit for average, Ted Kluszewski was chosen as the batting coach; Larry Shepard, "known to be a bit temperamental but he knew his stuff when it came to pitching," was in charge of the hurlers; George Scherger coached first base; and Alex Grammas handled chores at third.[19] This core of mentors was Anderson's support system, vital in its function to help the manager in his first turn with a Major League club.

Another key aspect of the earliest manifestation of the Big Red Machine was the "instant pitching" that general manager Bob Howsam seemed to develop rather quickly. Observing how painful it had been in 1969 to see "a sore-armed Red pitching staff repeatedly squander leads built by the most awesome array of sluggers assembled on one club since the Dodgers ... in the mid–50s," Cincinnati columnist Earl Lawson found a near-miracle in the foursome of Simpson, Nolan, Merritt, and McGlothlin.[20]

"A college kid could manage this club," was how Anderson brushed aside praise directed his way when Cincinnati reached the 1970 All-Star break with a ten-game lead in the NL West.[21] "And not even a rash of second half injuries (Wayne Simpson's shoulder, Jim McGlothlin's cheekbone and knee, Clay Carroll's ankle, Jim Merritt's elbow) could derail the machine," the club's media guide later noted.[22] The offense finished the season tied for first in batting average with three other teams at .270, placed third in the league in runs scored, and led the NL with 191 home runs.

Individual standout performances begin with Johnny Bench's MVP award-winning season, during which he won his third consecutive Gold Glove for his work behind the plate, batted .293, and led the majors with 45 home runs and 148 RBIs. Power-hitting was evident in the output of Pérez (.317, 40, 129), May (.253, 34, 94), Carbo (.310, 21, 63, along with 94 walks), Rose (.316, 15, 52), and Tolan (.316, 16, 80, and 57 stolen bases). On the mound, Merritt's 20 wins led the staff, followed by Nolan's 18, and McGlothlin and Simpson logged 14 each.

Defending its NL pennant would be a challenge unmet in 1971 as Cincinnati was hobbled by two significant injuries. Simpson had damaged his rotator cuff from too many innings pitched in 1969 and 1970, between his time spent in Triple-A, participation in the Puerto Rican Winter League, and then with the Reds in his rookie season. He would persist in his recovery, but Simpson never regained the form that heightened the expectations for what began as a promising career.

The sidelining of a quality starting pitcher was bad enough, but the other crushing loss happened in January 1971 when Bobby Tolan tore his right Achilles tendon in a basketball game, and it would cost the centerfielder the entire season when he suffered a second, partial tear four months later. The setback prompted GM Bob Howsam to look outside the organization for another outfielder, and he came up with a gem when he traded for San Francisco prospect George Foster.

Yet, the trying season remained just that. "Wherever Reds Look, They See Trouble," was the telling headline in the June 19 issue of *The Sporting News*, and when Howsam paid a visit to Anderson around that time, the manager had reason to feel as though his employment was in jeopardy. Anderson was relieved to learn that "Howsam was much more likely to get on his manager when the club was winning than when it was losing," but in the event, Cincinnati blundered to a fourth-place finish in the NL West.[23]

The sophomore jinx that haunted Sparky Anderson ran concurrently with Howsam's vote of confidence, and little time passed following the final Reds game before the manager quickly gathered of some of his players for immediate offseason work in the Florida Instructional League to iron out problems. Not least among those attending was Bench, whose drop in offensive output (from .293 / 45 / 148 to .238 / 27 / 61) was alarming. As Anderson and his coaches put the players through their paces, Howsam was beginning to work the telephone lines with other GMs to see what trades could be worked out as the 1971 Winter Meetings approached. As time would prove that he had struck it rich with the Foster trade, another deal was in the works with Houston in an attempt to recapture Cincinnati's gains of 1970 and better facilitate the Reds' switch from the natural grass surface at Crosley Field, their former home ballpark, to the artificial turf of Riverfront Stadium. The acquisition of Joe Morgan from Houston was pivotal to restoring the luster to the Big Red Machine but also helping to secure its place as one of the most feared teams of the 1970s.

In the wake of the retirement of pitching legend Sandy Koufax, the Los Angeles Dodgers entered a brief period of wilderness years, uncomfortably segueing from 1966 National League champions—and victims of an unexpected Baltimore sweep in the World Series—to eighth-place also-rans the following year with a 73–89 record, and rebounding only tepidly to seventh in 1968's "Year of the Pitcher" by going 76–86. The number of Dodger victories was not the only number in decline: attendance at Chavez Ravine plummeted from 2.62 million in 1966 to 1.58 million in 1968.

Through thick and thin, manager Walter Alston soldiered on, and 1969 saw a restoration of fighting spirit when the Dodgers battled for the top of the new NL West division with four other contenders but fell from the pack with two weeks left in the season. Los Angeles reporter Bob Hunter credited "a combination of the Mod Squad and veterans" with the resurgence, and he cited Bill Russell, Ted Sizemore, who would be named NL Rookie of the Year, and Bill Sudakis as heading up the youth movement of the "Squad" that also could have included Willie Crawford, who debuted in Los Angeles in 1964 when he was only 17 years old.[24]

The perked-up offense—Dodger runs jumped from 470 in 1968 to 645 in 1969—helped the club make up for the sudden retirement of ace pitcher Don Drysdale and the loss of playing time by Wes Parker and Willie Davis, while Bill Singer and Claude Osteen registered 20 wins each on the mound. Heading in the right direction once more, Los Angeles was feeling as though a return to competitiveness had been achieved heading into 1970.

The product on the field at Dodger Stadium looked favorable, and more seeds had been planted in the farm system. As Dodger executive Fred Claire observed of his recent joining the team's front office as publicity director, "My timing couldn't have been better from the standpoint of … the talent that had been injected into the organization as a result of the June draft of 1968, players such as infielders Steve Garvey, Ron Cey, Davey Lopes and Bobby Valentine, outfielders Bill Buckner and Tom Paciorek, catcher Joe Ferguson and pitchers Doyle Alexander, Geoff Zahn, and Sandy Vance."[25] The manager of the franchise's top farm team in Spokane of the Pacific Coast League who worked with this clutch of prospects was Tom Lasorda, Alston's future third-base coach and eventual replacement as Dodger skipper.

Upon the naming of the Dodgers as baseball's top organization for 1970, player personnel director Al Campanis said, "The success of our minor league clubs is a tremendous tribute to the fine job done by our scouts. We're all proud of them."[26] A crucial aspect was hiding in plain sight regarding the type of player the organization sought. According to Cey, "There was a lot of desire for flexibility; they wanted guys to be able to play more than one position. If there was a logjam, you could make it to the big leagues at another position."[27] This versatility enabled Garvey, Valentine, Buckner, Ferguson, and Russell, who was a 1966 draftee, to enhance their credentials in the eyes of Dodger management.

In 1970, Los Angeles placed second behind Cincinnati with an 87–74 record, a distant 14½ games out, but still the third-best win total in the league. A number 1968 draftees got at least a taste of life at the Major League level, and a new face, Billy Grabarkewitz, made the NL All-Star team as a rookie and finished with statistics (.289, 17 home runs, 84 RBIs, 19 stolen bases) that oddly earned him no votes in that year's Rookie of the Year voting. Los Angeles could hardly be thinking in terms of smelling blood in the NL West for the upcoming season, with the Reds featuring so many young players and an offense so productive. But the Dodgers sought to capitalize on their improvement while at once addressing a persistent weakness in home run power.

Since moving into Dodger Stadium in 1962, when the Dodgers hit 140 homers, they never approached that figure in the ensuing eight seasons, barely eclipsing the century mark only twice (110 in 1963 and 108 in 1966). But in early 1971 the team pointed optimistically to a remedy: "The Dodgers of 1970 had finished a ten-thousandth of a point, .2703 to .2702, behind Cincinnati's 'Big Red Machine' for the major league team batting championship but Los Angeles had finished last in the majors in home runs. The acquisition of [Dick] Allen, who hit 34 homers for St. Louis last year, and Duke Sims, who hit 23 for Cleveland, changes the Dodger image."[28]

Dick Allen, the controversial slugger, was a teammate of Grabarkewitz on the 1970 NL All-Star team, and as was the case with the snubbing of the Dodger rookie at award time, Allen also found that his .279 average, 34 home runs, and 101 RBIs rated not a single MVP vote. Yet, he was ready to put his one year with the Cardinals behind him after he was hobbled by a hamstring injury. Allen's unavailability added to the grousing by management and fans that the slugger was living up to his reputation as a malcontent, and his biographer, Mitchell Nathanson, wrote, "In the end ... his list of detractors seemed to be growing."[29] Thus, trading him to Los Angeles was the Cardinals' way of pruning a headache from the roster.

That Walter Alston was ready to take on Dick Allen and the baggage that he carried said much about the manager, and he discovered that a mutual show of respect between himself and Allen worked well for their relationship, at least in the early going. But there was a conflict at hand: the Dodgers already had a talented first baseman in Wes Parker, a Gold Glove fielder who in 1970 had led the majors in doubles, batted .319, and drove in 111 runs, which were also best on the team. After beginning his career as a third baseman with Philadelphia, Allen shifted to left field and finally to first base because of deficiencies with his glove, but with Parker having already staked his claim, Alston sent Allen to left field where he played until mid–June before returning to third base for most of the rest of the season.

Allen's bat justified the reason for the Dodgers having acquired him, and while his 1971 offensive output was solid (.295, 23 HRs, 90 RBIs), he was imbued with the attitude that the management and ownership of any team should not be forcing its values on any of

Beginning his career with the Philadelphia Phillies, slugger Dick Allen changed addresses in 1970 (St. Louis), in 1971 (Los Angeles), and 1972, when he landed with the Chicago White Sox.

its players. "Indeed," Nathanson observed, "even before the season ended there were whispers that Dick's time in Los Angeles was going to be brief," which turned out to be exactly the case.[30] When Los Angeles finished the year just one game behind San Francisco for the NL West pennant, a roster turnover commenced at Dodger Stadium. Even though an aging Frank Robinson was brought in via a trade with Baltimore, Allen was sent to the Chicago White Sox, and playing time increased for many younger men on the roster, such as Russell, Garvey, and Valentine, who could play nearly anywhere in the field.

The pieces of the stellar Dodger infield were slowly taking shape in these years, and by 1974, Cey (third base), Russell (shortstop), Davey Lopes (second base), and Garvey (first base) had become entrenched at their respective stations, and a host of their fellow 1968 draftees soon joined the Dodger ranks. This was a signal moment in the history of the franchise because it validated the process by which the club was selecting and grooming its new players, and it better prepared Los Angeles to face the Cincinnati Reds, who were coalescing to establish themselves as the team to beat in the NL West.

This growing rivalry had staying power throughout the 1970s: With the exception of 1971, when the San Francisco Giants won the division, the only other teams to do so were the Reds (1970, 1972, 1973, 1975, 1976, 1979) and the Dodgers (1974, 1977, 1978), with Los Angeles finishing in second place six other times in that decade. There can be little wonder that this level of competition defined the quality of baseball staged between two of the titans of the era as each sought to gain or maintain superiority in the division.

On the East Coast, New York was experiencing a curious version of a tale of two cities. One of its Major League teams—a former dynasty that was the most formidable of any in the world of sport—was trying to find a way out of its recent doldrums, while the other was reveling in the attention it garnered following its triumph in the 1969 World Series. This was the story of two franchises headed in opposite directions, to the chagrin of one and the delight of the other.

In the wake of their last World Series appearance in 1964, the New York Yankees had bottomed out by sinking to the basement of the American League in 1966, a once unthinkable occurrence, and they improved only the slightest bit to ninth place the next year. Following that were two seasons of .500 (or so) mediocrity, but the Bronx Bombers surged, relatively speaking, to 93 wins in 1970 and a second-place finish behind Baltimore in the AL East. A blend of young talent fronted by two recent Rookies of the Year, catcher Thurman Munson and pitcher Stan Bahnsen, also featured outfielders Bobby Murcer and Roy White, starters Fritz Peterson and Mel Stottlemyre, and a group of not-too-old but experienced veterans that included Danny Cater. This was hardly a squad of the dynastic Yankee standard and of little threat to the Oriole juggernaut, but it provided some return of respect to the Bronx.

The most public face of the Yankee front office at the time was one Michael Burke, the club's chairman of the board and president. Burke was 54 years old and well-educated; he served his country with distinction during World War II as an agent with the Office of Strategic Services. Post-war, he commenced an interesting and eclectic career as an executive with Ringling Brothers Circus, served as president of the Columbia Broadcasting System (CBS) headquarters in Europe before returning to the U.S. in 1962, and then became a vice president tasked with "developing new areas of business for the Broadcasting Company."[31]

CBS had purchased the Yankees in 1964, which Lee MacPhail, Jr., the team's general manager, thought may have been initiated by a proposal of Burke's to cater to CBS's desire to diversify its holdings. MacPhail was also aware that William Paley, the head of the network, enjoyed baseball and was a good friend of Yankee co-owner Daniel Topping. At the time of the purchase, Del Webb bowed out as Topping's partner, but Topping remained as the team's top executive until September 1966 when Burke assumed the presidency. MacPhail remembered that "Mike dressed with an elegant continental flair, but he was careful to combine this with a shirt with slightly frayed collar and cuffs.... He concentrated on the stadium, the public image, the broadcast, and the finances."[32]

Burke also grew his

Michael Burke's effort to return the New York Yankees to their dynastic glory days fell short during his tenure. His administration, however, was a stepping stone to the team's ownership under George Steinbrenner.

hair and sideburns stylishly long, as if to better assume a youthful identity. In a full-page photograph for the 1971 Yankee yearbook, he is posed in profile with furled shirtsleeves while staring out at the field of play, the gravity of his gaze unflinching. "The young Yankees are coming on," reads the accompanying inscription. "Ready now to challenge the best and to reward your loyalty in full. (Signed) Michael Burke."[33] The executive had been eager to acquire a Jewish native of the Bronx, Washington Senators first baseman Mike Epstein, for the Yankee lineup. Epstein, a lefthanded power hitter, would have been a valuable addition, both for his bat and as a gate attraction, but Burke's offer of an even-up swap of Joe Pepitone as well as a three-player package were rebuffed.

The Yankee president understood the value of a good public relations campaign, pointing out that the players were obliged to visit those in need and encourage children to stay in school, while ensuring that "hundreds of thousands of free admissions for deprived youngsters" would be available to ensure them "that someone gives a damn...."[34]

Despite this brave show of community spirit and a reminder that fresh players were on the way, the Yankees were a franchise skating on thin ice as a series of factors took form to conspire against them. Rumors began to circulate that a proposed sports complex in the nearby New Jersey Meadowlands would draw the team and their co-tenants at Yankee Stadium, the NFL's Giants, to a new home. This suggested change in venue was prompted by the conditions into which the area around the Bronx ballpark and many parts of New York City, generally speaking, had fallen.

"Once a tourist attraction in its own right, Yankee Stadium had become a deterrent to attendance, which barely exceeded one million in 1971. The temporary face-lift conducted at the start of Burke's reign couldn't rectify intrinsic design flaws such as view-obstructing pillars and rafters." But acting in concert against the edifice, "the aging ballpark stood in a crime-ridden slum no longer equipped to handle either the traffic or the parking.... Fans were also increasingly loath to ride the subway to 161st Street, especially at night."[35]

Burke's team was in unquestionable straits, and as the City of New York pondered a future without the Giants and the Yankees possibly also relocating, Hollywood would reinforce the negativism found in the Big Apple through the release of films like *The French Connection* (1971), *Serpico* (1973), and *Death Wish* (1974), which offered unflattering portrayals of a municipality awash in drugs, police corruption, and crime. Burke successfully partnered with Mayor John Lindsay, who used some bureaucratic finesse to cast the plan to renovate Yankee Stadium as "an urban renewal project," and with narrow approval by the City Planning Commission,

4. Teams in Transition, Mostly for the Better

the venture moved forward at nearly the same time that a new ownership group led by George Steinbrenner bought the team in early 1973.[36]

Meanwhile, as the Yankees struggled on and off the field, over in Flushing Meadows, the Mets were the hot ticket in town as evidenced by the nearly 2.7 million fans who swarmed into Shea Stadium in 1970. The season was replete with excitement because the Mets never fell out of contention; for most of the first half of the year, they were just a few games out of first place in the NL East and briefly held the lead on a number of occasions. In mid–September the defending World Series champions were tied for first but then won only five of their remaining 15 contests to finish in third with an 83–79 record. "Mets Close, But Lose 'Amazing' Tag" was beat writer Jack Lang's pithy assessment, and manager Gil Hodges expressed his disappointment by noting that the lack of "a little winning streak" derailed his team's chances for a repeat divisional pennant.[37]

There was little hangover from the Mets' previous postseason glory based on the focus the club demonstrated by staying in the race, but 37 blown leads did not help the cause nor was the shelving of starter Jerry Koosman for two months due to arm and shoulder issues. Cleon Jones lost his hitting form of 1969 but regained it with a 23-game hitting streak as the season wound down, and Tommie Agee and Donn Clendenon had overall good years as well. But Joe Foy, brought in via a trade with Kansas City in the quest to find an everyday third baseman, was a bust, and the magic of prevailing in one-run games was more elusive in 1970 (24 wins and 27 losses) than in the championship year (41–23).

Although some Mets fans rode a different line of the same subway system that serviced Yankee Stadium—and by extension were exposed to similar risks in taking this form of transportation—when they arrived at Shea Stadium there was a less imposing aura thanks to the absence of an immediate, decrepit neighborhood. For those who drove to the game, acres of parking awaited, and the thrill of seeing a contending team in person provided an alternative to the mediocre Yankees. The Mets' repeat of an 83–79 record in 1971, which gave them a tie with the Chicago Cubs for third place in the NL East, prompted a dip in home attendance to just over 2.26 million. When Gil Hodges died unexpectedly in the spring of 1972, he had only glimpsed Jon Matlack's pitching and John Milner's hitting his powerful bat, but these rookies would help the Mets return to the postseason in 1973 before the club fell into a decline that lasted for most of the ensuing decade.

In the short term, the Mets held sway over the Yankees in the earliest years of the 1970s, but as the Steinbrenner era took shape and while the reserve clause continued to benefit management, the Bronx Bombers used the trade route to assemble the essential pieces of a roster that would stir a dynastic renaissance beginning in 1976. Depending on where the loyalty of a particular New York baseball fan lies, there could be joy or disillusionment, possibly both emotions at once, but a baseball season in the nation's largest city almost guaranteed that there would be few dull moments.

The Orioles, Reds, Athletics and Mets were ultimately rewarded as they transitioned according to their particular circumstances. But at the onset of the 1970s the four most recent expansion clubs, as well as one created in 1961, were in various states of evolution. Two franchises held their ground and substantiated their viability, but in the case of the other three, ominous signs of outright failure dangerously became manifest, as the will to survive assumed priority to keep the enterprise afloat, let alone put a winning product on the field. While none of these teams folded up or otherwise went bankrupt, a facile glance at the paths they took hardly explains the plight they endured in maintaining the status of a Major League club.

In Kansas City, the new team made the most of the advantages they had in their favor. "The initial enthusiasm for the expansion Royals had to be built with positive play on the diamond," remembered public relations director Bob Wirz, "although it was refreshing for Kansas Citians to know there was local ownership from self-made drug magnate Ewing Kauffman and his family."[38] Credit also must be given to the supporting cast that allowed the relatively quick formation of a contender: general manager Cedric Tallis; minor league and scouting director Lou Gorman; and John Schuerholz, who served as Gorman's assistant farm director. When Charlie Metro was fired in early June 1970, Bob Lemon stepped in as the "velvet-glove, low key manager" who drew his inspiration and style of handling players from Al Lopez, who was the Cleveland Indians' skipper when Lemon was one of that club's top pitchers.[39] Lemon took the Royals to a second-place finish in 1971, carrying out his success with players who were mostly under the age of 28.

In August 1970, the Royals opened a new minor league complex in Sarasota, Florida, built on Kauffman's vision for a Baseball Academy that would "find superior athletes whose exposure to baseball may have been limited but who meet the extremely high standards as developed by the Academy staff."[40] Syd Thrift was in charge of the personnel that, besides baseball instructors, included a coordinator of classroom studies, a research psychologist, and a weight training advisor. The academy would produce a few prospects of Major League capability, yet this innovative concept was emblematic of the owner's entrepreneurial spirit.

Kauffman's deep pockets and willingness to spend earned him the nickname of "the twenty-million-dollar fan" as a nod to the money he spent to pay for the team initially, the losses he sustained in the course of establishing the farm system and the academy, plus the money he gave to Jackson County in advance of the Royals' move to the Truman Sports Complex so that it would "mak[e] the new stadium a showplace to attract maximum attendance."[41] The return on his investment justified the patient approach to building from within.

A second expansion club of 1969, the Montreal Expos finished with a dreary 52–110 record and would seem to have offered little attraction for the club's fans or encouragement for its players. Pitching was an acknowledged disaster, as the staff yielded a whopping 702 walks to lead the National League and its 4.33 ERA was the worst in the circuit. Despite the embarrassment of a horrific 20-game losing streak—there were a number of shorter ones as well—fans turned out at Jarry Park, which seated a modest crowd of 28,500, in numbers that ordinarily would not mesh with a poor, losing ballclub. Once a longtime minor league baseball outpost, the city of Montreal was not quite a stranger to America's national pastime, and a season-ending recap in *The Sporting News* described the exuberance that made the sport not just an occasion but a movement.

> The rebirth of baseball brought forth old fans from their backyard barbecues and managed to disengage the new generation from transistor radios.... Women turned out in their most clinging sweaters or items of high fashion. Men wore business suits with a familiar-shaped bulge in the hip pocket or set a world record for beer drinking while outfitted in Expo caps and jackets.
> One man played a fiddle on the roof of the Expos' dugout. Another brought a goose. One fellow bought $14 worth of peanuts and tossed them about his section, returned a week later in a Santa Claus costume and did it again. They danced in the aisles to the tempo of the best organist in baseball.
> They turned losing baseball into a carnival.[42]

Dreadful won-lost record aside, over 1.2 million fans, a stunning number, went to *Parc Jarry*. Boys were so taken by the sport that they were skipping the usual games of summertime street hockey in favor of action on a local diamond and clearing out sporting goods stores of baseball equipment in the process. "The birth of the Montreal Expos created a sudden resurgence in amateur baseball extending far and beyond anyone's imagination ... as new life was literally breathed into baseball programs throughout the City of Montreal, the Province of Quebec, other provinces of Canada, and even in the northeastern U.S.... In Montreal so many youngsters showed up for baseball at city playgrounds that an official of the Parks and Recreation Department remarked: 'It's becoming a new religion, a new way of life for young Montrealers.'"[43] This phenomenon heralded a cultural shift: "It is true that many of these clubs were in existence before the birth of the Expos. But it's equally true that in other years, coaches often had to scramble to field a team (usually 15 players). Now it's a problem of numbers and second squads often have to be formed to accommodate the overflow."[44]

Rusty Staub, a two-time All-Star acquired in a 1969 pre-season trade with Houston, achieved cult-like status through his skill as a batter and his red-haired pate that earned him the endearing nickname of "Le Grand Orange." His culinary talent as a chef and "confirmed gourmet" was featured in the Expos' 1971 yearbook, in which he revealed his recipe for an Oysters Rockefeller casserole.[45] Even the idols on National Hockey League rosters, including the hometown Canadiens, were competing for attention with the Staubs, Mack Joneses, and Coco Laboys who wore the quirky tri-colored Expo caps.

To show that their maiden voyage was no fluke, 1.4 million fans "stormed Jarry Park throughout the season to cheer along their darlings."[46] Manager Gene Mauch was delighted when his prediction claiming that the Expos would "Win 70 in '70" actually fell short of the 73 wins his team did register, a 21-game improvement that assuaged another finish in the basement of the NL East.

It can be left to speculation as to the degree of influence the team's new third-base coach, former Red Sox manager Dick Williams, had on the outcome, but the victory total proved a stunning gain for the second-year team. When Williams departed for Oakland in 1971, he may have taken some intangible to his new post: Montreal remained stuck in the 70-win range until Mauch's firing after 1975, and Dodger coach Tom Lasorda was given consideration as his replacement. Ironically or not, Williams returned in 1977 to manage the Expos for over four seasons, a period that proved to be among the more accomplished in the franchise's history.

The early 1970s spawned another in a series of what would later be known as Golden Ages, attended, as always, by nostalgia and the often misguided feelings that things were always better way back when. With the benefit of historical hindsight, it is easy to see that fans of the Orioles, Athletics, and Reds certainly had good reason to anticipate imminent success, and supporters of the Dodgers would not have too long a wait to see their team join the fray. The ephemeral ascendancy of the Mets proved the difficulty of staying on top, and as the Yankees had risen and fallen over the course of the 1960s, so too did the tenants at Shea Stadium follow a similar trajectory that is part of the game's ebb and flow.

As painful as the vagaries of the baseball world can be, that group of cities would retain their franchises through the remainder of the twentieth century and beyond, although the ride for them would not always be smooth. But new expansion teams in San Diego and Seattle, as well as the newer one in Washington, D.C., suffered calamities in which only the first of those three avoided the fate of relocating to a new home—and even in that case, it was a close call.

5

Teams in Transition, for the Worse

At best, formulas for success on the field are elusive to find, and at worst, intractable if not impossible to derive. The assemblage of a club's roster under the leadership of its manager and coaching staff presents an array of difficulties, to say nothing of a desire that some semblance of camaraderie among all the personalities brought together will foster a healthy, respectful work environment and result in far more wins than losses.

But when the basic structure of club ownership is compromised, the result of a rapidly crumbling foundation underpinning the operation can spell doom. From 1969 to 1971, three teams displayed glaring deficiencies in their finances—somehow these predicaments always relate to money— or problems associated with poor attendance. Two of these had been the companion expansion brethren of the aforementioned Montreal Expos and Kansas City Royals, the other was a slightly older newcomer barely a decade into its existence. For their respective magnates, the novelty of owning a Major League ballclub swiftly lost its luster.

Whereas Kansas City and Montreal fielded contending teams by the end of the 1970s, their contemporaneous expansion partners, the San Diego Padres and, of special concern, the Seattle Pilots, were wracked by difficulties almost from the moment they left the starting gate. In San Diego, where the Padres matched the Expos' dubious record by losing 110 games and winning only 52, attendance at San Diego Stadium fell woefully short of that north of the border. If the Expos had longed for a ballpark with a seating capacity of 50,000 to placate their fans, they would have been happy to trade with the Padres, who drew a mere 512, 970 in the first season of Major League Baseball in southernmost California. In fact, in San Diego's first two seasons, they totaled only 1,156,649 paid admissions, and nearly replicated that amount in their third and fourth years with a total of just over 1.2 million.

Trying to capitalize on the club's mildly positive finish to the 1969 campaign, the Padres also hoped for 70 wins in 1970, this optimism spurred by a 13–17 record in September and October when "the young and improving Padres collected themselves and accomplished a closing rush that knocked out two [NL West] contenders and staggered two others in its wake."[1] Manager Preston Gómez took pride in the maturing of his younger players in the closing weeks and believed there would be carry-over momentum entering 1970, but the increase of 11 more wins still found the Padres in the cellar of their division.

Citing the disappointment of 37 losses by a single run, the public relations department commented, "Considering the authors of such agony were sophomores assigned to a senior federation of excessively talented and tested antagonists, and considering their second-year record showed marked improvement (63 wins compared with 1969's 52), one is provoked to consider such slim margin of defeat indicative of substantial progress."[2] Parsing through other drivel on this same page of the team's 1971 media guide, one is hard-pressed to find other encouragement besides the names of Nate Colbert, Ollie Brown, and Clarence Gaston, the trio of home run hitters who delivered enhanced power that put San Diego third in the NL in homers. Yet, Padre run production was only 11th in the league, the team struggled at the gate, and as wins remained a scarce commodity, so too did financial deficits begin to mount.

Club owner C. Arnholt Smith "was one of San Diego's emerging financial leaders, turning a tuna cannery into the cornerstone of an empire that included real estate and U.S. National Bank. But his pockets weren't nearly as deep as baseball hoped."[3] Smith realized a dream when he leveraged his successful business career to garner a Major League team, but the entry price of over $10 million was far in excess of his estimated cost to join the ranks of ownership. Undeterred yet immediately behind a monetary eight ball, Smith was hamstrung by debt and the lack of crowds at San Diego Stadium, which despite its being practically brand-new failed to be an attraction in and of itself.

As events unfolded and Smith's position grew increasingly precarious, in May 1973 the Padres were conditionally sold to Joseph Danzansky, a grocery entrepreneur in Washington who intended to move the team to the nation's capital. After several National League owners expressed a reluctance to place a poorly performing expansion team in a city that had recently lost the Washington Senators to the Dallas–Fort Worth area—a clutch of players also indicated that they had little stomach for playing at Robert F. Kennedy Stadium—there ensued much confused legal wrangling, not least of which were law suits by the city of San Diego against the Padres and the National League to prevent the team from relocating.

Ultimately, a renegotiation of the club's lease at San Diego Stadium and the intervention of fast-food magnate Ray Kroc settled the issue when his purchase was approved by NL owners in late January 1974. The franchise was still far from stable, but the wealth of the McDonald's restaurant chain offered the financial cushion that Smith lacked and spared Major League Baseball from another embarrassing episode of a recent expansion team looking for a new home shortly after its formation.

Preceding the rollicking adventures of the Padres was the dramatic plight of the Seattle Pilots, who would spend a single season in the Pacific Northwest before transferring to Milwaukee to become the Brewers. The timing of this episode occurred at the beginning of the 1970 regular season: printed sometime after mid–January, the team's primary publication for the benefit of the press was their *Log Book, 1970 Press—Radio—Television*, and like the 1969 media guide, no city name was included on the cover, but the Pilots' winged helm logo was featured in an understated manner.

Having hosted the 1962 World's Fair, which allowed Seattle to expand in cultural and civic aspects, the city had a lot to offer as the decade progressed. "Seattle was already a major entrepôt on the Pacific Ocean," wrote historian William Mullins. "The region was growing. Seattle was the fifteenth-largest media market in the country, and metropolitan Seattle was the eighteenth largest urban area, surpassing the likes of Atlanta, Cincinnati, Milwaukee, and San Diego."[4] But situated as it was—bounded on the west by Elliott Bay and, by extension, Puget Sound, the city was surrounded by two national parks and a pair of national forests—Seattle's outdoor recreational opportunities abounded, and the locals were greatly attracted to powerboat racing and football games at the University of Washington. Simply stated, baseball assumed a lesser priority for passing one's leisure time.

Seattle was not necessarily an unattractive backwater in the eyes of the national pastime. The city had hosted a Pacific Coast League team for decades, and it had drawn the notice of the Cleveland Indians in 1964 as well as the Kansas City Athletics in 1967 as a possible relocation venue. At issue was the woebegone ballpark that served as the home to the Seattle Rainiers, Sicks' Stadium, which was far from Major League standards both in its seating capacity and physical condition. Bond issues in 1960 and 1966 that would have allowed construction of a new stadium failed before the Seattle electorate, and the mayor and two of the city's five council members were either lukewarm or firmly against allocating funds for any upgrades to the existing ballpark. The use of Sicks' would be a stopgap measure by any Major League team until a new stadium could be built.

By early 1968, a third bond issue finally passed with 62 percent approval, just two points over the minimum required, but "[it] appears that the stadium lagged among the blue-collar population, who probably saw little value in trading higher property taxes for the opportunity to pay hard-earned dollars to see baseball or football in a new sports facility."[5] Although the narrow affirmation of the voters enabled the landing of a Major League club, which was a matter of pride for the sporting community, the new stadium had yet to be designed and constructed, and boding worse than that was the shaky financial ground that supported the new Major League franchise.

Pacific Northwest Sports, Inc., was founded by brothers Max and Dewey Soriano, who were natives of the area and had strong ties to the former PCL team, and Cleveland-based William Daley, a former principal owner of the Indians who toured Seattle in 1964 when he considered moving the team there. Daley, already acquainted with the Sorianos, was to serve as the primary financier of the Pilots, and American League executives, knowing of his business acumen in wresting concessions from the city of Cleveland to keep the Indians from leaving, were comfortable with Daley's association with the new expansion club.

The Pilots had little time to get organized, both in the creation of the team they would field and the preparation of Sicks' Stadium to make it ready for the coming 1969 season. The former task yielded a roster comprised of the cast-offs from other AL teams with the predictable result of a non-contender, while the latter chore turned into a comedy of errors. This uncomfortable punch list included delays in beginning the refurbishing of the ballpark; uncompleted work on building new sections of stands; inadequate restroom facilities; squabbles between municipal officials and contractors charged with various repairs, construction, and landscaping; and once the ballpark was opened, reimbursement to fans whose "clothes had smears of blue primer from the not-yet-dry bleachers they sat in."[6] But the specter of a hard monetary reckoning ultimately doomed the Pilots rather than backed up toilets or inadequate supplies of some items at the concession stands.

If storm clouds were not already evident, they took on greater form mere weeks after Opening Day. Besides the funds that Pacific Northwest Sports expended for the franchise, the team's concession vendor, a company called Sportservice, gave the owners "a $2 million loan in exchange for a twenty-year concessions contract that would follow the team wherever it moved—presumably from Sicks' Stadium to the new domed stadium. The Sportservice loan essentially paid off $2 million of the $3 million in personal loans from the owners. The transfer of debt obligation to the concessionaire was a sign that ownership was getting jumpy about finances only a month into the [1969] season."[7]

On the heels of this monetary legerdemain, "[in] June, a worried Max Soriano, asked for an accounting department projection for the season. The accountants predicted a $2.2 million shortfall. 'That's when I knew we were in trouble,' he admitted. The Pilots longed for one million in attendance but had projected 850,000 to break even. They wound up with 677,944, leading to a loss estimated at $800,000."[8] In commissioner Bowie Kuhn's files, a memo dated the 19th of that month indicates that he and his associates were toying with the idea of restructuring the American *and* National Leagues into three divisions of eight clubs each, which would be a rapid update from the two-division split both circuits had just implemented. This arrangement of Western, Midland, and Eastern divisions featured a pair of two-week "inter-locking portion[s]" of the schedule when teams would play interdivisional contests. Curiously, the Seattle franchise was dropped in favor of one labelled "Milwaukee," hardly a vote of confidence from the highest office of the game regarding the status of the Pilots.[9]

William Daley went to Seattle in September to try to restore a semblance of calm with city officials over the manner in which Sicks' Stadium renovations had been handled. While in town, the chairman denounced insinuations in the press that the team might be on the move, yet he denied the Sorianos an infusion of extra cash to help the club regain its financial footing. When it appeared in October that a Seattle group headed by Fred Danz, a theater entrepreneur, had secured the purchase of the team, a California bank called in a loan to the Pilots that the American League knew nothing about.

Now on the hook for another $3.5 million and with a season-ticket campaign generating inadequate revenue, Danz backed out of the deal, and another Seattle consortium that included hotel mogul Ed Carlson and several high-ranking Washington State politicians proposed a community-based ownership group, but this gained little traction among AL team owners. Interests in Dallas entered the fray—this was actually a second bid for them—in the hope of purchasing and transferring the club, but this too was unsuccessful.

October proved a critical time as the Danz, Carlson, and Dallas parties were at work, for it was during the World Series that the Sorianos quietly reached an agreement with a group led by auto dealer Allan H. "Bud" Selig to purchase the Pilots and relocate them to Milwaukee. By the spring of 1970 when the Pilots gathered for spring training and were still calling Seattle their home, Jerry Hoffberger, owner of the Baltimore Orioles, indicated that the American League was willing to give $650,000 to the team as a down payment, of sorts, to help extricate itself from its peril. But Pacific Northwest Sports, alleging $2.3 million in losses from 1969 and already forecasting a dismal financial outlook in the new season, found itself in a bankruptcy hearing in late March.[10]

In the event, just a single bona fide offer was tendered to rescue the team, this coming from the Selig group. And so it was that "[t]he Seattle Pilots, seven days from the opening game of their second season, were going to Milwaukee."[11] There was obvious joy in Wisconsin's most populous city now that Major League Baseball was back after the departure of the Braves to Atlanta in 1966.

A quickly retooled team yearbook proclaimed, "Hello Brewers! Make yourselves at home," and the opening page displayed a message from Mayor Henry Maier wishing the team "good luck, always, and may you truly find a 'home' in Milwaukee!" There followed greetings from Milwaukee County Executive John Doyne, who noted that "Our Milwaukee County Stadium has been standing ready and waiting for a major league baseball team," while tactfully omitting any reference to the former National League tenants.[12] That pages 28 and 29 list an array of batting and pitching records devoid of any references to "Seattle" or "Pilots" mattered little—these were simply "Club Records" that were now part of the lore and legacy of the Brewers.

Yet, rather than closing the book fully on the sale and transfer of a baseball team, most years of the 1970s would contain one episode or another of action played out not at County Stadium but within the confines of courtrooms and law offices on the East and West Coasts. Miffed at being jilted by the Pilots' one-year stand, collective government interests in Washington State initiated a lawsuit against the American League (and other baseball defendants), which goes unmentioned in Bowie Kuhn's 1987 memoir. By the middle of the decade, Seattle had secured a new expansion team for the domed stadium that was at last being constructed—not primarily as an accommodation for baseball but instead for a new National Football League team to be called the Seahawks, who were formed in 1974 and were to begin play in 1976.

For baseball's part, there followed a complicated series of events involving the vacating of Washington, D.C., by the Senators in 1971 (discussed below) and the possible relocation of the San Francisco Giants to fill the void. But moving the Giants to Toronto was also an option, as was Seattle, the latter choice with the intention of stifling that city's legal action. In September 1973, Kuhn gave a deposition in the case of *The State of Washington, the County of King, and the City of Seattle v. The American League of Professional Baseball Clubs, et al.*[13] Revealing in the meeting at which Kuhn was called to depose—and, to be fair, this was roughly four years after some of the events had taken place—he was asked if, in his role as commissioner, he had "the power to prevent the transfer of a franchise from one city to another," and while stating that he had "no express power to do that," he elaborated: "However, it is my view that under certain circumstances the commissioner could determine that a proposed transfer is not in the best interest of baseball and could prevent a transfer."

Kuhn acknowledged sending a letter in 1969 to club owners asking "to report to [me] at the earliest stage of the preliminary discussions, any possible or suggested transfer of a franchise from one city to another," although he failed to recall the specifics of the note. Kuhn's questioner tried to get him to signal what current cities would be suitable for a new Major League Baseball team and what criteria should be followed in determining the awarding of expansion clubs, but the commissioner equivocated: "In other words, what I'm trying not to say is that I have made any determination that cities like Toronto and New Orleans are, under all circumstances, ideal locations for baseball. I am simply saying I think there is enough there that looks positive that they should be given serious consideration." It is noteworthy that he also felt Buffalo would be a favored location, but Denver, another potential site, would not.

Even three-plus years after the Pilots moved to Milwaukee, when questioned, "Is it still your view then, Seattle is definitely major league territory?" Kuhn stated, "Yes, it is." He confirmed that he was informed by Max Soriano during the 1969 World Series of "a handshake agreement that had been reached between Seattle owners and a group in Milwaukee providing for a sale of the Seattle franchise," but Kuhn had no recollection of "receiving a telegram from the mayor of Seattle asking your good offices in keeping the ball club there."

Disturbed by this lack of recall, attorney William Dwyer produced, for the record, a copy of the telegram, which had also been sent to Joe Cronin, president of the American League. Dwyer boldly asked Kuhn, "Do you have a document destruction policy in your office?" and when Kuhn affirmed that there was, the lawyer tried to pin down the culprit who may have made the telegram disappear and whether any other "Seattle material [had] been destroyed." Kuhn redirected by saying counsel for the American League had selected documents for him to review in preparation for the deposition hearing, and the issue of document destruction passed.

When October 1969 was brought up again, Kuhn gave his assurance that he desired to see the Pilots stay in Seattle, and he voiced no overt opposition to the Carlson proposal for community ownership, but later in the session he said that support for the Carlson group was "necessary" to keep baseball in Seattle. With nine votes among the 12 AL clubs required to allow the sale, the four negative votes cast by the Orioles, Athletics, White Sox, and Senators denied Carlson the chance to save the Pilots. The irony is that two of these owner-voters, Charlie Finley and Bob Short, had recently abandoned, or were soon about to abandon, their cities for supposedly greener pastures, while a good faith effort to keep the Pilots in Seattle was nixed.

Although Kuhn was not familiar with some of the financial aspects such as the Sportservice deal or the "large amounts of money that the City of Seattle had spent in refurbishing Sick's [sic] Stadium," there followed this compelling exchange.

Q: Did you know that what they had spent to refurbish the stadium was done in reliance upon an American League club being there and staying there until the new stadium was ready?

Kuhn: *No, I would not know that.* [Emphasis added]

Q: Nobody told you that?

Kuhn: No.

It is astounding that the commissioner of baseball could *not* have the slightest idea that such an important arrangement was in place. Pressed further—and again incredulously—Kuhn claimed no knowledge or concurrence with something that AL president Joe Cronin had been told in January 1970, namely that the funds being expended on a new domed stadium were predicated on a Major League team remaining in Seattle. Kuhn denied time and again knowing that, according to his questioner, "the state and county and city were asserting that they had made substantial investments and commitments based upon American League promises."

Q: Did you know that if the club were moved that the State of Washington and King County and City of Seattle would suffer financial damages?

Kuhn: No.

A similar degree of unknowing infused Kuhn on the issue of loss of business and tax revenues, yet he *was* aware of the American League's promotional effort that enabled the most recent bond issue to pass. The commissioner's deposition concluded with commentary on the Carlson situation, that in the time that elapsed from its initial offering until the Pilots were about to collapse in early 1970 that Carlson's "financial structure had changed so markedly for the worse that it was impossible to reactivate [its bid]...." Those four negative votes were apparently prescient, after all.

Granted that Kuhn had been in the commissioner's seat only since February of 1969, and not long thereafter the Pilots' drama began to unfold, if not commence spinning out of control. Had he been possessed of the same level of acumen as his predecessor, William Eckert, Kuhn might be excused for his cited lack of knowledge. Yet, as an attorney for the National League for over a decade prior to his naming as commissioner, he had to have been aware of at least some of the business implications of expansion as well as the problems with the Seattle situation, especially in light of the June 19 memo, written barely two months into the season, in which a three-divisional alignment of the American League shows Milwaukee, not Seattle. Although Kuhn's deposition was given several years after the Pilots had moved, his obfuscating does not stand up to scrutiny.

While Seattle and Toronto soon were awarded expansion franchises, the tears of joy cried by Bud Selig upon his purchase of the Pilots in 1970 were more genuine than some of the answers provided during the commissioner's hearing, and the Milwaukee Brewers were able to chart their own course that gained a modicum of success in the very competitive American League East by the end of the 1970s.

When Calvin Griffith moved the original Washington Senators to Minneapolis in 1961, the expansion team of the same name created to immediately fill the baseball vacancy in the nation's capital was as beleaguered as its forbear had been at times in its more recent past. The bromide "First in war, first in peace, and last in the American League" was especially true in Washington from 1955 to 1959 when the Senators finished in the AL basement four out of five years. Upon Griffith's departure to the Upper Midwest, a new franchise to keep baseball alive at old Griffith Stadium was imperative lest Congress be stirred to examine baseball's antitrust exemption.

The new Senators embarked on what became an inglorious 11-year journey that ultimately found them seeking a new home out west, albeit roughly 940 miles south of where the Twins were domiciled. A ten-member collective that created the expansion version of the Solons had dwindled to one solitary owner by the end of 1967, at which point James Lemon wanted to divest himself of the team. With Gil Hodges as field manager, Washington showed some signs of improvement, but during the Lemon years, attendance never surpassed 770,868, its total in Hodges's last year with the Senators.

Sale of the ballclub was agreed to in early December 1968, but it took nearly two months to finalize the $9.4 million deal.[14] The purchaser was Robert E. Short, former owner of the National Basketball Association's Los Angeles Lakers, who had made his fortune as a trucking company entrepreneur and hotelier. His work as the treasurer of the Democratic National

Committee also boded well for his status as a political insider. Short borrowed a page from Charlie Finley's playbook by becoming his own general manager, only with results far from spectacular compared to his counterpart in Oakland.

However, another past event in Short's career should have drawn closer notice among the American League club owners who approved the sale of the Senators: the Lakers were resident in Minneapolis at the time Short bought them in the mid–1950s, but after encountering money problems by 1957, he moved them to the West Coast in 1960. As events played out in his baseball venture, Short seemed to be afflicted with dysfunctional financial DNA at the same time he was trying to get a grip on his duties as an owner and GM, including player contract negotiations and basic operation of both the team and Robert F. Kennedy Stadium, formerly D.C. Stadium, where the Senators had played their home games since 1962.

Like Finley, Short liked the limelight when some dramatic flair was at hand, and as he contemplated who would be his field boss, "[t]he first Negro manager in the majors is a possibility. Short said he had given the matter a great deal of thought, and indications are that his thoughts have included Jackie Robinson, Elston Howard, Maury Wills and Monte Irvin," but the man he lured out of retirement, former Boston Red Sox legend Ted Williams, was handed the reins.[15]

Short was demanding an immediate turnaround in the club's performance on the field and at the box office, and he expected that his hands-on approach— some might have called it dictatorial—would bring the intended results. The owner was offended by the salary demands of his better players, including

With a habit of pleading poverty, Washington owner Bob Short set his sights on the greener pastures of the Dallas–Fort Worth area, where he moved the Senators after the 1971 season.

the behemoth slugger Frank Howard, who said, "I hate to do business with Short. He kills you with kindness and then you wind up making all the concessions."[16]

Spring training was underway in March 1970 when Short addressed a "sparsely attended luncheon" of Washington commercial and business interests, chiding those present for not purchasing more season tickets as a show of support for the Senators. "People are afraid to go to our games. And why shouldn't they be when you won't come?" he asked while trying to allay the fears of those reluctant to go to a stadium located in a less-desirable part of the city. "We said to the Interior Department [overseers of the stadium property]—put up fences around the parking lots and more lights. Make it daylight and that was done."[17] Short cited the work of eight Senator players who spoke to youth groups of every class and race in an effort to build community relations.

Yet, even at this early point in his tenure in Washington, "[t]he club president stopped short of threatening the loss of the franchise here but he did say, 'The future of the Senators is in this room.... I am not here to tell you our franchise may be sold. It is not going to leave here. But unless we get support it is going to be like Seattle. There is no way we can operate this year without community support.... We need every company in Washington on our season-ticket list."

In mid–September 1970, Bowie Kuhn spoke with Short and recorded some interesting notes of their telephone conversation. The owner pleaded poverty, portraying his financial condition and that of the Senators as weak: $300,000 losses for both cash flow and player procurement in 1969, with a $1 million deficit forecasted in the current year; Short paid himself no salary or dividends and "has taken out only expenses"; Short "cannot get a fair deal for [radio]-TV," claiming that the $315,000 received in 1969 "was the highest in club history" yet was near the bottom among AL clubs; "cannot sell season tickets ... [because] city is political & [business] lives in [Maryland and Virginia]"; the nearby Orioles, in regional geographic competition with Short's club, was "one too many" teams and claimed that the Senators could pull in $1 million more than the Orioles and still "go broke"; and he expressed a willingness to sell for $11 million, an amount that totaled his original purchase price plus additional funds to cover the losses he estimated for his two years of ownership.[18] Stating a preference to be a part of the National League—no record was made as how this might happen—Short also had spoken earlier that month with entertainer Bob Hope about becoming a part owner.

The following month, baseball's Executive Council learned that Short was trying to renegotiate his stadium lease to obtain more favorable terms. He liked the idea of a "Milwaukee-type contract, in which the club pays $1 rent for the first million in attendance," and he coveted the quarter-million-dollar parking fees that went to the D.C. Armory Board, the stadium's operator, rather than into his pocket.[19] Despite the rancor of his brief ownership tenure, he thought that the team deserved to stay in Washington rather than move to Toronto or Dallas, but if an effort to sell the team proved successful and he could recoup his investment, he was indifferent as to what city it called home.

Prior to the 1971 season, Short struck a deal for better radio-television revenue with two Washington outlets, but all the while the team continued to accrue unpaid bills to the Armory Board and other creditors. In March, he was notified by Francis Kane, the Board's chairman:

> Aside from the additional rent which was due October 27, 1970 in the amount of $84,847.93, the Armory Board expended the additional $28,010.81 due on your account, from July through November of last year on behalf of the Washington Senators, mainly to assure your having been provided with Metropolitan Police services and playing field lighting during the last two months of your 1970 season. We would, therefore, appreciate payment of this portion of your account as soon as possible.
>
> In the absence of any responsible statement from you concerning the payment, or anticipated payment, of your indebtedness dating back to October, 1970, *and earlier in the year*, the Armory Board is compelled to advise you that unless expeditious payment is forthcoming, it will be necessary to consider commencing action under Paragraph No. 31 of your lease agreement with the Armory Board.[20]

Just as the Armory Board was dunning Short for payment, so too was Kuhn scrambling to get reliable data to substantiate the owner's claim "that he only has sufficient funds to operate through the end of April [1971]."[21] The owner brought his case before a Congressional subcommittee because ownership of Robert F. Kennedy Stadium was to be turned over to the Department of the Interior, but not until the year 2007. If such a transfer could be done sooner, Short would have a better chance at renegotiating his lease, but he was "shocked" when the Interior Department rejected the bid.[22]

With his current lease due to expire at the end of the 1971 season, Short vowed to not sign another lease for the stadium unless modifications were made. Edward Bennett Williams, president of the National Football League's Washington Redskins, whose team also played at RFK, was opposed to any relief via transfer of the stadium's control for the benefit of Short, who was indeed reminded in mid–June that the Senators had the option of renewing the lease for five years beginning in 1972.

One AL owner who had little sympathy for Short was Milwaukee's Bud Selig. If the league chose to bail Short out of his predicament, which in turn meant each team paying a portion of the cost, the Brewers would not contribute, Selig told Kuhn. The "terribly concerned" Milwaukee owner said he received his favorable lease on County Stadium because the facility was already paid for—RFK Stadium still had $20 million in outstanding bonds along with $800,000 in annual interest payments—and that Milwaukee County kept the parking fees while covering the stadium's operating costs.[23]

Short's upheaval at this time was accompanied by another item that came to Kuhn's attention when a front-page newspaper story reported that in his role as a hotel magnate, Short "has purchased two major hotels in downtown St. Paul and adjacent properties for an estimated $2.3 million.... Taxes, which were paid by Short yesterday [March 31], amounted to about $90,000, city officials said."[24] Somehow, Short had access to funds apparently kept separate from his baseball business; the article also questioned the wisdom of such a venture, to which Short responded, "This isn't the first time that I've been in deep and gone in deeper to wade out."

The wading process in Short's baseball world was pockmarked by the poor roster adjustments in a failed effort to bolster attendance that only added to the team's debt load. Washington was now on an unrelenting slippery slope, as Shirley Povich reported in the *Washington Post*: "If the Senators' owner is disenchanted with Washington as a baseball town, then there is overwhelming evidence of the mutuality of it. Short blighted the current season before it began with his ghastly deal that stripped the team of the best side of its infield, Aurelio Rodriguez and Ed Brinkman, for Denny McLain. Again mistaking color for performance, Short brought Curt Flood out of retirement at a cost of 110,000 down-the-drain dollars in his team's financial crunch."[25]

Short tried to make peace with the Armory Board by forwarding a small check "for electrical services and bulb replacements through April 15, 1971, but the Board's manager was having none of it." In a letter—this was sent via registered mail with a return receipt requested—the Board returned the check for $5,636.99, threatened to "not permit the Stadium field lights to be turned on, nor will it suffer any further expense for the use of the public address system or for tenant purposes" unless $40,384.66 was remitted by July 14. The missive further advised Short that a lawsuit would be filed unless "some arrangements which are satisfactory to the Armory Board to pay the outstanding rental fees" were made.[26] For all previous unpaid rent and expenses since 1970, Short was in arrears for over $151,000—and counting.

At the end of June, Kuhn spoke with Ewing Kauffman, and they discussed the possibility of all teams (except the Senators) contributing to a fund, presumably under the auspices of the commissioner's office or the

American League, that would buy out Short and then find a new owner. Chapter 11 bankruptcy was another option they floated.[27] Through all the havoc, one thing finally went right for the Senators when American League president Joe Cronin notified AL executives on July 9 that the team and the Armory Board agreed on a payment schedule to keep the lights on at RFK Stadium and avoid any interruption of play.

But just as the front office was besieged with problems, the team on the field was suffering, too. "Mired in last place in the American League East," reported a July 14 story from the Associated Press, "[manager Ted] Williams has chosen to go with youngsters whenever he can: Shortstop Toby Harrah, second baseman Lenny Randle, third baseman Dave Nelson, outfielders Larry Biitner and [Elliott] Maddox and Dick Billings, who has caught and played third and the outfield."[28]

The root cause of this youth movement was placed at the feet of Bob Short, who traded away Aurelio Rodríguez, Ed Brinkman, et al., for the sore-armed Denny McLain, whose status by this point could only be labeled "has-been." At this time, the commissioner's office learned that the team had no actual television network: Only one station, WTOP-TV, carried any games, and the poorly performing Senators were generating little enthusiasm for any other outlets to pick up the broadcasts. Radio station WWDC found itself in similar circumstances as the lone carrier for that medium.

Détente, of a sort, was reached in August when the Armory Board agreed to some of Short's lease-renewal requests, such as free rent up to attendance of one million, but the Board would not relinquish all concession, advertising, and parking revenues—splitting was acceptable, full surrender was not—nor would they forgive the back rent still unpaid. The Board had its own finances to contend with and felt they had offered a fair deal, but Short wanted to extract as much as he could, and the predictable result was no agreement. During this wearying summer, he was denying rumors claiming that he was looking to move the team to Dallas, but there also emerged a possible new owner to purchase the troubled Senators.

Henry Fitzgibbon, the head of Kuhn's Security Division, conducted "a discreet investigation ... to develop information concerning JOSEPH B. DANZANSKY," and the findings were at once revealing and very encouraging.[29] Besides living in Washington and sitting on the board of several notable local businesses, Danzansky was the president of Giant Food, Inc., a regional grocery chain; he tended toward philanthropy, was a civic leader and "[o]ne of the most influential men in the Washington area, a very wealthy man whose reputation is beyond reproach." As Kuhn was learning about the food magnate, the Washington City Council Chairman, Gilbert Hahn, filed a law suit against the Senators to collect unpaid rent of nearly

$137,000, an action that Short laughed off by mocking Hahn as an unemployed lawyer looking for easy money.[30]

Appearing to bring a lot to the table, Danzansky found favor to the extent that a draft of an asset purchase agreement was created, and the commissioner's administrative officer, John H. Johnson, evaluated the Senators' Major League roster and minor league teams. Johnson found an organization hardly in shambles: "The farm system has benefitted (since 1965) in the free agent draft by drafting fairly high, enabling them to acquire some of the better prospects that are now coming to fruition," and the Triple-A team in Denver as well as the Double-A club in Pittsfield, Massachusetts, were in first and second place, respectively, in their leagues as of August 30.[31] Slugger Frank Howard was flagged as the only "outstanding major leaguer," but Johnson noted that Dick Bosman, Del Unser, and Paul Lindblad—along with the failing McLain—were "good," and he marked a 20-year-old Jeff Burroughs among those having "good future potential."

The middle of September featured more negotiations between the principals, and the *Washington Star* reported that "an associate of Short who attended yesterday's 90-minute secret meeting with the Armory Board told The Star today: 'I can only say this. He is trying terribly hard to stay here.'"[32] Yet, at the same time, the mayor of Arlington, Texas, indicated that a group of buyers in the Lone Star State was "ready to pay the $12 million price" for the ballclub.[33] Radio and TV rights in northern Texas were estimated by Kuhn's director of broadcast media to bring in about $700,000, an amount that may have sounded good compared to the Senators' current deal but was, in actuality, negatively impacted by "the strength of its competition (for example, Houston, St. Louis, Kansas City, and even Atlanta)" from other Major League teams already broadcasting their games in Texas.[34]

However sincere Short may have been in trying terribly hard to stay in the nation's capital, when the 12 owners of the American League clubs convened in Boston on September 21, an air of uncertainty abounded. Danzansky was given the floor to state his case for purchasing the team at a price of $8.4 million, and he was met with an initially favorable reaction. But when he was called back for serious questioning, "Danzansky admitted that he did not have his financing arranged and at this point was willing only to put up $50,000 which he would use to pay for a purchase agreement, *i.e.*, an option to buy."[35] The supposedly affluent grocer intended to take out a $6.6 million loan that he expected the AL to underwrite, thereby putting the league rather than himself at risk for any losses. Counsel for the American League present at the same meeting "also pointed out that such an undertaking would probably not be possible in

5. Teams in Transition, for the Worse 121

light of existing contractual commitments of the Clubs" and "might jeopardize the tax exempt status of the League."[36]

Needless to say, the offer disintegrated quickly. When Danzansky said that "a mysterious man" he had met the day before—and to whom he was sworn to secrecy not to identify—was willing to participate in the purchase, the owners may have wondered about the potential buyer supposedly, in the words of Henry Fitzgibbon, beyond reproach.[37] One last-minute, last-ditch effort by Charlie Finley to enlist Ed Daly of World Airways, Inc. to fill the Danzansky void failed, but a record of the meeting provides what could be seen as the crux of the matter at that moment:

> It was recognized that the critical inquiry was: in which of the two cities would the presence of an American League Club best protect and advance the interest of the League, without regard to Mr. Short's personal interest. Viewed from this point of view, it was observed that Dallas–Fort Worth had the potential of providing two new cities to support a single club, while the Washington–Baltimore area has been marginal or less as the locations for two clubs.[38]

The owners preferred potential over the woes of the current angst, and on a second ballot, Short was given ten approving votes to transfer his team to Texas, with Baltimore and the Chicago White Sox voting against.

A contrite Danzansky shortly thereafter addressed another meeting of AL owners, blaming himself for his earlier proposal being "inadequate," and he offered the support of the Washington Board of Trade, which he chaired, should there be another attempt to put a new team in RFK Stadium.[39]

Short delivered an apology to the fans in Washington over an inability to remain in town—one may wonder how sincere he was—but Walter O'Malley, owner of the Los Angeles Dodgers and a man never bashful about leveraging a good opportunity, fired off a letter to Bob Carpenter, president of the Philadelphia Phillies. Baseball could keep a tentative presence in lieu of the Senators, and O'Malley acknowledged that "[t]here is some logic in the thought that Baltimore would play up to half of its games in Washington.... If by chance Baltimore does not take advantage of the situation, I suggest that you consider playing 11 games there."[40] O'Malley cited an ability to more easily market partial season-ticket plans compared to those for a full season, so he believed it possible for baseball to capitalize in some way even without a regular tenant at RFK Stadium.

But where O'Malley quickly saw dollar signs, editorial comments on the Senators' transfer were tinged with more than bitterness. Dick Denham, program manager of NBC Radio affiliate WRC 980AM, told listeners two days after the owners gathered in Boston,

> It all sounds so hollow now doesn't it? We're speaking of the line that "the nation's capital deserves the national game." Obviously, 10 of the 12 American League owners couldn't have cared less when they voted to strip Washington of a team for the second time in a decade, this time sending the Senators to a Texas turnpike somewhere between Dallas and Ft. Worth....
>
> All the franchise needed here was loving care from a competent doctor. In Bob Short it got a quack!⁴¹

The Senators' now former TV broadcaster evinced more sympathy than its radio counterpart.

> Bob Short leaves Washington neither all right nor all wrong. He was flamboyant, surely. It may be that he was downright inept as the club's overseer. Be that as it may, Short has been pilloried far beyond his due. The sportswriting fraternity in this town has been naive to the point of childishness in expecting Short to pay his bills with wishful thinking. It's also true that Short was underfinanced when he bought the Senators, but he also had to contend with an economy which turned sour and with civic and governmental leaders who cheered him on but who backed him up with precious little tangible support.⁴²

With the nation's capital now confirmed to be losing its baseball team, the nation's number-one fan, President Richard Nixon, reverted to the AL club closest to his hometown of Yorba Linda, California, by throwing his support behind the California Angels.

On the evening of Thursday September 30, 1971, the Senators played their final game at RFK Stadium before 14,460 fans, and the home team was one out away from ending its run in Washington with a 7–5 victory over the New York Yankees. That is, "until several kids jumped the fences in left and right as Joe Grzenda was pitching to Horace Clarke in the ninth and the place erupted."⁴³ The finale was fertile ground for many fans to vent their anger at an owner they had come to despise while at the same time there was much sorrow expressed for the players, especially Frank Howard, who were crowd favorites never to be seen again.

All the love shown the greatest slugger in expansion Senators' history, however, was countered by the display of tension and hatred directed at the club's owner, including chants of "Bob Short Stinks" and outsized bed-sheet banners that echoed those same sentiments, some in obscene terms. When the field was stormed in the ninth inning, "[t]he fans took the bases, tore up the mound, snatched lights off the scoreboard, leaped on the dugout roofs, and tore up the turf."⁴⁴ Many players beat a hasty retreat to their clubhouses as the mayhem grew worse and the 50 extra police assigned to the stadium that night became overmatched. The game was forfeited to the Yankees as an ignominious ending closed out a chaotic chapter in Washington's baseball history.

In an interview with Chicago-based sportswriter Jerome Holtzman, White Sox owner John Allyn said that Short was receiving what amounted to a $7.5 million advance from the Arlington Park Corporation, which operated as a municipal non-profit organization, in exchange for the radio and television broadcast rights of $750,000 annually over a ten-year period. In response to the question of "Where does this organization get its money?" Allyn replied, "It's all taxpayers' money. It doesn't belong to anybody. None of it is coming from individuals who are putting money where their mouths are and who could be sued."[45] This last point was an important legal safety-valve, for example, should objections be raised to funding the necessary improvements to Arlington Stadium, the team's new home. When Holtzman opined, "This is quite a deal for Short, isn't it. Especially for an owner who was supposedly bankrupt last week," Allyn concurred with the writer's additional comment, "In other words, Short takes the $7.5 million, pays all of his debts and winds up with 100 percent equity, that is, a completely paid-up club."

Outrage by the fans during RFK Stadium's swansong was predictably accompanied by critical comments from several prominent Washington political figures. A staunch antitrust advocate, New York Congressman Emanuel Celler, demanded a review of baseball's antitrust exemption, and House Republican Leader Gerald Ford sought the placement of another team to fill the vacancy created by the Senators' move.[46] The name of Joseph Danzansky appeared in the record of the United State Senate signaling his interest "to explore the possibility of a major league franchise being allocated to Washington by the 1973 season."[47]

A dubious, twisted punch line to this episode was disclosed in galling fashion near the end of 1971. Economists Roger Noll and Benjamin Okner conducted a detailed review of data that Short provided to his accounting firm, Arthur Anderson & Company. A startling discovery showed that Short had paid a mere $1,000 for the baseball team, supposedly all that was needed to handle some paperwork establishing the bureaucratic framework for his ownership of the club. Between tax write-offs for player depreciation, loans taken from other businesses he owned, and creative accounting methodology employed to blur the lines distinguishing/defining losses and profits, Short could be thought to be laughing all the way to the bank rather than running away from creditors. "If figures don't lie, they don't always tell the truth, either," observed *The Sporting News* in an editorial, adding, "The losses Short claimed were mainly of the bookkeeping variety, not cash leakage."[48]

"Nothing, the economists point out in their analysis, shows that Short did anything unethical or improper—merely that he was a shrewd business operator at work in the lucrative byways of professional sports and its extraordinary tax setups," reported Shelby Coffey III in his front-page story in the *Washington Post*. "Like many shrewd businessmen, he was out to make money with other people's money—even though he often complained that he was handicapped in his work with the team by 'servicing' his debts."[49]

Once the team settled into Arlington as the new Texas Rangers, they were as hapless, if not more so, in their new home—the AL West division—as they had been in the AL East. Finishing in last place in 1972, the Rangers won 54 games, lost 100, and despite their manager being one of the greatest hitters who ever lived—Ted Williams did accompany the team in the move—the collective team batting average was a pathetic .217, 12 points less than 11th-ranked Baltimore and firmly at the bottom of the league. *The Team That Couldn't Hit: The 1972 Texas Rangers*, published by the Society for American Baseball Research, was a book dedicated to the latest club to find its way from the greater Northeast to supposedly greener pastures out west.

Fans at Ranger home games saw little to be thrilled about: Texas drew just under 663,000, good for tenth among the 12 AL teams and not much more than the 655,156 at RFK Stadium the previous year. And chaos in the front office still held forth even though Joe Burke was brought in as an advisor and technically served as the general manager, "although his influence with [Bob] Short was limited as long as the dominant Ted Williams was manager."[50] The Rangers finally found their footing in 1974 with Billy Martin at the helm, and he guided the club to a second-place finish in the AL West—attendance surged along with the win total—but Short was already in the process of bailing out. By striking a deal to sell the team to Brad Corbett, Short thereby "len[t] credence to the accusations that he was just interested in the tax write-offs that were available for [the five years he owned the team]."[51]

Attempts to install baseball again in Washington arose in the first year of its absence there in seven decades. Buzzie Bavasi, president of the San Diego Padres, wrote to Bowie Kuhn, confessing, "I am not too familiar with the situation in Washington. However, I have been approached by several members of the National League asking if the Padres will be of a mind to relocate the franchise in Washington. The people in Washington are ready to offer a rather attractive arrangement and from a baseball perspective, I would have to listen."[52] As described earlier, this effort would come to grief, and the Capital remained without a Major League franchise until several years into the next century.

Blame for the downfall of the Washington Senators can easily be laid at the feet of Bob Short due to his troubled financial affairs and, in

5. Teams in Transition, for the Worse

his role as the club's general manager, his acquisition of pitcher Denny McLain from Detroit did nothing to counteract the disorder occurring in the front office. Despite the possibility of trades like this not ending well, the exchanging of players between Major League teams was in a golden age thanks to the built-in constraints of the reserve clause, and until that bit of legalese was voided, the wheeling and dealing among GMs, whether they were swapping stars or figures of lesser stature, was a source of debate and discussion both in-season and during sessions of the Hot Stove League.

6

The Trading Post

Bob Short's failure as a general manager was not unique in the handling of baseball personnel. When a trade works to the spectacular benefit of one team and the extreme detriment of its trading partner, there will always be commentary rife with ridicule as results of the exchange play out.

Yet, any club will execute a deal with the expectation of improving its lot by fixing an extant problem: The need for more pitching, whether in the form of another starter to bolster the rotation, or a reliable closer capable of holding a late-inning lead; a position player to address a problem area, such as the New York Mets' perennial issue of finding an everyday third baseman; or possibly simply someone to serve as a quality backup who can enter the game in a pinch. Paul Richards, the GM of the Atlanta Braves when they won the National League West in the first season of divisional play, refused to be complacent and sought improvement for his pitching staff because he knew that he could not rely solely on the club's surplus of power-hitters. Another means of improvement can be sought simply through the removal of an unwanted or undesirable player, which can be a prime motive for a club to deal him away.

That said, the team seeking change obviously needs to surrender one or more players. Will it trade from a surplus of pitching or a small pool of extra position players? Or sweeten the deal with a minor league prospect? Or attempt to package a player who has worn out his welcome with his current team—the process of addition by subtraction, as it might be wryly called—in the hope that a new home will re-invigorate his career and thereby entice the trading partner? The early 1970s saw an active trade market that featured no shortage of star players changing addresses for one reason or another, and the decade commenced with a new policy affecting the exchange of players, this amendment occurring during the December 1969 Winter Meetings held in Fort Lauderdale, Florida.

Before they even played their first ever exhibition game in 1969, the expansion Montreal Expos traded first baseman Donn Clendenon to the

Houston Astros for a pair of outfielders, Jesús Alou and All-Star Rusty Staub. Initially exhibiting little difficulty with the January 22 trade, the 33-year-old Clendenon suddenly balked about switching teams just as spring training was set to begin. The newly minted Expo would have been reunited with Harry "the Hat" Walker, one of his former managers in Pittsburgh, a pairing that Clendenon did not relish based on his past encounter with a skipper whom he considered bigoted. "Although [Clendenon] never said his refusal to report was because Harry Walker was manager of the Astros, many insiders assumed that was the case. Joe Morgan argued in his autobiography that Clendenon's motive was a refusal to ever play for Walker again."[1]

Announcing his supposed retirement, yet soon after expressing a desire to return to the field—but not with the Astros—Clendenon caused an uproar that involved commissioner Bowie Kuhn and initiated much negotiation between the player and the two ballclubs. When the dust settled, it was ultimately decided that Houston would receive two other players as compensation for Clendenon, while Clendenon would remain with Montreal, where he signed a two-year contract for $100,000 and netted him a $14,000 pay increase through all the machinations.

The ripple effect was swift: "Immediately, the players realized that Kuhn had opened a Pandora's Box. Hearing the news [of Clendenon's outcome], Ed Kranepool of the Mets announced in exultation, 'Great! If the Mets trade me, I'll retire before I report to the other club.'"[2] And the subject of another trade, Ken Harrelson of the Red Sox, drew attention because he too chose to "retire" in order to better maintain the various business relationships beyond baseball that he had cultivated in Boston since his arrival there after being released by the Kansas City Athletics in late August 1967.

When the BoSox traded him to Cleveland in mid–April 1969 mere weeks following the decision in the Clendenon case, Harrelson, the most modish dresser of his era, cited the huge financial interests he had fostered in less than two years in Boston: a sandwich shop, a nightclub, real estate holdings, and the proposed venture of a "'Harrelson's of Boston,' a four-story clothing store and men's boutique."[3] Reluctant to step away from this portfolio with an estimated value of $750,000, Harrelson chose retirement and the forsaking of his $50,000 baseball salary, but the tide turned remarkably when the Indians gave him a $100,000 contract. Officials with his new and former teams, as well as Kuhn's office, convinced him that "the outside opportunities in Cleveland are as good as they are in Boston," thus facilitating his return to the diamond.[4]

Clendenon and Harrelson were back in the baseball fold, but the maneuvering of both players created a huge amount of apprehension in every front office. Was retirement now an ad hoc means to leverage a pay increase? Would this scheme become an issue with each attempted trade from now on? Finally at the 1969 Winter Meetings, baseball sanctioned a "caveat emptor" rule in which "all trades, once agreed upon, would stand. It was up to the teams themselves to persuade their [newly acquired] players to report to work."⁵

Whether this amendment *en*couraged or *dis*couraged future trading can only be left to speculation, but as the decade of the 1970s progressed, the wheeling and dealing continued.

By using the threat of retirement as leverage to block what they felt were trades that went against their best interests, Donn Clendenon (top) and Ken Harrelson (right) forced front offices to adopt a "buyer beware" policy when swapping players.

6. The Trading Post   129

"You have to trade value to get value." This was the simple trading philosophy of Cincinnati Reds general manager Bob Howsam, and he demonstrated this quite well in the course of enhancing the emergent Big Red Machine.[6] As his club was preparing to move into Riverfront Stadium midway through the 1970 season, the GM recognized the need for a faster-running team to take advantage of the artificial turf at the new ballpark, and he took a gamble by trading longtime outfielder Vada Pinson, a dependable veteran, to St. Louis for Bobby Tolan, a young prospect who was only a part-time outfielder for the Cardinals, along with reliever Wayne Granger.

Given a steady job upon his acquisition for the 1969 campaign, the speedy Tolan thrived in his first two years in a Red uniform before his unfortunate Achilles' tendon injury, while Pinson remained a steady outfielder beyond his lone season in St. Louis, playing six more years for Cleveland, the California Angels, and the Kansas City Royals. But as was noted earlier, Howsam did well in filling the void caused by Tolan's absence when he obtained George Foster from San Francisco in late May 1971, and the general manager went even further six months later in pulling off one of the best trades ever.

The Reds sent the right side of their infield—second baseman Tommy Helms and first baseman Lee May—plus reserve outfielder Jimmy Stewart to the Houston Astros for a package of five players, three of whom became regulars that were vital to Cincinnati's lineup: Joe Morgan would replace Helms and later win consecutive National League MVP awards; Denis Menke took over at third base and allowed Tony Pérez to move to first base; and centerfielder César Gerónimo became one of the Reds' best defensive outfielders, winning four straight Gold Gloves in the mid–1970s. The other figures in the trade added to the rotation—Jack Billingham was a key starter for the nascent championship clubs—and gave manager Sparky Anderson a new spare outfielder, Ed Armbrister. As the changes jelled in Cincinnati, they brought an NL pennant in 1972 and served as a springboard for the dynastic Reds of three years later.

Ray Shore, an advance scout for Cincinnati, recognized the importance of retooling with the new playing surface in mind. "I started bearing down in my scouting on outfielders' defense because of AstroTurf. At Crosley [Field], you could get by with slower guys, but boy, the minute you moved to turf, if you don't have speed, you can get killed."[7] While Shore's comment was directed toward the outfielders, he certainly anticipated the potential of Joe Morgan, who had played on turf in the Astrodome for several years, to quickly adapt to Riverfront Stadium's field.

Another infield prospect, Dave Concepción, broke in with the Reds in 1970 and soon gained a foothold as the mainstay at shortstop.

On the other side of this trade, the Astros gained only marginally, moving from fourth place in the NL West to third in 1972, and although the addition of Helms and especially May enhanced Houston's offense, the pitching staff ranked in the bottom half of the National League in runs allowed and ERA. Whereas Houston mired in mediocrity for most of the decade, the deal helped the Reds progress from being a good team to a great team.

Houston's Joe Morgan was a two-time National League All-Star with the Astros, but his career flourished after he was traded in late 1971. He became one of the vital cogs in Cincinnati's "Big Red Machine" of the 1970s.

The New York Mets blundered into a pair of lopsided deals during Gil Hodges's last years as their manager. In an attempt to put a halt to the revolving door at the hot corner where an uncomfortable number of third basemen failed to become a bona fide regular, the Mets' recent acquisition of a member of the famed 1967 Boston Red Sox, Joe Foy, did not yield the intended result. Foy had fallen out of favor in Boston, was left unprotected in the 1968 expansion draft, and was subsequently acquired by New York from the Kansas City Royals in exchange for pitcher Bob Johnson and Amos Otis, a young prospect who played well at third in the low minor leagues but soon made a name for himself as a standout centerfielder for the Royals.

Meanwhile, Foy, in the midst of enduring drug and alcohol-related issues, was sold to the Mets' Triple-A team after the 1970 season and later picked up by the Washington Senators. In mid–July of 1971, he was released, never to play again, while Otis became a five-time American League All-Star and winner of three Gold Gloves during his 14 years in Kansas City.

Persisting in their search for another third sacker, the Mets made an even bigger mistake in the trade market. In 1971 New York's young but veteran hurlers were Tom Seaver and Jerry Koosman, and filling out the rotation were Gary Gentry, Ray Sadecki, and Nolan Ryan. Over two dozen other starts were handled by Jim McAndrew (10), Charlie Williams (9), and Jon Matlack (6), while Danny Frisella and Tug McGraw—the latter also had one start—were being groomed as closers.

Featuring the best team ERA (2.99) in the National League and with Sadecki and reliever Ron Taylor the only pitchers age 30 or older, the Mets felt comfortable dealing from a position of surplus pitching strength to bolster their weakness at third base. Ryan, who threw hard but lacked the control of Seaver, Koosman, and Gentry, was dangled as trade bait in the autumn of 1971, and in Anaheim, general manager Harry Dalton was mere weeks into his new job with the California Angels and had acquired shortstop Leo Cárdenas from Minnesota as a successor to Jim Fregosi. At the Winter Meetings in Phoenix, Dalton ran into his opposite number with the Mets, Bob Scheffing, who expressed his desire to obtain "a hitter," whereupon Dalton offered Fregosi.[8]

The Angel executive at first sought Gentry, Matlack, or another prospect, Buzz Capra, none of whom Scheffing considered parting with, so Ryan, still viewed as untamed, became the pitcher of choice that Dalton was willing to take a chance on. Three other minor players were packaged with Ryan in the four-for-one swap for Fregosi, who lasted but one-and-a-half seasons at Shea Stadium and "served to remind New York fans of the bad deal the Indians got when they parted with Manhattan Island for assorted trinkets."[9] Ryan matured from thrower to pitcher under the tutelage of coach Tom Morgan and was immediately on his way to becoming baseball's all-time strikeout king and, like the Reds' Joe Morgan, a Hall-of-Famer.

For all the acclaim garnered by Nolan Ryan, the Angels under GM Dick Walsh, Dalton's predecessor, had a spotty record in the trading market, and Dalton himself was also hampered by less fruitful transactions that failed to help the club. Aurelio Rodríguez, Jay Johnstone, and Pedro Borbón were among Walsh's castoffs who, after 1970, went on to enjoy serviceable careers in other cities, while Dalton later sold Rudy May—to be fair, the southpaw endured problems with his back—and would swap Ed Figueroa and Jim Spencer, who continued to play well elsewhere, for players who did not pan out well in return.

Entering the 1970 season, other players of moderate stature were changing teams, including former AL Rookie of the Year Curt Blefary, who was sent from the Houston Astros to the New York Yankees for Joe Pepitone, who, like Joe Foy, was a native of the Bronx. Two players who hit their stride in the new decade were part of the same trade when the Cleveland Indians sent pitchers Luis Tiant and Stan Williams to the Minnesota Twins for hurlers Dean Chance and Robert L.

By trying to solve their perennial problem at third base, the New York Mets traded some of their surplus of pitching in search of an answer. In what turned out to be one of the most lopsided deals in baseball history, Nolan Ryan (top) emerged with the California Angels as a dominant power pitcher and eventually the game's all-time strikeout leader. Although Jim Fregosi (left) was one of the American League's better shortstops, he did not meet the Mets' expectations at the hot corner and spent fewer than two seasons at Shea Stadium.

6. The Trading Post

Miller, outfielder Ted Uhlaender, and third baseman Graig Nettles. The new addresses for Tiant and Nettles became waystations before the former landed in Boston to achieve great success on the mound and emerge as a fan favorite, while the latter solidified the Yankee infield during the resurgence of the Bronx Bombers in their World Series victories of 1977 and 1978.

In late April 1970, the Angels traded outfielder Rick Reichardt and third-base prospect Aurelio Rodríguez to the Washington Senators for veteran infielder Ken McMullen. This deal signaled that California had given up on Reichardt, who, at the time he was signed just prior to the creation of the amateur draft in 1965, commanded a record bonus of $200,000.[10] His unfulfilled expectations led to squabbling between Reichardt and several Angels: The former bonus baby remarked, "I don't think the Angels can win," while Jim Fregosi countered that Reichardt, who had been benched, "couldn't even play regular for a third-place team," and manager Lefty Phillips called the outfielder's comment "bush."[11] McMullen helped the Angels a bit, yet he only lasted in Anaheim through 1972, while Rodríguez, with his cannon-like arm, went on to become a stalwart at the hot corner through the 1970s, arguably second only to Nettles with his glove work.

As the winter of 1970 began to set in, Dick Allen was on the move from St. Louis to Los Angeles, with Ted Sizemore and Bob Stinson heading to Busch Stadium, while, as noted earlier, Senator owner Bob Short was quite active in importing Curt Flood and peddling Rodríguez and Ed Brinkman to Detroit for Denny McLain, along with other players.

For some time, a slow dismantling of Boston's "Impossible Dream" team had been occurring, the departures including Ken Harrelson, Dalton Jones, Joe Foy, Gary Bell, and Jerry Adair by the end of the 1960s. An almost unthinkable addition to this list was made when the popular outfielder Tony Conigliaro, along with pitcher Ray Jarvis and catcher Jerry Moses, was traded to California in October 1970 for pitcher Ken Tatum, outfielder Jarvis Tatum, and second baseman Doug Griffin. "Tony C," as he was affectionately known by Red Sox fans, had seemingly recovered from the August 1967 beaning that nearly cost him sight in his left eye. Missing the entire following season, he earned "Comeback Player of the Year" honors from *The Sporting News* in 1969 when he hit .255 with 21 doubles, 20 home runs, and drove in 82 runs. Even better production came in 1970 as Conigliaro batted .266, with 36 home runs and 116 RBIs, apparently laying to rest any doubts about his recovery.

But as Boston faltered in the American League East standings—manager Dick Williams lost his job after the 1969 season—and Conigliaro butted heads with teammate Carl Yastrzemski, Yaz emerged as a greater favorite of club owner Tom Yawkey. General manager Dick O'Connell sought a solution to this problem of dissension while at once capitalizing on Conigliaro's trade value based on his most recent output. Trading a hometown hero—Tony C was born in nearby Revere, Massachusetts—raised the hackles of Boston fans, but as events transpired in Anaheim, he proved to be only a shell of the player he had once been.

In the course of trying to establish himself with the Angels in 1971 and despite the comforts and glamour of living on the West Coast, Conigliaro developed a variety of ailments that led some teammates to believe that he was afflicted with hypochondria more than anything else. As the hoped-for production from Tony C's bat went missing, this angst partnered in an unfavorable manner with the tempest surrounding his teammate, Alex Johnson, whose erratic and combative behavior bred its own brand of discontent.[12]

Dating to his first years as a professional player, Johnson had a penchant for leaving his potential unfulfilled. Johnson hit well in the minors but was a defensive liability, yet when he was promoted to the Philadelphia Phillies, his first big league manager, Gene Mauch, grew "increasingly frustrated by Johnson's *perceived* lack of effort and poor attitude."[13] Traded to St. Louis in October 1965, Johnson grated on Cardinal management for two seasons before being dealt in January 1968 to Cincinnati, where he seemed to at last stabilize and become a full-fledged ballplayer. The Reds general manager, Bob Howsam, traded Johnson to the California Angels because he believed that his club was overstocked with hitters and sought pitching help in exchange.

Johnson captured the American League batting title in 1970, his average of .32899 barely edging out Carl Yastrzemski's .32862 for the honor, but the upheaval he caused among teammates and with management led to a serious rift both on the field and in the clubhouse. Multiple fines, benchings, and suspensions all failed to bring the troubled outfielder in line, and his problems, which were ultimately linked to mental illness, spilled over to the 1971 season.

Suspension by the Angels occurred in late June for Johnson's lack of giving his best effort as well as the demeanor with which he carried himself. This action came days after California attempted to trade him to the Milwaukee Brewers, whose general manager, Frank "Trader" Lane, considered acquiring with the hope of reuniting him with field manager Dave Bristol. It was Bristol, in his role as the Reds skipper, who was able to coax solid play from Johnson when they were together in Cincinnati in 1968 and 1969. But when Dick Walsh, the California GM, asked for Tommy Harper, one of the Brewers' best players, in return, Lane demurred and the trade fell by the wayside.

Just weeks after Johnson was banned—he did not play the rest of the season when commissioner Bowie Kuhn placed him on his office's restricted list—Conigliaro stepped away from the club and returned to his family in Boston in early July. Claiming his exit to be a retirement, he cited lingering headaches and vision that never fully recovered from his beaning as the reason for his departure. With Conigliaro gone and the Angels still saddled with the suspended Johnson, Walsh ended up trading Johnson—a perfect case of addition by subtraction—and Jerry Moses to the Cleveland Indians in early October for pitcher Alan Foster and outfielders Frank Baker and Vada Pinson.

California ended up paying for more than the

Tony Conigliaro (top) seemed to have recovered from a horrific beaning in 1967 and gave the Red Sox the chance to capitalize on his trade value when they sent him to the California Angels after the 1970 season. He was expected to pair up with defending American League batting champion Alex Johnson (right) to give the Angels an offensive boost, but Johnson's personal problems carried over from the previous season, and both he and Conigliaro were finished with the team by early July 1971.

disruption in their clubhouse when Johnson won his grievance against the team—he claimed that his condition should have been treated as a disability rather than punished by a suspension—and Conigliaro also filed a grievance to receive the salary he said he was owed because his retirement had been hastened by a medical condition. Despite the absence of Johnson and Conigliaro, a pall remained over the Angels for the rest of the season and ultimately cost manager Lefty Phillips and his coaching staff their jobs.

The October 1971 hiring of Harry Dalton, late of the Baltimore Orioles, as the new Angel general manager was intended to give the team a fresh start, yet the ensuing years were fraught with their own peril that did not produce a winner on the field. It was hard to believe that of the four players honored by their appearance on the cover of the 1971 Angels' media guide, only pitcher Clyde Wright remained with the club heading into the following season. Johnson and Fregosi had been traded, while Conigliaro remained the technical property of the team—but for whom he never again played—until he was released in November 1974.

One of baseball's top pitchers, who dominated the American League just as Sandy Koufax lorded over the National League, was Sam McDowell, whose strikeout totals from 1965 to 1971 were unsurpassed. "Sudden Sam," as he was nicknamed, debuted with the Cleveland Indians in 1961 at the age of 18, but he did not hit his stride until three years later when he started 24 games, was victorious 11 times, logged a 2.70 ERA, and fanned 177 batters in 173.1 innings. In 1965, he earned his first All-Star berth, won 17, and led the AL with 325 strikeouts (his 17 wild pitches were a league high, and the 132 walks he issued topped the majors). But McDowell was now an established ace, and he again was an All-Star in 1966 as well as from 1968 to 1971. In each of these seasons he was the supreme strikeout artist: 225 K's in 1966 to lead the league, 283 during 1968's "year of the pitcher," 279 in 1969, and 304 in 1970, these last three figures being the best in all of baseball.

But by 1971, McDowell's bases-on-balls had ballooned to 153 in 214.2 innings, and a demon that plagued him for years could not be harnessed. Years after he left the game, he admitted, "People said I had a drinking problem. No! I had a stopping problem."[14] Outsized at 6-foot-5, McDowell was no stranger to a brawling lifestyle when inebriated, and while he controlled his intake of alcohol when it was his turn to pitch, "[o]ther than that, I was unrestrained."[15] Having grown weary of these escapades, Cleveland general manager Gabe Paul was unsuccessful in trading his pitcher to the Houston Astros for outfielder Jimmy Wynn or second baseman Joe

Morgan, but he worked out a deal in late November 1971 that sent the troubled southpaw to San Francisco for shortstop Frank Duffy and starting pitcher Gaylord Perry.

Twice an All-Star as well as a two-time 20-game winner since 1962, Perry was in the process of refining his practice of doctoring the baseball, but by most practical measures, his age was thought to be catching up with him. The Giants believed that the 28-year-old McDowell, who was four years Perry's junior, would be a better fit in their rotation, but McDowell's performance declined in part due to a shoulder problem, which, besides his drinking issue, was exacerbated by a burgeoning addiction to pain medication.

Whereas Sudden Sam was firmly on the downside of his career, Perry in 1972 paid a remarkable dividend by winning the AL Cy Young Award while also embarking on a desultory journey that lasted over a decade but earned him later induction to the Baseball Hall of Fame. Including the time he spent in an Indian uniform, the spitballer would pitch for six other teams before finally retiring after the 1983 season. Ironically, the trade that sent Perry away from San Francisco was girded by Gabe Paul's belief that Frank Duffy was "the key man in the deal ... and we told the Giants that we would not close the deal without him."[16] So it was that a light-hitting but dependable shortstop was involved in two of baseball's more storied transactions, made just six months apart at that:

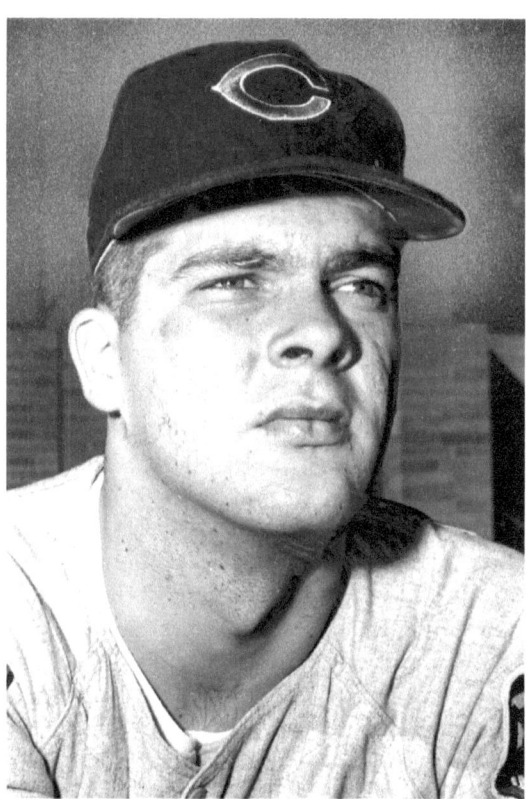

Sam McDowell's dominance as a strikeout artist was attended by his struggles with alcoholism. He was traded in late 1971 to the San Francisco Giants for Frank Duffy and Gaylord Perry, who would go on to win a pair of Cy Young Awards.

Cincinnati's landing of slugger George Foster, and Cleveland's acquisition of Gaylord Perry.

On the same day that the McDowell–Perry exchange was completed, the Oakland Athletics bolstered their starting rotation by sending outfielder Rick Monday to the Chicago Cubs for lefthander Ken Holtzman. History shows this trade as one of mutual benefit to both clubs. Monday was the first player selected by the former Kansas City Athletics in the new amateur draft instituted in 1965, and the alumnus of Arizona State University became the Athletics' centerfielder. But in the years following the franchise's shift to the West Coast, the team had accumulated a surplus of outfielders, and with Reggie Jackson, George Hendrick, Angel Mangual, and Joe Rudi on hand, Oakland was faced with "a trade that had to be made."[17] Monday was hampered by inconsistency at the plate, and when starters Chuck Dobson and Blue Moon Odom were thwarted by elbow injuries at the close of the 1971 season, Oakland had little choice but to seek help for the mound.

For their part, the Cubs, and in particular their manager, felt stymied by Holtzman's inability to build upon the 17-win seasons he had in 1969 and 1970, falling to a 9–15 record in 1971 with a career-worst 4.48 ERA. Skipper Leo Durocher complained of Holtzman's reluctance to use his fastball more frequently and had exhausted his patience hoping for the southpaw to come around. In Monday, the Cubs gained a solid defensive outfielder with some pop in his bat—he would average 21 homers during his five years in Chicago—while averting their eyes from his strikeout total. After jettisoning Holtzman, the Cubs saw him blossom as a vital cog in the Oakland rotation, where he won 77 games over his four years with the Athletics and helped them capture three straight World Series from 1972 to 1974.

On the move once more was Dick Allen of the Los Angeles Dodgers, who in early December 1971 was sent to the Chicago White Sox for lefthander Tommy John and infielder Steve Huntz. Billing Allen as "one of the greatest sluggers of modern baseball," the ChiSox eagerly anticipated a lineup featuring their new acquisition and another power hitter, All-Star third baseman Bill Melton, but when the latter was derailed by a season-ending back injury in late June, Allen had to carry most of the load.[18] Picking up the slack, Allen earned AL MVP laurels by hitting .308, leading the league in home runs (37), RBIs (113), walks (99), and slugging percentage (.603), as well as topping the majors in on-base percentage (.420) and on-base-plus-slugging percentage (1.023). Victorious 87 times, the Sox finished second to Oakland in the AL West, just five and one-half games behind.

The circumstances surrounding Tommy John's post-trade success took a far different path after he donned a Dodger uniform. He attained renown in 1972 and 1973 by winning a total of 27 games as a solid starter, but in 1974 as he was again pitching most effectively—his 13–3 record yielded a Major League–best winning percentage of .813—disaster struck when he ruptured the medial collateral ligament in his left elbow. Agreeing with Dr. Frank Jobe to undergo radical surgery to repair the damage, John missed the 1975 season but recovered to pitch from 1976 until the end of the following decade. The eponymous "Tommy John surgery" has now been performed countless times in efforts to save the careers of players who have suffered similar injuries, and in turn has led for calls to induct John, who ultimately won 288 games, into the Hall of Fame. (To a lesser extent, there have been calls also to induct Dr. Jobe for his pioneering work that has contributed greatly to the game in the medical sense.)

Frank Robinson was a two-time MVP and the AL Triple Crown winner in 1966, and he had been the subject of a previous trade for having fallen out of favor with Cincinnati Reds owner Bill Dewitt. The mogul believed that by the end of 1965 Robinson's best years were behind him, even though the future Hall-of-Famer had recently turned just 30. Packed off to Baltimore, where Robinson became a central figure in the Orioles' dynasty from 1969 to 1971, he was now 35 years old but still productive, having placed third in the 1971 voting for AL MVP. But with young talent in the form of Don Baylor and Merv Rettenmund ready to play at the Major League level, the time had come for Baltimore to move the elder statesman.

In December 1971, Robinson and pitcher Pete Richert were sent to the Los Angeles Dodgers for pitchers Doyle Alexander and Bob O'Brien, catcher Sergio Robles, and outfielder Royle Stillman. Of the quartet that Baltimore received, only Alexander would go on to a notable career, ultimately playing for 19 seasons with eight different teams. At his new address in Chavez Ravine, Robinson at first seemed to validate the critics who believed his decline was inevitable when he set a new personal low for batting average (.251) and hit only 19 home runs with 59 RBIs, his least output since 1968 when he continued to suffer the effects of a concussion sustained in a base-running collision the previous season. And as if to mirror Dick Allen's one-year term in Los Angeles before being sent to a club in the AL West, Robinson was traded to the California Angels in late 1972 before yet another deal landed him in Cleveland, where he famously became baseball's first African-American manager in 1975.

Dismissed as the general manager of the St. Louis Cardinals in 1964, Bing Devine was rehired by owner August A. "Gussie" Busch, Jr., after the team won the 1967 World Series. Devine was central to the Cards' acquisition of outfielder Lou Brock, but lost his job for failing to placate the cantankerous Busch over a dispute between manager Johnny Keane and shortstop Dick Groat that had long been settled and need not have bothered the owner. Upon his return to St. Louis, Devine executed several trades, not all of them popular: In 1969, he sent Orlando Cepeda, the 1967 NL MVP who led St. Louis to victory in the Fall Classic, to Atlanta for Joe Torre, then in October 1969 he packaged Curt Flood and Tim McCarver in a trade to Philadelphia for Dick Allen, which triggered Flood's legal action against the baseball establishment.

By 1971, St. Louis pitcher Steve Carlton had settled in as a solid veteran starter but had recently experienced wavering won-lost totals, losing a Major-League high 19 games in 1970, then winning 20 the next season. Devine admitted that "Carlton had a high opinion of himself. Rightly so, as it turned out," and in his retirement the GM reflected, "I'd like to think that I could have kept Carlton around to see how great he would become."[19]

But Carlton and fellow Cardinal lefthander Jerry Reuss did not conform to Busch's standard of subservience that was expected of his players, especially when contracts were being negotiated. (Busch also abhorred facial hair, which sprouted on more than a few players around both leagues.) After the 1971 season, when both pitchers had earned some leverage based on their performance—to be fair, Carlton outpaced Reuss, as the latter went 14-14, the third-highest win total on the staff, but with a relatively steep ERA of 4.78—contract wrangling for 1972 irked Busch and prompted him to order both pitchers traded.

Complying with his boss's wish the following spring, Devine dealt Reuss to Houston, setting him on a peripatetic journey that lasted for nearly two more decades in a Major-League uniform during which he compiled 220 victories, while Carlton wound up in Philadelphia, swapped even-up for pitcher Rick Wise. Carlton blossomed into baseball's dominant workhorse from the early 1970s until the early '80s, winning a total of 329 games and four Cy Young Awards as well as earning his induction to the Hall of Fame.

Many transactions involve just a handful of players, yet there can be the occasional trade in which the number of those involved might approach double digits. In the fall of 1971, one such bargain was completed between the Boston Red Sox and Milwaukee Brewers. "The deal was bigger than had been expected," *The Sporting News* informed its readers, and the Red Sox players shifting west were first baseman George Scott, outfielders Billy Conigliaro and Joe Lahoud, pitchers Jim Lonborg and Ken Brett, and catcher Don Pavletich.[20] Headed east were outfielder Tommy Harper, pitchers Marty Pattin and Lew Krausse, and minor leaguer Pat Skrable. As the beat writer for the Red Sox pointed out, "The trade was a direct result of dissension on the team throughout the season.... There were so many cliques that Boston sports writers were hard-pressed to keep track of them."[21]

After four straight seasons of being unable to reclaim the AL pennant or at least the AL East—during the last three of these, it was unlikely that *any* team could surpass the Orioles of this period—Boston was frustrated at fielding an ostensibly competitive team yet unable to move above third place. For the 1970 season, the BoSox brought in lefthander Gary Peters from the Chicago White Sox (in a deal populated mostly by reserves) and Sonny Seibert from Cleveland (the big player exchanged here was Ken Harrelson). The December 1970 trade of Mike Andrews and Luis Alvarado to the Chicago White Sox for Luis Aparicio, the elderly but effective shortstop, forced Rico Petrocelli to move from short to third base and strengthened the infield, yet the personnel changes did not yield a better finish in the divisional standings.

Besides ridding themselves of a malcontent like Billy Conigliaro—he complained about playing time even during spring training and felt that Yastrzemski had much to do with the earlier trade of his brother Tony—Boston resorted to a purge of some players in whom they felt disappointment, lost patience with hoping that they would mature, or believed lacked a level of performance that had gained them fame in 1967. General manager Dick O'Connell also sought room for newcomers Rick Miller, Cecil Cooper, Ben Oglivie, and a young New England-bred catcher named Carlton Fisk, all of whom he hoped would provide a fresh start and an air-clearing quality.

The executive was happy to land Pattin for the Boston rotation as a replacement for Lonborg, while Krausse could serve in relief or as a spot starter, and Harper was a speedy, well-rounded player who would play centerfield and force Reggie Smith to move to right field. But in another trade that proved to be disastrous, O'Connell sent reliever Sparky Lyle to the New York Yankees for first baseman Danny Cater during spring training of 1972. Lyle became a fan favorite and the Yankees' invaluable closer in winning the 1977 AL Cy Young Award.

For all the trades in which Boston engaged in the earliest part of the 1970s, they reaped little reward but did finish in second place in the strike-marred 1972 season, one-half game behind Detroit. In the near future they would contend thanks to an infusion of young stars, outfielders Fred Lynn and Jim Rice among them.

In an age when the reserve clause remained unshakable, owners and general managers enjoyed the luxury of having the upper hand in personnel matters. The purported retirements of Donn Clendenon and Ken Harrelson prompted a quick revision to baseball's bylaws—in management's favor, of course—yet the players received a modicum of authority in determining their place of employment: With the latest collective bargaining agreement, in 1973 a player had earned the right to refuse a trade if he was a ten-year veteran who had spent the last five seasons with the same ballclub. Only when the Seitz decision opened the door to true free agency after 1975 did the pendulum start to swing demonstrably in favor of the players, who then earned much freedom in choosing their venue of employment.

Trades knew almost no time limit, save for the deadlines for interleague deals and determining which players would be eligible for the postseason roster. In any given calendar year, dozens of trades could be made, yet this chapter has focused on those involving the most significant players. Often by the time the regular season had concluded, clubs could evaluate their most recent performance and come to grips with what problem areas needed to be corrected. The subsequent Winter Meetings then became fertile ground for consummating trades already under discussion or for laying the foundation for future deals. Untethered by any restrictions and with executives of all teams under one roof, GMs were at liberty to shop and bargain as they saw fit, and such settings provided plenty of kindling for the Hot Stove season.

As shown in the above pages, big-name trades were in vogue, and fans were tantalized by the possibilities of how the new faces would contribute to the success of their team. On paper at least, there would always be hope.

7

All-Stars and Hall-of-Famers

Each year, Major League Baseball honors players both active and retired, in some cases extending laurels to past contributors such as front-office executives, owners, and umpires. The creation of the All-Star Game and the founding of the Baseball Hall of Fame in the 1930s furnished reasons to celebrate the achievements of the sport's leading figures, and the introduction of both further enhanced the image of the national pastime as it labored through the Great Depression.

In 1971, a watershed moment occurred when the first former Negro League player was inducted into the Hall of Fame, thereby opening the doors of that institution to players of color who had toiled in segregated leagues both before and after the integration of the national pastime upon Jackie Robinson's debut with the Brooklyn Dodgers in 1947. This induction was the result of a lobbying effort by one of baseball's most renowned hitters, whose own heritage included minority lineage.

All told, stars continued to shine in their various galaxies, making for good press and enhancing baseball's appeal to fans of all stripes.

Beginning in 1933, save the exception of 1945 as World War II was thankfully nearing its end, the All-Star Game was staged in ballparks rotated among American and National League cities and featured the best players of the two circuits.[1] The contests of 1970 and 1971 provided a pair of legendary big hits that resonate to this day, the former year also marking the return of All-Star balloting to the fans.

Voting by fans to determine the starting lineups drew scrutiny in 1956 when five members of the Cincinnati Reds were elected as NL starters, and when balloting in 1957 repeated the same sin even more egregiously—this time seven Reds were chosen—commissioner Ford Frick was compelled to intervene. "Reds fans clearly rigged the election of starters for the National

League All-Star team—jamming the ballot boxes with pre-marked ballots published in the Cincinnati Enquirer newspaper," wrote one sports journalist. "Cincinnati bars also joined the campaign to get Reds voted into the starting lineup."[2]

A "late deluge of 550,000 votes from Cincinnati had raised the prospect of an all-Redleg team, except for the pitchers," *The Sporting News* reported in an editorial.[3] Stan Musial, the St. Louis first baseman, narrowly edged Cincinnati's George Crowe, and Frick was having none of it, as he supplanted a pair of Red outfielders, Gus Bell and Wally Post, with Hank Aaron and Willie Mays named as their replacements. Managers had picked the lineups from 1938 to 1946, but it was felt that the fans should have a voice in picking the starters. Catering to this sentiment worked for a decade until the debacle of 1957 when Frick revoked the fans' privilege in favor of having players, coaches, and managers make the selections.

By the time Bowie Kuhn assumed the role of commissioner in 1969, he "was determined to give the voting back to the fans in 1970." Admitting that there was the likelihood of possible controversy over some of the players ultimately chosen, Kuhn nonetheless recognized that "fan voting made too much marketing sense to ignore," and Baltimore Orioles general manager Harry Dalton also supported the restoration of the balloting.[4] This marketing sense translated into the revenue stream fueled through appealing to the fans, whose dollars were spent on all manner of baseball goods from game tickets to ballpark concessions and team merchandise. Kuhn's arrival in February 1969 left little time to formulate the strategy for an All-Star balloting system with the game just five months away, but the main thrust to implement it the following year was initiated.

The Gillette Company, famous for its shaving products and significant as a longtime sponsor of Major League Baseball, was instrumental in creation of the ballot and, not least, for its willingness to "finance the high-road system" that the commissioner relied on to prevent a replay of the Cincinnati fiasco of 1957.[5] In March 1970 as Kuhn announced the return of fan participation in the voting process, he stated that "the major concern was to obtain the widest possible distribution of ballots so that any fan would have a chance to vote."[6]

By enlisting a prominent national business to aid in the broad circulation of 26 million ballots—these would be made available at 156 major and minor league ballparks across the country and Gillette would also have display stands at 75,000 retail outlets—the theory was that a far-reaching network of distribution points would thwart any ballot-box stuffing and lead to a more equitable outcome in the voting. "This year you elect the All-Stars," read an advertisement from the Boston-based company. "Pick up your official All-Star ballot today. If your team loses, you have nobody to blame but yourself."[7]

Once a fan had voted by punching out the chads corresponding to the players' names chosen, the ballot could be placed in a collection box at a ballpark or stamped and mailed to the election tabulator. Although some skeptical fans believed that the choices should remain the responsibility of the players, coaches, and managers who best knew the deserving All-Star Game participants, this methodology would not prevent any fan from voting multiple times. But the cost of postage per ballot—a six-cent stamp was the going rate for mailing such an item—or the need to purchase a ticket to any professional ballgame to access a ballot box would create enough of an obstacle to rigging the system in favor of one player or a select group of them.

The ballot itself was a modified version of the ubiquitous Hollerith computer card, which was a standard means of feeding data into computers of that era's information technology. Allowing for 80 characters (alphabetic, numerical, or special symbols such as asterisks, dollar signs, and the like) across its width, the ballot's 48 player names for each league were categorized by their primary position, with the exception of pitchers, who along with reserve players would be chosen by the team manager. A separate chad could be punched if a fan wanted to write in the name of a player not listed, and blank lines for each individual position were provided for this purpose. "Managers and player representatives were polled to prepare the lists of ... nominees," explained *The Sporting News*.[8]

This was cleverly devised and comprehensive, yet the challenge for the coders charged with creating the computer program to properly

The humble computer punch card was used to configure the new All-Star ballot that fans would use to vote for each league's starting players (Paul Hensler collection).

tabulate the votes—this also needed to account for managing write-in candidates—had to have been daunting. Checks and balances needed to ensure that only one vote per position per league was cast, with the exception of three outfield slots, which were lumped together rather than specifically delineated by left, center, or right field.

Technicalities of handling the ballots notwithstanding, the entire process was further steeped in controversy almost from the moment the 1970 versions were printed. To be sure, the familiar names of perennial All-Stars such as Roberto Clemente, Willie Mays, and Brooks Robinson were included, yet conspicuous by its absence was that of Detroit's Al Kaline.

The Tiger legend was an All-Star from 1955 through 1967 but was not a member of the two most recent AL squads, and when ballot nominations were submitted to meet the printing deadline of February 1970, Kaline was bypassed. (Note that Detroit was still very well represented: first baseman Norm Cash, second baseman Dick McAuliffe, catcher Bill Freehan, as well as a full outfield complement of Willie Horton, Jim Northrup, and Mickey Stanley.) Frustration over Kaline's omission was evident when Detroit's player representative, Jim Price, tore up his ballot and said, "How can you select who's going to be on the All-Star team during spring training?"[9]

But when Kaline showed he had not lost his touch—he was the Tigers' best hitter (.329 through May 31) when voting commenced at the end of May—there were cries asking how he could have been left off the ballot. Likewise with Houston Astro third baseman Doug Rader, who was weak in batting average but with 83 RBIs in 1969 was one of the NL's best run-producers at the hot corner. For his part, Rico Carty of the Atlanta Braves was blistering National League pitching at a .436 clip, but his circumstances were complicated. Having contracted tuberculosis during spring training 1968, Carty missed that entire season, and upon his return in 1969, he suffered injuries that prevented a return to fulltime status, yet his bat remained dangerous: Carty hit .342 in 103 games, and he even earned some votes for NL MVP.

In 1970, the write-in option of the All-Star ballot accomplished its purpose, as sympathetic fans took the time to ultimately ensure Carty's place as a starter in the NL's outfield. He garnered 552,382 votes, surpassing Pete Rose by 67,000 to claim the left field spot.[10] Not least among Carty's support were the 48 write-in ballots cast from those associated with the Southeast Florida Tuberculosis Hospital in Lantana, Florida, where he had received treatment. One of his attending physicians indicated that Carty "caused quite a commotion" through his post-illness performance, and the doctor noted further that the outfielder had become an inspirational figure: "Some people feel that after they have TB, they will never be the same," but Carty was dispelling those doubts in a most definitive way.[11]

Yet, there was concern as to the sustainability of this type of grassroots justice. "How many fans actually will bother to write in a player's name (no matter how deserving) when it is so much more convenient to check or punch the names listed?" was the complaint of one fan.[12] To advance this point, write-ins had to be processed separately to discern what player was receiving a vote.

Running counter to these slights, several potential All-Stars such as St. Louis Cardinal third baseman Mike Shannon and Cleveland Indian outfielder Ken Harrelson had their names printed on the ballot but ended up on the disabled list and had yet to play when voting was opened. And although Aurelio Rodríguez may have been a fine prospect for the California Angels after his first full season in 1969, the strong-armed third sacker had his name altered in casual fashion on the ballot to "Leo Rodriguez."

In 1970, the first year that All-Star voting was returned to the fans, they responded to the omission of Rico Carty's name by using the write-in feature of the ballot to elect him as a starting outfielder for the National League.

Another complaint went to the root of what constituted the honor of selecting the players who actually deserved to be a part of the All-Star team. When players, managers, and coaches made their selections absent the voice of the fans, those choices were supposedly grounded in merit based on a player's current performance, *i.e.*, those with the best batting averages or pitching statistics were worthy of inclusion. But one sports editor detected more than a whiff of bias that mirrored the chaos generated in Cincinnati in 1957.

"I take objections to ads like the one appearing recently in a New York paper, which read: 'Send Your Favorite Mets and Yankees to the All-Star Game,'" wrote Daniel Schlossberg. "The All-Star team is supposed to be based on outstanding all-league performances, not on home-town heroes. Perhaps New York–area fans should be prohibited from voting for their home-town favorites, and likewise around the league...."[13] Without saying how this prohibition was to be enforced, this comment nevertheless obviously seethed with annoyance.

Lastly, the Boston Red Sox inadvertently introduced an unanticipated wrinkle to the voting process. Shortstop Rico Petrocelli had a banner season in 1969, reaching career highs in batting average (.297), on-base percentage (.403), slugging (.589), OPS (.992), doubles (32), home runs (40), and walks (98). In the process of compiling this impressive trove of data, he also was named an American League All-Star, so his appearance on the new All-Star ballot as a shortstop seemed a foregone conclusion. However, in mid–May of 1970, "Red Sox manager Eddie Kasko accepted Petrocelli's voluntary suggestion that he be moved from shortstop to third base for the possible good of the team."[14] At the time, Petrocelli was hitting a weak .222 and the Sox were struggling to reach the .500 mark, having won only 16 of their 34 games so far that year. Part of Boston's problem was at third base, where Luis Alvarado, a promising youngster, was not performing well, his poor defense leading to several recent defeats.

With Boston still in its post—"Impossible Dream" wilderness, Petrocelli believed that his shifting positions would allow Alvarado to play a more natural position in the middle infield, so Kasko was receptive to the idea. This trial lasted about three weeks but failed to yield the hoped-for benefit. However, with regard to the All-Star voting, the regular Red Sox shortstop unexpectedly playing a different position from the one listed on the ballot caused confusion as to what position Petrocelli would play should he prevail in the voting.

In the event, there would be only a modicum of drama: Luis Aparicio, shortstop of the Chicago White Sox, narrowly edged out Petrocelli, 532,825 votes to 521,024, and a *Sporting News* survey among players showed Aparicio as the favorite over runner-up Petrocelli by a wide margin, 130 to 75.[15] (The same players' poll put Hank Aaron and Rico Carty in the National League outfield, but rather than Willie Mays, who drew a mere 16½ votes, completing the trio, the final slot went to Roberto Clemente with 132.) Meanwhile, the affair had an ironic coda in early December when Boston sent Alvarado and Mike Andrews to Chicago in a trade for the 37-year-old Aparicio. Little Louie played his final three years in a Red

Sox uniform and relegated Petrocelli to third base, where he played for the remainder of his career.

Table 7.1 1970 All-Star Game Voting Results

American League		National League	
Bill Freehan, c	Detroit Tigers	Johnny Bench, c	Cincinnati Reds
Boog Powell, 1b	Baltimore Orioles	Dick Allen, 1b	St. Louis Cardinals
Rod Carew, 2b *	Minnesota Twins	Glenn Beckert, 2b	Chicago Cubs
Harmon Killebrew, 3b	Minnesota Twins	Tony Pérez, 3b	Cincinnati Reds
Luis Aparicio, ss	Chicago White Sox	Don Kessinger, ss	Chicago Cubs
Frank Robinson, of	Baltimore Orioles	Hank Aaron, of	Atlanta Braves
Frank Howard, of	Washington Senators	Willie Mays, of	San Francisco Giants
Carl Yastrzemski, of	Boston Red Sox	Rico Carty, of	Atlanta Braves

*Replaced by Davey Johnson (Baltimore Orioles)
Source: The Sporting News, July 18, 1970, 7.

Another lineup change was forced when Rod Carew of the Twins suffered a knee injury on June 22 and was sidelined for three months; he was replaced by Baltimore's Davey Johnson.

In a broad sense, and despite the tempests that reared up during 1970's inaugural computer-based balloting process, the pluses far outweighed the minuses. "Commissioner Bowie Kuhn has 2,034,724 reasons to show that he was right in letting fans select the starting lineups for the All-Star Game in Cincinnati July 14," crowed *The Sporting News*, which pointed out that despite the flaws that cropped up, those casting their ballots acquitted themselves well, especially in the case of rallying to support Rico Carty.[16] Kuhn admitted that "a number of kinks" hampered the enterprise, but he defended the venture because "far from damaging the process, [it] fostered fierce debates and actually popularized the new voting."[17] Hank Aaron of the Atlanta Braves was the most popular choice, being selected on 1,394,847 ballots in 1970, a feat that he would duplicate the following year with 1,119,306 votes.[18]

However, some notes that apparently did not make it into the commissioner's 1987 memoir are revealing. Kuhn privately cited the unevenness with which ballots could be cast, especially when a team was on an extended road trip, as a cause for controversy. For example, a quality player who was expected to rank high in the voting "might be somewhere in the middle" because his team was not playing at home, meaning that thousands of local fans were unable to cast their ballots at the ballpark and "the press would be screaming that the system didn't work."[19] By the time *all* the votes were collected—they included those mailed in and gathered from retail outlets as well as major and minor league stadiums—a clearer picture would emerge after the submission deadline that ultimately validated the fan voting procedure.

Columnist Bob Addie observed that the fans' choices, generally speaking, mimicked the All-Stars as favored by the players themselves, noting that "[b]oth lean heavily to sentimental favorites and those who have big names in the past." He also suggested delaying the game until August "when interest in baseball could lag with the intrusion of exhibition football," this being an age when NFL teams played six preseason contests prior to the opening of the regular season.[20]

Taking some of the recent complaints to heart, Major League Baseball made several key improvements in the 1971 ballot. By way of conspicuous reformatting measures, the updated version moved the position headings ("1st Base," "2nd Base," etc.) into the margins of the ballot and also used a light blue background shading to alternately denote the first base, shortstop, and catcher positions. Besides the card being a bit easier on the eye, the space-saving measure allowed for an increase from six infielder and catcher candidates to eight, and the outfielder choices grew from 18 to 24 (yes, Rico Carty was among those listed). The write-in feature remained, but instead of allowing one line for each position, only six unlabeled spots were available, and fans had to indicate the position of the player they wrote in. Ballots printed for Canadian fans in Quebec conformed to bilingual French-English regulations.

The second round of computerized fan voting again was accompanied by complaints from various corners. Ralph Garr of the Atlanta Braves was the latest subject of a write-in effort based on his batting average of .324 through the month of June, but unlike Rico Carty he failed to gain a spot on the NL squad. Willie Davis of the Los Angeles Dodgers lacked support despite hitting even more robustly (.367) than Garr, while Davis's teammate, Maury Wills, said that he had "outplayed every shortstop in the National League.... The All-Star Game should be a showcase for the men having the best years, not the men with the biggest names."[21] San Diego Padre slugger Nate Colbert belted 17 home runs through the conclusion of voting to support his case, while Pittsburgh Pirate catcher Manny Sanguillen, who was trying to establish himself in the shadow of Johnny Bench, averaged .320 by June 30.

One American League second baseman, Cookie Rojas of the Kansas City Royals, was left off the ballot—batting .317 at the end of June, he griped, "Maybe they should put everybody's name on the list along with the statistics"—while another, four-time NL All-Star shortstop Leo Cárdenas now with the Twins, had a batting average (.289) far superior to rival Luis Aparicio (.184).[22] Saying he was "embarrassed" by his lead among AL shortstops in the voting—a recent 0-for-44 slump also saw his average plummet to .154 at the end of May—Aparicio believed that Mark Belanger of Baltimore was a more deserving All-Star.[23]

And while the computerized regimen was successful in keeping the ballot-box stuffing at bay for the most part, it did not deter fans of St. Louis Cardinal catcher Ted Simmons from giving it a try. For Simmons, a native of the Detroit suburb of Highland Park and a graduate of nearby Southfield High School, the All-Star Game in the Motor City would have served as a homecoming of sorts. The Southfield High principal "estimated that the students had cast nearly 10,000 ballots for Simmons by June 12," even with the postage rate now increased to eight cents.[24] Simmons eventually became an eight-time All-Star, but he would have to wait until 1972 for his first such honor.

For the cases cited above, Ralph Garr, Maury Wills, Ted Simmons, and Mark Belanger were not selected as starters or reserves, but Willie Davis, Nate Colbert, Manny Sanguillen, Cookie Rojas, and Leo Cárdenas at least had the opportunity to suit up in Detroit.

Table 7.2 1971 All-Star Game Voting Results

National League		American League	
Johnny Bench, c	Cincinnati Reds	Ray Fosse, c *	Cleveland Indians
Willie McCovey, 1b	San Francisco Giants	Boog Powell, 1b **	Baltimore Orioles
Glenn Beckert, 2b	Chicago Cubs	Rod Carew, 2b	Minnesota Twins
Joe Torre, 3b	St. Louis Cardinals	Brooks Robinson, 3b	Baltimore Orioles
Bud Harrelson, ss	New York Mets	Luis Aparicio, ss	Boston Red Sox
Willie Stargell, of	Pittsburgh Pirates	Frank Robinson, of	Baltimore Orioles
Willie Mays, of	San Francisco Giants	Tony Oliva, of ***	Minnesota Twins
Hank Aaron, of	Atlanta Braves	Carl Yastrzemski, of	Boston Red Sox

* Replaced by Bill Freehan (Detroit Tigers)
** Replaced by Norm Cash (Detroit Tigers)
*** Replaced by Reggie Jackson (Oakland Athletics); Bobby Murcer (New York Yankees) named as starting centerfielder
Sources: The Sporting News, July 12, 1971, 8; The Sporting News, July 31, 1971, 10.

Disputes and debates always a constant companion, the discussion was further fueled by former Minnesota Twin Bob Allison. After his recent retirement, he suggested that "the players should have some kind of voice in the selection of the All Star team," and the commissioner's director of radio and television agreed with Kuhn that implementing a "weighted vote" that combined fan balloting and a canvass of the players might lead to more equitable selections.[25]

While the wrangling over which players deserved All-Star honors would remain part of what drew attention to one of baseball's signature events, the logistics of staging the game itself was of prime importance to the highest offices of the game. "Since both the World Series and the All-Star Game serve as showcases for Baseball, there can be no overemphasis on preparation and attention to detail."[26] So declared the American League to its officials in an effort to put its best foot forward in dealing with events of the highest profile.

The most recent expansion of the American and National Leagues meant the creation of a new tier of playoffs to determine the World Series participants, and the junior circuit had codified some of the procedures that were involved in preparing for the most special occasions. Authored by the publicity directors of four Major League clubs, the booklet they produced allowed them to share their collective experience in these affairs and inform their fellow PR brethren with other teams as to the benefits of careful planning.

The fluid and intractable nature of knowing what sites would be hosting league championships and the World Series—think of the three-team scramble for the American League pennant on the final weekend of the 1967 regular season—can be a nightmare for any team's traveling secretary and its media relations staff. By contrast, preparations for the All-Star Game have an inherent advantage: the host city is determined a few years in advance, thus allowing plenty of time for agendas to be formulated and action plans to be executed.

For the 1970 Midsummer Classic in Cincinnati, the Reds reserved about 500 hotel rooms, and those with experience in handling other arrangements suggested securing "space for a Hospitality Room which will accommodate approximately 800 persons, working press facilities, [and] an area for press conferences and luncheon sites to accommodate anywhere from 200 to 500 persons."[27] Floor plans for dining space was a knotty problem for a luncheon honoring the players because it could not be known how many of them would actually attend. Issues at the ballpark related to the assigning of press credentials and reserving areas to accommodate members of the media, whose number could run between 500 and 600.

7. All-Stars and Hall-of-Famers

In an age before such a thing as the internet and wireless communication were even dreamed of, the host team was advised that "[a]pproximately 50 typewriters should be made available. These can be secured from a rental service," while Western Union was to be provided space near the press room for the wire transmission of game accounts and news.[28]

"Assigning working positions to photographers is always another problem to wrestle with," warned the American League office, "especially in ball parks not equipped to handle the deluge of photographers usually associated with the All-Star Game."[29] While the 1970 game was held at brand-new Riverfront Stadium, the 1971 contest would be at Detroit's Tiger Stadium, an old, cramped facility that was showing its age even though it would remain in service through 1999. Building temporary camera stands on the field were an option as a stop-gap measure, but one point that was immutable concerned security to ensure that intruders would not be able to access "functions taking place at the hotel, ... clubhouse entrances, dugouts, entrances to the playing field, working press areas and any special areas such as luncheon or dinner sites."[30]

Access to the postgame clubhouse and an "interview area used for the WINNING team only" were important considerations for those in the print media who needed to complete their stories and file them in a timely manner before their respective newspapers went to press.[31]

Round-trip bus transportation between the hotel and the ballpark as well as limousine service for those requiring it needed to be considered, and the public relations department, charged with creating the program for the game, was advised to begin assembling the framework of this publication so as not to be too overwhelmed with "a considerable amount of near last-minute work" to be done when the rosters of each team were finally announced.[32]

Hal Middlesworth, one of the authors of the American League special event primer, was the public relations director for the Detroit Tigers, and his feedback on the 1971 All-Star Game was of particular interest to the commissioner. "Fans, sponsors, and PR men very cooperative. Most aspects went smoothly," Kuhn was informed, although there were some glitches: Not all of the players attending the luncheon were seated at the head table, which had been the preference; it was recommended to hold a workout at the ballpark on the eve of the game so that they can "be at the same place at one time for press and publicity value"; and the timing of a youth Pitch, Hit & Throw competition at Tiger Stadium proved a disadvantage for paying customers. Because of this scheduling conflict, "The fans went to see batting practice and couldn't," reported Middlesworth.[33]

Minor gaffes notwithstanding, the hard work of the organizers, which occurred mostly out of public view, paid off, and the first two All-Star

Games of the 1970s each produced memorable moments that old-time fans still recall with great nostalgia.

The publicity office of the American League served up some tantalizing trivia for the 1970 Midsummer Classic, pointing out that the contest slated for Riverfront Stadium would be the fourth night game in All-Star history, following the ones held in 1943 at Shibe Park in Philadelphia, the next year at Pittsburgh's Forbes Field, and most recently at the Houston Astrodome in 1968.[34] Meanwhile, the host club Cincinnati Reds produced an All-Star Game program with a cover honoring all 24 Major League teams and featured a new eye-catching "Bannermark" logo. Fans who purchased this souvenir publication could read the fine print inside and learn that this new symbol "abstractly suggests a flag spiraling out of a baseball ... connotes action and excitement ... and reflects not only the banners and pennants so indigenous to the atmosphere of the Game, but also is intended as a flag of its own, a banner to unfurl proudly over the world of Baseball."[35]

On the steamy, summer evening of July 14, a robust crowd of 51,838, which included President Richard Nixon, witnessed a contest that began with five innings of whimpers but ended with a 12th-inning bang. National League starter Tom Seaver of the New York Mets and his American League counterpart, Jim Palmer of the Baltimore Orioles, each logged three shutout innings of one-hit pitching. Their respective replacements, Cincinnati's Jim Merritt and Sam McDowell of Cleveland, continued the scoreless skein through the fifth inning until the AL broke through with a run in the top of the sixth against the San Francisco Giants' Gaylord Perry. Perry's brother Jim of the Minnesota Twins allowed one run in his two innings of work while Gaylord surrendered the AL's second run in the seventh. St. Louis ace Bob Gibson was touched for a pair of runs in the eighth on a Brooks Robinson triple.

But with a 4–1 lead entering the bottom of the ninth, the American League could not close out the Nationals, as an ineffective Catfish Hunter was charged with three runs in just one-third of an inning before Mel Stottlemyre of the Yankees finally retired the side with the score even at 4–4. Neither team scored in the 10th or 11th inning, and the AL was also blanked in the top of the 12th. Clyde Wright, one of four California Angels named to the junior circuit squad, had taken over for Stottlemyre and held the NL at bay in the 11th and got the first two batters out in the 12th before fate intervened when hometown favorite Pete Rose singled to centerfield. Rose advanced to second base on a hit to left by Los Angeles third baseman Billy Grabarkewitz, bringing Jim Hickman, "the Cubs' vagabond outfielder-first baseman," to the plate.[36]

A lanky native of Tennessee, Hickman was making what would be his only appearance in an All-Star Game, and after replacing Rico Carty in left field, he later moved to first base. Going hitless in his first three trips to the plate, Hickman made good his fourth time up when he got a base hit to centerfield. Rose, one of the most determined players—and baserunners—ever to step on the field, made a mad dash for home as Amos Otis of the Kansas City Royals, himself a skilled outfielder and future Gold Glove winner, picked up the ball and threw home.

Defending the plate was Cleveland's Ray Fosse, and when the ball and runner arrived at the same instant, the Indian backstop was on the receiving end of a thunderous hit by Rose. Rose's left shoulder-to-left shoulder contact with Fosse bowled the catcher over into a backward somersault. "You know, Ray Fosse is a friend of mine," Rose later recalled. "On the evening before the game, Ray visited our house in Cincinnati, but when I saw that the play at home was going to be close, with Ray blocking the plate, I had no choice except to knock him over.... If I'd tried to slide, I might have been tagged out."[37] Rose indeed scored the winning run as he touched the plate with his right hand and rolled on his side after the impact, rising quickly from the ground, while the stunned Fosse righted himself but remained kneeling on the ground.

Besides this jarring play making for one of the most memorable moments in the game's history, it cemented Rose's reputation as his generation's premier hell-bent-for-leather ballplayer as well as creating a myth that lingers about the fallout with respect to Fosse. "It is often written that Rose severely injured Fosse and ended the catcher's career as an effective player. Although one can certainly argue that Rose was wrong to smash into Fosse the way he did, the claim that Fosse's career was ruined is simply not supported by the evidence," especially when the facts show that Rose's next game on July 19 saw him appear only as a pinch-hitter, while Fosse played in Cleveland's first nine games after the All-Star break, beginning two days after the collision.[38]

Fosse's right foot had been burned the previous month by a cherry bomb thrown on the field at Yankee Stadium, but the catcher from Marion, Illinois, and nicknamed the "Marion Mule" for his tenacity, continued on in that game.[39] There were more repercussions from the All-Star hit when it was later revealed that Fosse had suffered a fracture and separation of his shoulder, but his grit and persistence often carried the day for the remainder of his career that ended in 1979. He won two Gold Gloves and was a key member of the Oakland Athletics championship teams in 1973 and 1974.

The 5–4 National League victory was its eighth straight in All-Star competition, and though the American League seemed poised to fall again after trailing early in the 1971 contest, the tables were turned in dramatic fashion on a windy night the following July in Detroit.

With Detroit hosting the 42nd Midsummer Classic, the game program included a paean that recognized the city's blue-collar framework and touched on several aspects of its recent past. Born in South Carolina but proud to make his journalistic mark after moving to the Motor City, Bob Talbert of the *Detroit Free Press* wrote,

> I first met my Detroit when she was at her best, … when ribbons cascaded from Tiger caps, and crowds of happy people were descending on Tiger Stadium. She was on her way to a baseball pennant and a World Series championship in the summer of 1968—a glorious, grabbing, sock-it-to-'em time of unity and oneness that big cities rarely seem to enjoy today.… While some sophisticated cities don't even perspire, the nation's fifth largest city sweats a ton.… Its labor force is the I-beam that supports this giant machine of a city.… Detroit, I had been warned, is full of big city ills—crime in the streets, racial tensions, Mafia underworld and hippie underground. All this is true.… But I've found people committed—not committed [*sic*]—to make today's solutions the textbook for the big city's future … the real "center" of Detroit lies in its people.…[40]

Where some people had vivid recollections of Detroit in flames during the summer of 1967, others like Talbert exuded confidence in a city he saw reborn and inspired by a great baseball team. He embraced the city's diversity of "dozens of cultural and ethnic backgrounds.… Afro-style Dexter Boulevard … the rampant rhythms of Motown soul music … and natives speaking enough Yiddish to confuse white gentiles."[41] The deadline for Talbert to submit his essay in time for the printing of the program was well in advance of the naming of the All-Star Game starting pitchers, but based on the sentiments he expressed, he likely found reason to celebrate that announcement.

As chosen by the All-Star team managers, who were automatic selections by virtue of having led their respective clubs to the World Series in the year prior, the starting pitchers in the 1971 contest were two Blacks, Vida Blue for the American League and Dock Ellis for the National, the first matchup of its kind in the All-Star Game. Beforehand, Ellis, the Pittsburgh ace, famously said, "They'll never start one 'brother' against another 'brother,'" his statement shot through with racial overtones indicating that he felt baseball—and, by extension, White America—was not ready to accept a pair of Black pitchers being purposely scheduled to start the national pastime's premier summer event.[42]

But the manager of the National League, Sparky Anderson, pointed to Ellis's excellent won-lost mark of 14–3 with a 2.11 ERA and the fact that the pitcher would have six days of rest entering the contest in Detroit, making him a superb candidate to be honored with the starting assignment. Blue was the natural choice of Baltimore skipper Earl Weaver to take the mound for the AL, his merit clearly evident in his dazzling record of 17–3 and accompanying ERA of 1.42 at the All-Star break.

On the evening of July 13, Blue and Ellis pitched their allowed maximum of three innings each, yet only in the opening inning did either display the quality that earned them their designations as All-Stars. The Oakland ace retired the NL in order in the top of the first, while the Pirate honoree yielded only a single in the bottom of the frame. But in the second inning, Blue hit Willie Stargell with a pitch and Johnny Bench belted a two-run homer to the upper deck in right-centerfield. This clout portended how the rest of the scoring would unfold: "There was a substantial wind blowing out to right field this night in Detroit, reaching gusts of thirty-one miles per hour. As a result, there were plenty of suggestions that the home run barrage was a little tainted."[43]

Ellis set the AL down in order in the bottom of the second, and in the top of the third, Blue was tagged again, this time by Hank Aaron for a solo home run to give the NL a 3–0 lead. But more fireworks were in the offing when the American League batted in the bottom half. Luis Aparicio opened with a single, and Weaver went to his bench, selecting Reggie Jackson to pinch-hit for Blue.

Unloading what many still consider the longest homer hit in an All-Star Game, Reggie swung on the second pitch and made perfect contact to send the ball soaring into the light tower atop the stands in right-centerfield. Estimated to have traveled over 520 feet, the ball was thought by some observers to be still on the rise when it struck the lighting's framework, and after the game, Jackson said, "Two years ago, I hit a couple of tape-measure jobs well over 500 feet in Minneapolis and Kansas City, but I think this would have to be the longest one I ever hit."[44]

Instant replay was not exactly a novelty of sports television in the early 1970s, yet this indelible moment may not have received all the acclaim in terms of the NBC Television broadcast. Columnist Dick Young wrote, "Fans are still screaming that Reggie Jackson's taper didn't get an encore. I'm told the cameras missed it. If the networks would stop straining for gimmicks and concentrate on following the ball, we'd all be better off."[45] Fueling Young's angst was the decision to put a microphone on umpire Frank Umont yet NBC's inability to adequately capture the visual highlight of the game.

Shortly after Jackson's heroic feat, Frank Robinson hit his own two-run homer to right field—less dramatically, this reached only the lower grandstand—to give the AL a 4–3 lead. Harmon Killebrew's two-run shot in the sixth completed the scoring for the American League, and Roberto Clemente's solo homer in the eighth accounted for the final NL run in the 6–4 American League win. Despite giving up three runs in as many innings pitched, Vida Blue was credited with the victory, while Dock Ellis took the loss, which was the only National League defeat between 1963 and 1982. This period of utter domination—19 wins in 20 contests—was countered by a surge in victories by the American League as the pendulum swung in favor of the junior circuit, but this stretch did not begin until the late 1990s.

All-Star heroics aside, notable candidates were voted into the Baseball Hall of Fame in 1970 and 1971, including a most significant induction that, in the manner of Jackie Robinson, broke a color line of baseball albeit related to a different matter. Controversial at times in its own way, the selection of those enshrined in Cooperstown is a two-part process: Recently retired players, managers, and executives could remain on the ballot used by members of the Baseball Writers' Association of America (BBWAA) for up to 12 years, during which time they were either elected to the Hall or dropped from consideration, while those figures who had failed in the past or otherwise been ignored in the voting were reviewed by a select Veterans Committee that would reconsider their past credentials.

Whereas the voting body of the BBWAA numbered in the hundreds—in 1970, "300 ballots were submitted by veteran writers with ten or more years as members of the [BBWAA], plus honorary members (who pass the ten-year restriction)"—the Veterans Committee was a mere dozen.[46] Candidates were elected based on a 75-percent vote. In his tenth year on the BBWAA ballot, Lou Boudreau, player-manager of the 1948 World Series champion Cleveland Indians, garnered 77.3 percent of the vote to earn his Hall-of-Fame plaque, and he was the only player chosen by the writers. The Veterans Committee added three members to the Hall's roll: former New York Yankee centerfielder Earle Combs, who was a sparkplug for the Babe Ruth–era teams; Jesse Haines, a longtime St. Louis Cardinal pitcher and three-time 20-game winner in the 1920s; and Ford Frick, whose lengthy service as president of the National League (1934 to 1951) and baseball commissioner (1951 to 1965) took place "during trying days for the game [that included] rising costs, entry of TV into baseball, integration and expansion."[47]

Boudreau's path to the Hall of Fame was seemingly lengthy given his credentials: He compiled a lifetime .295 batting average, during the 1940s he was named an eight-time All-Star, and on eight occasions he received American League MVP votes that placed him the top ten, including

7. All-Stars and Hall-of-Famers   159

winning that award in 1948. Frick's tenure was marked by several notable achievements, not least of which was "the saving of the National League in the 1930s when four [of eight] clubs were bankrupt. Through Frick's efforts, the failing franchises in Brooklyn, Philadelphia, Cincinnati and Boston were salvaged."[48]

The transfer of teams from their original cities to new destinations— the westward movement in the 1950s of the Braves from Boston to Milwaukee, that of the Athletics from Philadelphia to Kansas City, as well as the migration of the Brooklyn Dodgers and New York Giants to the West Coast—broadened baseball's horizons under Frick's watch. After Frick, in his role as NL president, approved Jackie Robinson's contract with the Dodgers in 1947, he laid down the law by quashing a potential strike by St. Louis Cardinal players who were poised to sit out rather than engage a Black player on the field. As a founding father of the Baseball Hall of Fame itself, Ford Frick proved that he was hardly an idle executive.

The BBWAA balloting in 1971 produced no past player who met the necessary three-quarter majority. Although Yogi Berra would easily gain admission to the Hall the following year, in his first year of eligibility he showed that even his impeccable résumé of three AL MVP awards, 10 World Series championships, and 18 All-Star appearances were no guarantee of a debut-year election, his 67.2 percent being 28 votes short. (Pitcher Early Wynn, just two votes behind Berra in 1971, succeeded the following year as well.) Despite the shutout of the writers, the Veterans Committee would be able to elect one non-player and two former players, this total of three being the standard quota, but the annual meeting of the Hall of Fame's Board of Directors included a "motion duly made, seconded and carried" that "in 1971 only [the Committee] may elect an additional four players from those eligible … from among the real old timers."[49]

With a temporary spate of seven electees for the Class of 1971, the Veterans group tabbed one executive and six players: New York Yankee and Met luminary George Weiss was an architect of the Bronx Bombers' dynasty of the late 1940s and '50s who was also instrumental in "assembl[ing] the front-office infrastructure that would create the 'miracle' 1969 World Series champion"[50]; Dave Bancroft, a 16-year National League shortstop who won four pennants; NL first baseman Jake Beckley, who played from 1888 to 1907; Chick Hafey, a bespectacled outfielder with a .317 lifetime average in his time with the Cardinals and Reds beginning in the mid–1920s; AL standout Harry Hooper, who was part of the Boston Red Sox "Million-Dollar Outfield" of the 1910s; Joe Kelley, whose career spanned the late nineteenth century into the twentieth, and, like Hafey, batted .317 for his career; and Rube Marquard, a southpaw who won 201 games in an 18-year stint in the National League that commenced in 1908.

Several decades after the 1970 and 1971 honorees had their moment in the sun on Induction Day, historian Bill James published an excoriating analysis regarding the worthiness of some of them. In doing so, he cited the undue preferential treatment that became evident when a member of the Veterans Committee pleaded the case for a past teammate to be elected to the Hall of Fame. Although not every past player nominated received such biased treatment, James paid particular attention to Frankie Frisch, a committee member beginning in 1967 who had already earned his plaque in Cooperstown thanks to his stellar performance as a player with the New York Giants and St. Louis Cardinals in the 1920s and most of the '30s. "Frisch very quickly became a central figure on the Veterans Committee," wrote James. "Everybody liked him, but everybody wanted to stay on his good side," and when Frisch proposed the names of one-time Giants and Cardinals with whom he played or managed, the results were predictable.[51]

When former Giant star Bill Terry joined the panel in 1971, it was little coincidence that "the Veterans Committee made a series of appalling selections, littering the Hall of Fame with Frisch and Terry's old cronies" from their past clubs.[52] James determined that Dave Bancroft was possibly worthy of the Hall, but indicated that the same could not be said for Haines, Hafey, and several other old-timers who were chosen in subsequent years. In future years, the composition of the committee would continue to spark debate when similar connections between its members and those nominated and elected could be easily discerned. Such impassioned discussions continue into the twenty-first century, with some inductees elating fans and others raising eyebrows, Gil Hodges and Harold Baines, respectively, serving as prime examples.

One aspect of damage control, of sorts, was built-in since the Hall of Fame Board granted the increase of four extra players—or six in total—only for 1971, thereafter reverting back to two players and one non-player. Before the decade was out, the number was set at two men regardless of their status as player or non-player.

Rightfully immune from James's poison pen was one Leroy "Satchel" Paige, the great pitcher from the Negro Leagues who joined the Cleveland Indians in 1948 and pitched for parts of six seasons in the American League. Paige's biographer, Larry Tye, noted that he "pitched his heart out during twenty years in the Negro Leagues, then reminded the Majors of all that he could do at an age when most players were feeding beer bellies and watching from the bleachers."[53] Paige was born in 1906 in Mobile, Alabama, to a typically poor family and was raised in a segregated South. Misdeeds as a youngster landed him in the state's Reform School for Juvenile Negro Law-Breakers, where he spent most of his teen years, but "[t]he good news was that his new home gave him endless time for his favorite pastime: pitching a baseball."⁵⁴

Shortly after his release from the reform school and by the time he was 20 years old, Paige embarked on a career playing for numerous Negro

Negro League star Satchel Paige was rightfully honored with a plaque that was installed in the Hall of Fame's Gallery rather than placed in a separate display. Pictured with commissioner Bowie Kuhn on Induction Day in 1971, Paige later resented his treatment by the baseball establishment, yet he broke ground that allowed other great Black ballplayers from the past to be honored in Cooperstown.

League teams, rapidly gaining a reputation as the foremost pitcher in Black baseball. Spectators flocked to see him pitch, and he was never at a loss for words, this loquaciousness endearing him even more to his fans as well as a press corps looking for quotes. Paige's actual statistical record is murky because he controlled the narrative: His personally maintained "almanac" was fluid, and he was wont to adjust the numbers to suit whomever he was trying to impress at the moment.[55]

Regardless of what the true data was, Paige's performance on the mound was where it counted, and the many eyewitnesses in the stands and the opposing players who were victimized by his pitching add to the legacy he forged. By the time Paige ultimately retired in 1965—to all intents and purposes, he had finished his career with the St. Louis Browns in 1953, but Kansas City Athletics owner Charlie Finley brought him back for a three-inning cameo appearance in late September 1965—it was accepted that there was substance to back up the boasting about his achievements. As acknowledgment of Paige's feats gained acceptance, so did those of another past Negro Leaguer, catcher Josh Gibson, whose prodigious home-run hitting—"he was the best hitter in the universe of black baseball," wrote one biographer—put him in the forefront of Black position players.[56]

Given the accomplishments of Paige and Gibson, it is most fair to speak of them in the same breath, but through the 1960s as the civil rights struggle continued, the lack of Negro League inductees at the Hall of Fame became increasingly conspicuous by their absence. A compelling moment occurred during his own enshrinement speech in late July 1966 when Boston Red Sox star Ted Williams bravely threw down the gauntlet in an effort to set a precedent for the inclusion of players of color in the Hall.

After commissioner William Eckert introduced the "Splendid Splinter" to the crowd and presented him with his Hall-of-Fame plaque—the former Air Force general also read its inscription for the benefit of the gathering—Williams thanked a host of people who helped him over the course of his baseball career, from those who influenced his learning of the game of baseball to the sports writers who elected him to the Hall. His relationship with the reporters was often contentious, yet he acknowledged that he appreciated having received so many votes; of the 302 ballots that were submitted, only 20 did not include his name. After noting his own good fortune in the game, Williams laid bare a glaring omission.

> Inside this building are plaques dedicated to baseball men of all generations and I'm privileged to join them. Baseball gives every American boy a chance to excel, not just to be as good as someone else but to be better than someone else. This is the nature of man and the name of the game and I've always been lucky

to wear a baseball uniform, to have struck out or to have hit a tape-measure home run. And I hope that someday the names of Satchel Paige and Josh Gibson in some way can be added as a symbol of the great Negro players that are not here only because they were not given a chance."[57]

In a similar vein, outfielder Billy Williams of the Chicago Cubs used the dais during his 1987 Hall of Fame induction to push for greater minority representation "as third base coaches, as managers, as general managers, as executives in the front office, and yes, [as] owners of major league ball clubs."[58] These expanded opportunities would naturally lead to the likelihood of better chances that people of color serving in roles beyond that of players could anticipate entry into the Hall of Fame should their deeds warrant it.

Renowned as baseball's greatest hitter, Ted Williams was uniquely qualified to advocate for players of color and express his pathbreaking desire: "The news that Ted Williams had Hispanic blood—that he really was the first Latino inducted into the National Baseball Hall of Fame— takes a lot of people by surprise."[59] So wrote Red Sox historian Bill Nowlin, and with Mexican ancestry from his mother's side, Williams understood the plight of minorities. Having played in an era when Jackie Robinson and Larry Doby broke the color line in their respective leagues shortly after World War II, Williams's "awareness of discrimination led to his welcoming of black players" into Major League Baseball.[60] Neither did he shy away from counting his blessings as a ballplayer, noting, "A chill goes up my back when I think I might have been denied this [opportunity] if I had been black."[61]

Leigh Montville, one of Williams's biographers, observed of the Hall-of-Famer's encouraging comments, "No one had said this from the podium," and although Williams's "politics always would be aligned with conservative, Republican men," his moral compass was guided by "a liberal social conscience.... He was—and even his worst critics would have admitted it—a constant ally of the downtrodden and neglected."[62]

The slowly-turning wheels of the baseball establishment took no immediate action to address the slight that Ted Williams pointed out. By the time Eckert was deposed as commissioner and his replacement, Bowie Kuhn, took office in February 1969, the new head of the game recognized that "a lively debate was percolating over whether stars of the old Negro Leagues, particularly Satchel Paige and Josh Gibson, should be considered for the Hall of Fame."[63] There was growing recognition that had Blacks not been excluded from Major League Baseball, the top tier of those players would clearly have earned their rightful place both in the game and in the Hall.

As a youngster growing up in Depression-Era New York, sportswriter Leonard Koppett "accepted the prevailing view that Negroes were 'not qualified' to be major league baseball players," yet he thought it curious that "while the Yankees and Giants were on the road, all-black teams played in those same ball parks."[64] Which was to say that if the Negro League talent was of sufficient quality to earn the right to use a big league field, then why not allow those players to occupy the same space *at the same time* as their white counterparts?

In his memoir, Kuhn recounted that a meeting convened to discuss the admission of Negro Leaguers to the Hall of Fame was "heated and unpleasant."[65] Present for the session were Dick Young and Jack Lang of the Baseball Writers' Association of America; three officials from Kuhn's office, including the former standout Black player Monte Irvin; Hall of Fame president Paul Kerr; and Ford Frick, who was president of the National League at the time Jackie Robinson became a Brooklyn Dodger and was a founder of the Hall of Fame. Strong opinions for and against Negro Leaguer inclusion were raised—interestingly, Frick was among the naysayers—and despite his support for the initiative, Kuhn felt that the board of directors of the Hall of Fame would not accept the proposal.

So, in February 1971 the commissioner established a special Negro League panel to pick the best former Black players who would then "be honored *with a display* at the Baseball Museum in Cooperstown."[66] The committee members were former players Eppie Barnes, Roy Campanella, Monte Irvin, Judy Johnson, and Bill Yancey; two prominent writers in the Black sporting press, Sam Lacy and Wendell Smith; and three past Negro League executives, Frank Forbes, Ed Gottlieb, and Alex Pompez. They were tasked with determining the candidates and, each year through 1977, would ultimately pick one or two players from the 1930s–1940s timeframe for each position on the diamond.

Yet, the initial "display" of several Negro Leaguers would not be on equal footing with the venerated individual plaque, such as that given to Ted Williams. Once made public, the issue generated more controversy because of its segregationist nature and physical separation from the Plaque Gallery. Finally relenting, the Hall's board agreed to allow Negro League inductees to assume their rightful place, and due to "the public weigh[ing] in with outrage at the spectacle of a segregated baseball museum," plaques for inductees were to be installed in the same gallery as held all the others.[67]

With Satchel Paige perhaps the most visible face of the former Negro Leagues, he was named to be the first honoree from those circuits. The timing of the announcement of this achievement came in early February 1971 while the uproar over the plaque location remained an issue. Paige deflected any hurt or resentment—"As far as I am concerned, I'm in the Hall of Fame. I don't know nothing about no Negro section. I'm proud to be in it. Wherever they put me is all right with me," he said at a press conference in New York—and he "[q]uieted his competing instincts by siding, as he always had, with moderation over militancy."[68]

On a hot afternoon in early August, he delivered a rambling, entertaining speech to a crowd of about 2,500 people, recalling his barnstorming days of yore: "We played up in Canada, and if I didn't pitch every day, they didn't want the ball club," he said of developing his stamina as well as citing the demand by fans to see him on the mound.[69] He paid tribute to Bill Veeck, owner of the Cleveland Indians who signed Paige to his first Major League contract in 1948, and shared his timeless source of inspiration: "The little poem I wrote about don't ever look back something might be gaining on you, that kept me going." Ironically or not, the last speaker of the day to accept George Weiss's plaque—unlike the previous year, inductees were introduced alphabetically by last name—was none other than Ford Frick.

The Indians proudly devoted a section of their 1971 yearbook to members of the Hall of Fame "whose exceptional talents helped to attain national prominence for the game of baseball and the city of Cleveland."[70] Paige now joined past greats Cy Young, Nap Lajoie, Tris Speaker, Jesse Burkett, Elmer Flick, Bob Feller, Stanley Coveleski, and Lou Boudreau as full-fledged members of the Cooperstown institution. Yet, as honorable as his membership was, and as glib as parts of his Hall of Fame speech were, Paige nonetheless harbored resentments that he was less reluctant to suppress in the afterglow of his Hall of Fame induction.

Paige still viewed baseball's white-dominated landscape as a place where men of color were less likely to receive consideration for positions in management or advanced levels on the playing field. "When he was invited back to Cooperstown for a luncheon following the induction of other ex-players, he was even less inclined to deflect his hurt with humor." When he vented his perception that "young black ball players were being kept in the minor leagues instead of being brought up to the majors," an aide in Bowie Kuhn's office "interrupted me and said, 'Satch, sit down. This is no place for that kind of talk.' I sat down. They kept asking me to come back but I've never been back to Cooperstown."[71]

Dick Young of the New York *Daily News* was a proponent of the Black cause, and his opinions were swayed in a discussion with Brooklyn Dodger great Roy Campanella. The former catcher, who played with Negro League teams in Washington, Baltimore, and Philadelphia, believed that "there were at least eight or nine players with Hall of Fame credentials," so it was obvious that Satchel Paige was only a harbinger of what could follow.[72]

Besides changing the hardened attitudes of those who demurred about the cause of Negro League Hall of Fame candidates, another major obstacle impeding their progress was the lack of substantial and reliable statistics to back up the claims of how great any Negro Leaguer supposedly was. As the *New York Times* reported in a detailed essay about worthy Black players, any fan was able to:

> consult the record book for [Babe] Ruth's 60-home-run season, [Joe] DiMaggio's 56-game hitting streak, and [Marty] Marion's fielding averages. His intuitive certainty of their greatness is reinforced by the printed word.
> But for Negro baseball stars, no such reinforcement is possible. The old fan can bring to mind Josh Gibson standing loose and easy in the righthand batter's box at Yankee Stadium during a Negro League doubleheader in 1934 and almost effortlessly propel the ball over the third tier next to the left field bullpen, the only fair ball ever hit out of the Stadium. He cannot go to a record book and find Gibson's career home-run total, which in his 17 years in black baseball probably surpassed Ruth's 714. He cannot even be certain about the top figure for a single year, which was reported to be 89.[73]

Defaulting to the example of an extreme case when making an argument can foster great doubt among those less inclined to believe a potentially tall tale. However, one baseball writer advanced the case of the "mythical figure of Babe Ruth, who did things on the diamond that had not been done before in the majors," and asked, "[I]f there can be a bigger-than-life figure in Ruth, why couldn't there be the same in the Negro Leagues, especially since we have had transcendent black players throughout baseball as well as in all sports they have participated in?"[74] Boxer Jack Johnson, the first Black heavyweight champion, and football legend Jim Brown are but two other superlative African-American athletes who demonstrate the validity of this idea and lend credence to the possibility that Josh Gibson's feats *were* accomplished and should not be easily dismissed as fiction.

The Negro League panel charged with choosing the inductees "worked without benefit of any statistics and was therefore relying upon word of mouth of the Committee members."[75] Another vexing piece of data related to the requirement of a nominee's having played for at least ten years, although this limit was loosened.

Indeed, just two years prior to Paige's induction, the first edition of Macmillan's *Baseball Encyclopedia* had been published, and that endeavor required a monumental effort to track down the records of all Major League players intending to be added to this massive tome. The record for most players of the post–World War I era could be validated with relative ease, but such was hardly the case for those with careers in the nineteenth century (or prior to World War I) whose deeds may have been recorded in long-lost, obscure newspapers that now required vigorous research in the quest to create an official record. (In May 2024, after decades of compilation, investigation, and analysis, Negro League statistics were at last sanctioned and added to the official corpus of Major League data.)

Over half a century has passed since the Rose–Fosse collision, the herculean home run by Reggie Jackson, and the watershed moment of Satchel Paige's entry into the Baseball Hall of Fame. In this time, a home run–hitting contest has been added to the All-Star Game festivities, and fan balloting on punch-cards has been supplanted by online voting, which is now a two-tiered process to ultimately choose the starters, and the players also have a say in determining who makes the squad.

As fans both serious and casual can appreciate, the annual Hall of Fame election and its results incite emotions and debate. The Induction Ceremony, formerly held behind the main building of the Hall, has long been moved to the Clark Sports Center, located about one mile south of Main Street in Cooperstown. This change in venue was necessitated by the burgeoning crowds that rendered obsolete the quaint aspect of the limited physical space—perhaps the size of a football field—that remains Cooper Park. And through the doors of the Hall have passed dozens of minority players—Negro Leaguers and more—who have made their respective marks on the national pastime.

Not least among this group was one Bud Fowler, who was born in 1858 in Fort Plain, New York, and grew up in Cooperstown shortly after his family moved there. He toiled on ball fields across the United States and even in Canada as a pitcher and infielder, fighting racial prejudice nearly every step of the way. In his post–playing career, Fowler was instrumental in the formation of Black barnstorming clubs, and he supported associations that would later take shape as the Negro Leagues in the early twentieth century.

Although not exactly a native-born son of Cooperstown, Bud Fowler's youthful roots in this village, when conjoined to his work in advancing the sport of baseball, earned him induction into the Hall of Fame as part of the Class of 2022. Yet, another tribute was already in evidence to those passing just outside the first-base side of Doubleday Field only a few blocks down the street from the Hall of Fame. Since the spring of 2013, vehicles and pedestrians have been traveling on a Cooperstown thoroughfare dedicated as Fowler Way.

8

There Used to Be a Ballpark Here

Slowly but surely, the modern outdoor stadium began to encroach on the American sporting landscape when Candlestick Park opened in San Francisco in 1960 and was joined by Dodger Stadium and Washington's DC Stadium two years later. This trio of venues had much company by the middle of the decade: Shea Stadium, the Houston Astrodome, Atlanta Stadium, Busch Stadium, and Anaheim Stadium soon followed, with the Oakland–Alameda County Coliseum and San Diego Stadium hosting big league baseball by the close of the decade.

The feature that distinguished most of these structures—but not all of them—was their design as multipurpose sports facilities, and as the calendar turned to 1970, the wave of cookie-cutter stadiums reached a crescendo of sorts. Riverfront Stadium, Three Rivers Stadium, and Veterans Stadium joined the fray, further extended the use of artificial turf, and became as emblematic of their timeframe as the polyester clothing then being worn by so many people across the country.

Fitting of the period covered in these pages, this trend of modernity spelled the end of several old-school ballparks, namely Pittsburgh's Forbes Field, Connie Mack Stadium (née Shibe Park) in Philadelphia, and Cincinnati's Crosley Field. More by coincidence than design, the demise of three legacy National League ballparks swept away decades of any nostalgia that accrued to these venerable sites whose days had become as numbered as those of Ebbets Field and the Polo Grounds. Each of them hosted a team that had captured a World Series championship at some point in its lengthy past, yet the passage of time did them few favors as age, maintenance issues, and the evolution of the surrounding neighborhoods demanded new facilities to replace the old.

◆ ◆ ◆

8. There Used to Be a Ballpark Here

When the Philadelphia Athletics began play in 1901, they established themselves as one of the more competitive teams in the nascent American League. Their modest fourth-place finish in the AL's inaugural season was just nine games behind the pennant-winning Chicago White Sox, and 1902 saw Connie Mack's team capture the league crown by five games over the St. Louis Browns. The sudden success created a pleasant problem when local fans caught an early version of baseball fever and attendance surged at little Columbia Park in North Philadelphia, which had a seating capacity of 9,500.[1] First-year attendance at Columbia totaled 206,000, but the title-winning club drew 420,000, far outpacing the turnstile count of the rival Philadelphia Phillies of the National League, who played at the Baker Bowl.

Benjamin Shibe, the owner of the Athletics, knew he had to take action to accommodate his supporters: The pennant-winning team in 1905 drew more than half a million fans, and two years later when well over 600,000 flocked to the park, "[t]he team often had to barricade the gates and turn away thousands."[2] With great foresight, Shibe not only sought to oblige the crowds but to do so in a prudent and modernistic way. Finding land at Lehigh Avenue between 20th and 21st Streets that was also bounded by Somerset Street, he embarked on a project that delivered "the first baseball stadium constructed of steel-reinforced concrete. In 1909, all existing ballparks were made of wood, and they were all firetraps—all of them," wrote *Boston Globe* columnist Bob Ryan in commemoration of the stadium's centennial. "Shibe thought the time had come for baseball to enter the 20th century in terms of stadium construction."[3]

Taking just under one year to complete, Shibe Park occupied an entire city block, and its rectangular shape naturally meant that the grandstand and playing field would follow suit. The original distance to center field was an enormous 515 feet, with pitcher-friendly dimensions of 378 feet down the left field line and 340 to right. The practicality of the construction techniques was masked by aesthetically pleasing architectural appointments that faced directly on the streets outside, among them "rusticated bases, composite columns, arched windows and vaultings, ornamental scrollwork and a fabulous French renaissance tower, with cupola."[4] Beneath the dome of this last adornment was the location of offices for team officials and Connie Mack, whose duties included that of team treasurer and field manager.

Shibe Park's opening on April 12, 1909, was a spectacular event that was overwhelming in the number of people that it drew. The official attendance for the Athletics' game against the Boston Red Sox was listed at 30,162, as "[a]bout 7,000 rooters watched the game from the outfield, standing seven-deep and held back by a rope stretched across the entire

With its beautiful exterior and dome behind home plate, Shibe Park—later known as Connie Mack Stadium—saw the departure of the Philadelphia Athletics after the 1954 season, but the Phillies called it home until 1970 before they moved to Veterans Stadium.

expanse of the outfield. Another 6,000 fans looked in from the rooftops around the block."[5]

Unpaid admissions, or at least those that did not contribute revenue to the team, were a persistent problem. "Almost from the beginning there were other seats that didn't net the club a cent, only more spectators— the long-familiar 'peep' bleachers atop the 20th Street row houses. These homes, with their big bay windows, provided perfect rooftop and porch viewing spots for fans outside the park."[6] The 12-foot-high concrete wall in right field could not obstruct the elevated sightlines from beyond, and not until 1935 was Mack able to install an additional 22-foot corrugated metal barrier—this was labeled *Connie Mack*'s "Spite Wall" even though Ben Shibe's son Jack was the instigator—to end the free viewership.[7]

The size of the field had its own ebbs and flows over the years as seating sections were built or otherwise amended. As if to mimic another Major League ballpark that began operating that same month, Shibe Park "had slopes in front of the outfield fences in the early years," but as the inclines vanished, more accommodations for paying customers were constructed.[8] "[L]ike so many [stadiums] of the day, [the field] was ludicrously large, with dimensions of 378–515–340. In what you'd have to call its '50's

8. There Used to Be a Ballpark Here

prime, it was 334–447–329."[9] Various projects were initiated in which formerly open bleacher areas were replaced with two-tiered sections, and another salient feature was built: A massive scoreboard 50 feet high was installed in 1950, soaring another ten feet with the addition of a sign for Ballantine Beer in 1956. By this point, the Phillies were the ballpark's lone tenant. Although it took several decades, Shibe Park ultimately became a fully enclosed venue.

For the first season at Shibe Park, 674,915 spectators came to see the Mackmen finish a close second behind AL champion Detroit, the performance of the home team presaging the first phase of Mack's dynasty that commenced in 1910. Not until 1925 was that total number eclipsed as the second dynastic phase loomed on the horizon, and the Athletics unseated the New York Yankees as the cream of the American League crop by capturing three consecutive pennants, including winning the World Series of 1929 and 1930. Fan enthusiasm was shown in home attendance, which peaked at 839,176 at the end of the Roaring Twenties. But by 1932's nadir of the Great Depression, Mack, already in his late sixties, found himself financially strapped due to his club's league-leading payroll. When he "sold off his stars to owners with deeper pockets, ... his team returned to the nether regions of the American League."[10]

The Athletics never recovered, not at the box office or in the standings. The introduction of night baseball in the spring of 1939 had little overall beneficial impact to the team. In fact, residents in the immediate neighborhood were irked about the presence of the ungainly light towers, and the Phillies, having vacated the dilapidated Baker Bowl a year earlier, had become co-tenants at Shibe Park. Cellar-dwellers themselves, the National League team began forging its own legacy of poor attendance by drawing an annual average of fewer than 237,000 fans from 1939 to 1942. Yet a post–World War II stretch from 1946 through the early 1950s offered encouragement as spectators—1.2 million of them in 1950—flocked to see the "Whiz Kids" capture their first NL pennant in 35 years.

Try as they might, both the Athletics and the Phillies simply did not have the ability to match up with the Yankees, in the case of the former, or the New York Giants and Brooklyn Dodgers, in the case of the latter, as those three Gotham-based clubs began dominating the Major Leagues in 1949. Connie Mack, now well into his 80s and at last retired from the game, saw his sons Roy and Earle gain controlling interest in the Athletics by "heavily mortgag[ing] the club through the Connecticut General Insurance Company" in the summer of 1950, but the operation was in a new version of a death spiral from which it could not recover.[11] Even the honor of renaming Shibe Park to Connie Mack Stadium in 1953 provided no salve to a now hopeless situation.

After the Athletics bottomed out in 1954 with a last-place finish 60 games behind the AL champion Cleveland Indians, the Mack brothers sold the team to Arnold Johnson despite their desire to maintain the franchise. Owner of the Yankee minor league affiliate in Kansas City, Johnson won approval to transfer the Athletics, who had become second-class citizens in a town no longer capable of supporting two baseball teams, to the Midwest.

By fielding a more competitive team and now the lone baseball occupants of Connie Mack Stadium—the Eagles of the National Football League called Shibe Park home from 1940 to 1957—the Phillies also had an owner who was aggressive in implementing updates to the ballpark. Bob Carpenter installed billboards on portions of the outfield wall and brought in the huge scoreboard. The capstone of this period moving into the 1960s occurred in 1964 when the Phillies notoriously collapsed coming down the stretch, ultimately falling short of a National League pennant that seemed all but in their grasp when a 10-game losing streak torpedoed their 6½-game lead in late September.

Coincidentally, this debacle was representative of the state of affairs as they pertained to the stadium proper, as aptly summarized by noted Philadelphia baseball historian Rich Westcott: "Although it had been a favorite place of players and fans, Connie Mack Stadium was not destined to go on forever. Not with its rundown condition and obsolescence. Not with the surrounding neighborhood becoming increasingly dangerous. Not with an influx of modern venues appearing throughout the country. By the 1960s, the old ballpark was ready to go."[12]

The replacement for Connie Mack Stadium, Veterans Stadium on the south side of the city, was supposed to be ready for Opening Day of 1970, but a variety of problems related to municipal bureaucracy and construction issues forced a delay of one year that cost the team an estimated $2 million.[13] With the 1970 season commencing at the old address, the pre-game ceremony brought an unexpectedly poignant moment for Frank Lucchesi, the Phillies rookie manager of Italian heritage:

> Lucchesi was given a warm reception as he was introduced and headed toward home plate ... [he] doffed his cap after the first wave of applause and the noise grew louder.... He waved his cap again and then blew a kiss to the stands and now, the entire crowd rose to its feet, saluting the manager who had yet to manage his first major-league game.... During the National Anthem, Frank stood there a few seconds and dabbed his eyes with a handkerchief.... "We hadn't even played a game and they give you this ovation. It has to choke you up—must have been all the Paisanos in the park," Frank remarked after the game.[14]

Yet, the love shown to the home-team manager could not mask the ill physical state of the ballpark, a condition compounded by a locale in the city that had turned "ominous." "Crime was a major problem. Robberies and felonies were common. Frequent crimes were committed inside the ballpark. People were robbed in the bathrooms. Women had their pocketbooks snatched. Fights occurred regularly. A woman was raped. There was even a murder in the stands," noted Westcott.[15]

Some naive fans were their own worst enemy, hanging around the stadium too long after a game in the hope of getting an autograph, only to leave the area well after the crowd had thinned. What can only be described as urban decay on a number of fronts was given gallows-humor treatment by Lucchesi, who, almost certainly with dry eyes, said that Connie Mack Stadium "was in such a tough neighborhood that we had to give away two policemen with every admission."[16]

A local police officer fixed the blame for much of the crime on an age-old problem: "It's not the neighborhood people. Ninety-nine percent of the people who live here are wonderful. It's that one percent ... the gangs," and one city newspaper proudly pointed out that "most of the 700,000 fans came and rooted and went home in safety. For that[,] the men who protected them deserve credit.... They were the real heroes of this [1970] baseball season."[17]

In their final year at Connie Mack Stadium, the Phillies scheduled more day games in an attempt to keep some crime, cloaked by darkness, at bay. Although this strategy prompted a slight bump in attendance, the team nonetheless attracted just 708,247 fans—only the San Diego Padres drew fewer, with 643,679—and the last game played at the once-venerable ballpark devolved into a chaotic scene that was consistent with if not the exact equal of the mayhem about which Westcott wrote.

Over 31,800 fans came to see the end of Connie Mack Stadium on October 1, but Amos Strunk, an outfielder with the Athletics' first dynasty of the 1910s, was not among them. In the company of a reporter for the *Philadelphia Inquirer*, Strunk visited the ballpark one last time and was "a little wet eyed as he look[ed] around the place." The last surviving member of that long-ago championship squad brushed aside any pangs of nostalgia about a place he called "just another old building. I haven't any sentimental feelings about the place. It's just a ball park." Declaring what he deemed to be the *real* ending for a venue he believed now devoid of any significance, Strunk said, "As far as I'm concerned, Connie Mack Stadium died when the A's moved to Kansas City in 1954. It should be torn down."[18]

There was one last bit of Major League business at the old ballpark, and the good news was that Oscar Gamble drove in Tim McCarver in the bottom of the tenth inning to give the Phillies a 2–1 victory over Montreal.

Yet what immediately followed almost obscured the fine accomplishments of the many great past players who competed on the park's diamond. Fans were given slats from the wooden seats as souvenirs, a gesture meant to give them a keepsake of the stadium, but for many who came, this was not enough. "All this was incidental to the main event of the evening, a destructive rampage on the part of those who attended and a substitute for [stadium owner Jerry] Wolman's proposed auction [of artifacts]."[19]

What ensued after McCarver crossed home plate was unfettered havoc as "the crowd ripped up whatever it could, including souvenir sod.... Some people brought their own tools," including those fastened to toolbelts, to better dismantle everything from entire rows of seats, urinals, toilet seats, and turnstile machines.[20] All of this booty was hauled away with the exception of home plate, which the vandals, apparently lacking a shovel, failed to dig up.

Some remnants that escaped the plunder—not all the seats and field sod were looted—were later repurposed by the team for use in the farm system. The team also gave fans the chance to win "one of hundreds of items—stadium equipment, uniforms, and special prizes—for which the Phils held a drawing after the final game Thursday night."[21] This unique trove included the three infield bases—not including home plate, which was unearthed and brought to Veterans Stadium—the uniform of the last Phillies pitcher, locker seats belonging to Tony Taylor and Jim Bunning, several rest room signs, a home plate rake and sprinkling can, Frank Lucchesi's office chair, and the rubber from the pitching mound.

As had been the case in years gone by when fire laid waste to old wooden ballparks, the demise of Connie Mack Stadium came in similar fashion in August 1971 when two youths "snuck into the building to watch a [revivalist] tent go up. They lit a small fire for the hell of it and ran from the park when it did not go out."[22] The ensuing five-alarm conflagration burned and collapsed portions of the main grandstand, including "the domed office of the late Connie Mack, which occupied a tower above the grand entrance on Lehigh Avenue."[23] Rather than hasten the arrival of the wrecking ball, the venue devolved into the apotheosis of blight.

Visiting "the Grand Old Lady" in the summer of 1974 was Phillies infielder Tony Taylor, who broke into the majors with the Chicago Cubs but became a much-loved fan favorite when he was traded in 1960 to Philadelphia. Presently in his second tour as a Phillie and taking some time to see his former place of work, Taylor was stunned "as he walked across an outfield that once looked like golf course greens. Now, the weeds were chest-high, the ground uneven and littered with twisted pieces of metal.... Like bombed bunkers, the concrete dugouts were like tombs ... [and] the most eerie sight was that of the right field scoreboard, which once had flashed like a pinball machine [but] was now stripped bare, its guts of wires and bulb sockets exposed below the peeling Ballantine beer sign."[24]

"My last game here, I'll never forget the ovation," recalled Taylor with a sigh, before departing the site. A reporter who was with Taylor somberly noted, "The old lady, who now has a tree growing where home plate used to be, should have been buried the day she died. It would have been the proper thing to do."[25]

Not until June of 1976, after years of public wrangling with Jerry Wolman, who still owned the property, was the lot finally cleared of its decay.

Less than three months after the debut of Shibe Park, Forbes Field opened its gates to fans of the Pittsburgh Pirates, the event of June 30, 1909, marking the launch of a ballpark that was "ahead of its time" and the construction of which "dwarfed the highly touted project in Philadelphia."[26] Pirate president Barney Dreyfuss sought to vacate Exposition Park, his team's previous venue, because "a lease could not be obtained making it possible to rebuild the wooden park[,] ... at least six floods hit the park every year [that] ruined the field and parts of the stands, as Exposition Park was located in Allegheny, PA, about fifty yards from the Allegheny River ... [and] because of the floods, the field was always damp until midsummer" and thus susceptible to being wrecked by the players' spiked shoes.[27]

In mid–October 1908, Dreyfuss secured a seven-acre plot next to Schenley Park in the Oakland section of Pittsburgh, and two months later he contracted with architect Charles Wellford Leavitt, Jr., to design a new stadium. Leavitt's bona fides included the building of New York horseracing tracks at Belmont and Saratoga. Some may have believed the Forbes Field locale to be less desirable since it was at a remove from Pittsburgh's business district, but access to 15 nearby trolley lines and the ballpark being situated in "an emerging upscale neighborhood" were prime considerations in Dreyfuss's decision.[28] A potentially destructive fire affecting this new concrete-and-steel ballpark would be nearly impossible since the site was one mile distant from local cinder-emitting factories.

Just days before Christmas, construction by the Nicola Building Company started and moved apace at a rate that is hard to fathom.[29] On New Year's Day 1909, the process of filling in Pierre Ravine commenced and lasted for nearly two months in order to first sculpt the area for the playing field; on March 1, Nicola embarked in earnest on construction of the facility, the same month that grandstand-supporting piles were driven into the ground. Also working in the contractors' favor were the lengthening daylight hours, which permitted crews to be employed in two eight-hour shifts as the month of March came to a close. "By May 12, 1909, all steel girders were in place and all grandstand and bleacher seats were received," with installation of the seats beginning eight days later.

Forbes Field, named in honor of General John Forbes, who commanded British troops in the French and Indian War in 1758 as they captured Fort Duquesne and renamed it Fort Pitt, was replete with features that were novel in their day and earned Dreyfuss the distinction of being "a baseball pioneer."[30] A protective tarpaulin to cover the field, telephones—at this point in time, these had not been in existence all that long—were available for the public's use on all levels of the stands; season-ticket holders and players were accorded the luxury of separate entrance gates; elevators took patrons to the third deck of the stadium, where "posh seating locations" served as a "precursor to modern skyboxes."[31] Ramps were built in place of stairways to allow easier movement between levels, "men's and ladies' restrooms were more modern and comfortable than was available in other ballparks," and clubhouse attendants enjoyed the use of laundry equipment that eliminated having to send uniforms out for cleaning.[32]

When the Pirates vacated the third and final version of Exposition Park in favor of their new home, opening day on June 30, 1909, at "Forbes Field was a sight to behold":

> Fans enjoyed the view of Schenley Park over the outfield fence.... The stands stood majestically, 74 feet high and 889 feet in length. Flags lined the roof of the grandstand. Potted plants and palms were in the foyer and in the club offices.... At 2:30, two processions started, one from each foul line in the outfield. Each was led by a band and consisted of the two teams and dignitaries. Both processions went to home plate where they joined together and marched to the centerfield flag pole. When the flags were raised, a cheer swept the stands.[33]

By paying for the ballpark himself at a cost of about $1 million, Dreyfuss warded off the troubles of possible disputes had multiple parties been involved in various decision-making processes. Further aided by clement weather and a lack of labor disruptions, the owner achieved the delivery of a remarkable new ballpark in less than seven months. The Pirates capped a memorable season by placing third in National League attendance, due in no small part to the opening of the new ballpark, and hurtled through a September winning streak of 15 games that put them in the World Series, which they won in seven games over the Detroit Tigers.

In the ensuing decades, second- and third-level sections—the latter behind home plate was nicknamed the "Crow's Nest"—were added that ran the seating capacity from its original 23,000 up to 35,000, while the field dimensions experienced some fluctuation.[34] Left field opened at 360 feet and underwent some minor adjustments over the next 60 years,

8. There Used to Be a Ballpark Here

Courtesy of Pirates owner Barney Dreyfuss, Pittsburgh's Forbes Field was built with amenities that were ahead of their time. Shown here moments after the game-ending out was recorded in the final game played at Forbes, the ballpark was the site of Bill Mazeroski's famous World Series home run.

except when "Greenberg Gardens" (1947)—this was also known as "Kiner's Korner" from 1948 to 1953—were constructed to assist power-hitters Hank Greenberg and Ralph Kiner in their quest for increased home-run production. (Left-centerfield also dipped from 406 feet to 355 during the Gardens/Korner era.) A cavernous distance of 462 feet extended to the farthest corner to the left of straightaway center, right-center settled in at 408 feet by 1942; a section of right-field stands built in 1925 cut the foul line from a whopping 376 feet down to a more reachable 300 feet for lefthanded pull-hitters, with a screen, climbing to just under 28 feet in height, installed in front of the right-field stands in 1932. The backstop, starting at 110 feet behind home plate, was shortened to 84 feet in 1938 and ultimately to 75 feet by 1959.

Despite the opulence and amenities at Forbes Field, attendance seemed to correspond almost in direct proportion to the fortune of the Pirates in their first 15 seasons there. When Pittsburgh secured its next NL pennant—and World Series win over the Washington Senators, to boot—in 1925, they finally topped the league in attendance with just over 804,000 fans. Another NL title followed two years later, but after being swept by the New York Yankees in the Fall Classic, the Pirates fielded only a few contending teams: From 1929 to 1938 they managed to finish in second place on four occasions, third one time, and in fourth place another time just eight games behind the pennant-winning New York Giants.

When Barney Dreyfuss died in 1932, his widow, Florence, assumed ownership of the Pirates, and she recruited her son-in-law to run the team. In the summer of 1946, she sold the club to a consortium that included two notable figures, the entertainer Bing Crosby, and John W. Galbreath, a real estate magnate. The post–World War II era in Pittsburgh saw not only this changing of the guard in the Pirates front office but also in the city's desire for urban renewal, "a major effort to revitalize the region. [The] efforts resulted in the redevelopment of the Golden Triangle, the lower Hill District, and the near North Side. The latter included construction of Three Rivers Stadium, an idea first proposed by the Allegheny Conference for Community Development in 1955."[35]

For better or worse, the Pirates "never publicly solicited for a new stadium. Instead, the combined needs of Pittsburgh's urban renewal and the ever-increasing appetite of the University of Pittsburgh for Oakland real estate made it easy for the Pirates to rid themselves of a costly maintenance liability."[36] When the school purchased the ballpark in 1958 and leased it back to the baseball team, this arrangement was intended as a short-term measure but ended up lasting for the years that the Pirates remained at Forbes Field.

The dark spell of 1950 to 1957 saw the Pirates place seventh or eighth— the latter being the basement of the National League at the time—but relief was on the way when Branch Rickey, the erstwhile general manager of the Brooklyn Dodgers, joined the Pirates front office at the onset of this nadir in 1951. Though his tenure would last but a handful of years, "[i]n 1955 Rickey sent Howie Haak, his best scout, to begin scouring the Caribbean for talent. This move would bear immense fruit for the Pirates in the 1960s, but by then Rickey was gone."[37] One such gem was future Hall-of-Famer Roberto Clemente, whom Rickey plucked from his former employer in Brooklyn.

Pittsburgh's return to glory in 1960 was a watershed moment in Major League history when Bill Mazeroski's home run in the bottom of the ninth inning of Game 7 of the World Series propelled the Pirates to a thrilling victory over the New York Yankees, despite the Bronx Bombers having outscored the Bucs 55–27. Yet, beyond 1962 when the Pirates drew just over one million fans to Forbes Field, the old ballpark was showing its age, and those plans for a new multipurpose stadium that had been afoot since 1955 were slowly moving closer to becoming a reality. That new facility soon hosted a homecoming of sorts: The Pirates' Exposition Park had been located at nearly the same spot where Three Rivers Stadium would later be built.

8. There Used to Be a Ballpark Here

Although Three Rivers fit the criteria of being a multipurpose facility, one historian noted that Forbes more than held its own when it came to versatility:

> Besides hosting professional baseball, Pitt, Carnegie Tech, Duquesne University, and the Steelers played football at Forbes. It was the place where one went to see a boxing match. The Pittsburgh Symphony, Civic Light Opera, and various popular music entertainment acts played there. The park saw numerous political rallies, religious congregations, prayer services for departing GIs, and even the circus which used to play at Exposition Park. This broad scope of events meant that just about every Pittsburgher experienced its special feel.[38]

It was inevitable that Forbes Field would reach the end of its service life given the above circumstances. When the Pirates issued their media guide prior to the 1969 season, the cover of the publication featured an artist's rendering of a righthanded Pirate batter clad in the familiar tank-top uniform, but also along the bottom of the front were two images of significance. To the right was a plain baseball, its wide sweet spot noting that "1969 is the 100th Anniversary of Professional Baseball," and on the left was a three-dimensional sketch of Forbes Field, with each of its light towers artistically topped with a tapered candle flame. "JUNE 30, 1969.... FORBES FIELD'S 60th (and probably last) BIRTHDAY," read the ballpark's caption, and this would indeed prove true because June 28, 1970, marked the final Pirates home game there.[39]

After hosting the St. Louis Cardinals for a five-game series that included the makeup of an earlier rainout, the Pirates were riding a short four-game winning streak when the Chicago Cubs arrived for a single game on Saturday June 27 and a doubleheader the next day. Dock Ellis bested Fergie Jenkins in the weekend opener, 2–1, when three straight singles brought in the winning tally in the bottom of the ninth inning. In the first game on Sunday the 28th, a bases-loaded walk in the home half of the eighth inning plated the winning run as the Bucs were victorious, 3–2, and in the back half of the twin-bill, each team traded single runs in the first inning but Pittsburgh scored twice in the fifth and once more an inning later, holding on for a 4–1 victory to push its winning streak to seven games.

A relatively unknown pitcher, Jim Nelson, hurled eight innings for the win in the nightcap before an overflow crowd 40,918 fans, and the final out was recorded when second baseman Bill Mazeroski fielded Don Kessinger's grounder over the mound and stepped on second for a game-ending force-out. Broadcasting the game on the Pittsburgh Pirates Radio Network, Gene Osborn and Nellie King closed out their time on the air noting the importance of the recent wins: Osborn linked the sweep of the Cubs with the good fortune of the 1909 Pirates who went all the way to a championship, while King observed, "I got more goose bumps during the [final] ball game because the ballclub has kinda attracted a lot of enthusiasm or brought some enthusiasm back to Pittsburgh and to sports, and I'm happy to see that."[40]

"Auld Lang Syne" was sung as the Pirate players took a final Forbes Field bow in front of the home crowd, and "[t]he plan was for an orderly handing out of mementos, orchestrated by Pirate broadcaster Bob Prince."[41] At his own expense, Roberto Clemente bought baseballs, autographed and penned the date of the final game on them, and handed out the balls to young fans prior to the opening of the doubleheader. In fact, seekers of souvenirs had purchased so much merchandise that even before the second game was over, "park officials had [one vendor] close ... for fear of robbery."[42]

Prince then supervised a drawing in which Clemente's and Mazeroski's clubhouse chairs were offered as prizes, along with game-worn caps used that day by the players. Home plate, sets of bases, and some bricks from the outfield wall were among the swag for other lucky fans. But the levity of the drawing ceremony soon took on more threatening tones.

> The crowd edged down to the box seat area, all the way to the foul lines, as Prince began to read off the names of the winners. However, as the process plodded along, some impatient fans started walking around the back of the diamond as well, so that eventually Prince was totally engulfed. Somewhat nervously, the veteran broadcaster pleaded with the fans to back off, but they edged closer and closer. Prince took off before he was overwhelmed, and all hell broke loose.[43]

As local columnist Phil Musick described what unfolded, "mostly it was like having a kindly, old uncle thrown to the piranhas."[44] Quickly the "Grand Old Lady of Schenley Park" became the target of blatant looting and plundering as fans dispensed with the niceties and took matters into their own hands. Telephones, electrical wiring, grandstand seats, all manner of pieces of the scoreboard beyond left field—herbivores grabbed portions of the ivy that covered its wall—were part of the trove either carted away or gleefully vandalized. "Kids ripping and hacking and tearing while old Dad stood there and smiled at the ravage," wrote a dismayed Musick. "If you had any class you were wondering how long it would be before you lost your lunch."[45]

Photographs that appeared soon after in the newspapers proved his point: Hundreds of so-called fans mingled near the base of the scoreboard as the braver ones climbed it, using vacant spaces normally used to hold the number placards as a makeshift—and built-in—ladder to ascend to the top. Tiers of concrete that moments before had secured the seats in place were strewn with bent, broken segments of same. "A county psychiatrist

Dr. M.L. Aronson, shook his leonine head. Sick scenes are his business, but suddenly he was on a busman's holiday. 'Yes, I anticipated this,' he said. 'I guess it's a sign of the times ... but it scares me.' Why would people strip a public place to its skeleton, destroying stuff of no conceivable value?"[46]

Some assets that survived the mob scene did eventually find their place on the memorabilia market, where individual seats, or rows of them, and other hardware sold at varying prices. The Pirates had plans to use artifacts, such as seats and window frames, in the Allegheny Club at the new Three Rivers Stadium. "[One] plan calls for removing a dozen Romanesque window frames from the outside of Forbes Field, replacing the panes of glass with mirrors, and installing the frames behind the 100-foot bar and in the cocktail lounge."[47]

Before Forbes Field was torn down in the fall of 1972, a local citizens' group objected to the encroachment of the University of Pittsburgh on the stadium's site and commissioned "its own architect-designed proposal to turn Forbes Field into a combination of housing, shops, classrooms, concert space and even a community garden."[48]

Yet, the most valuable remnant of the ballpark was the portion of the outfield wall over which Mazeroski's memorable World Series home run traveled. An 8-by-12-foot section of the brick wall was disassembled and restored at the Allegheny Club's cocktail lounge, and when Three Rivers Stadium later was razed, the section was again transferred, this time in 2009 to PNC Park, the next—and current—home of the Pirates. In early July 2006, the *Pittsburgh Post-Gazette* informed its readers that a commemoration would take place to officially mark the restoration of "[a] portion of the old park's wall and its center-field flagpole, dedicated as a monument in 1976."[49]

Although the grass-roots effort failed, a compromise was reached to save home plate; it was later installed in the University of Pittsburgh's Posvar Hall. The flagpole and some bricks from the wall were repurposed as part of the walkway of what came to be known as Center Field Plaza, behind the former location of Forbes Field's left field wall. A blue metal placard placed by the Pennsylvania Historical and Museum Commission furnishes visitors with a brief overview of the site's significance.

There could be any number of ghosts of great past Pirates lurking about where Forbes Field once stood, not least those of Barney Dreyfuss and Bill Mazeroski. As is the case with other relics that end up on the receiving end of the wrecking ball, little of the original physical plant is ultimately saved, yet a pair of tributes will forever stand the test of time. Besides the indelible image of a joyous Mazeroski doing his World Series romp around the bases—preserved in photos and on film—plaudits for the Pirate second baseman and the club owner, whose vision created the once magnificent ballpark, will remain, courtesy of their plaques found at the Hall of Fame in Cooperstown.

When Cincinnati's Redland Field was dedicated in April 1912, it provided no small amount of inspiration for the home team domiciled at the corner of Western Avenue and Findlay Street. The Reds burst from the opening gate and ran up a record of 20 wins and only five losses before being engulfed in mediocrity for much of the remainder of the season; they finished in fourth place at 75–78. Redland's site had been occupied from 1902 to 1911 by the opulent "Palace of the Fans," a structure lush with hand-carved wooden pillars and columns that incorporated elements of Greek and Roman architecture, and where "[w]aiters roamed 'rooters row,' along the first and third base foul lines, selling beers, 12 for $1."[50]

Fire being a primary enemy of wooden buildings, newer construction methods employed concrete, brick, and steel in various combinations to ward off the flames. The replacement for the Palace—outdated after 1911, its seating capacity was only 6,000—would consist of these better materials as had recently been used to create baseball stadiums in Chicago, Pittsburgh, and Philadelphia. Inheriting the grounds-keeping duties from his father, Matty Schwab was already a ten-year veteran who served at the Palace and moved to Redland Field upon its completion. "For 60 years, no one touched a blade of grass without Matty's permission and oversight," wrote one historian of the caretaker who administered to both ballparks.[51]

Redland was generously proportioned for turnstile counts and the benefit of pitchers: the grandstands now accommodated about 20,000 fans, and the foul lines on both sides ran 360 feet, while center field measured 420. By 1927, more than 5,000 box seats were added "in foul territory, requiring a readjustment of home plate that shortened the fences by approximately 20 feet [and] the park's capacity jumped to 26,060."[52]

Through no fault of their own, the Reds became permanently attached to the infamous Black Sox Scandal that befell the 1919 World Series, yet Cincinnati's victory over Chicago nevertheless instilled a competitive spirit that carried forward in the near term. Although 20 years would pass before the Reds secured their next National League pennant, between 1920 and 1926 they finished in third place twice and second place on three occasions.

Changes in team ownership and the onset of the Great Depression did the club few favors. In 1929, the Reds began a woeful stretch in which they quickly sank to the bottom of the National League and faced the possibility of bankruptcy. Powel Crosley, Jr., a native of Cincinnati whose first businesses related to the pioneering automobile industry, gravitated toward another nascent business when "[a]round 1920 Powel Crosley III asked his father for a radio, an innovation that was becoming popular."[53]

Stunned that the cost of a radio could be $100 or more, Crosley embarked on an enterprise to bring far a more modestly priced product to consumers, and soon his radio manufacturing company became a huge success. Encouraged by this endeavor, Crosley launched radio station WLW, which grew into a 500,000-watt broadcaster of top-flight musical entertainment in 1934.

Crosley's achievements seeming to know no bounds, as the manufacture of home appliances, notably the refrigerator, became part of his stable. He also sat on the board of the financial institution that stood to lose out on a $100,000 loan to Sidney Weil, a major partner in the Cincinnati Reds' ownership but a man with little baseball acumen who suffered greatly when the stock market crashed in October 1929. When Central Trust Company foreclosed on Weil in 1933, Crosley and his wealth were poised to fill the breach as the bank sought a new owner. Larry MacPhail, a minor league executive in Columbus, Ohio, was hired to operate the team on behalf of Central Trust and find a local buyer willing to keep the club from being sold to out-of-town interests.

Not only was Crosley's purchase of the Reds consummated in 1934—at this point, Redland Field was rechristened Crosley Field—but MacPhail also convinced the team's new owner to air the team's games on WLW. Continuing in his role as vice president and general manager, the innovative MacPhail drew on his previous work with Columbus and installed a lighting system in the spring of 1935 to make Cincinnati the first Major League city capable of hosting night games. By activating a switch from the White House in Washington, D.C., President Franklin D. Roosevelt had the honor of turning on the lights for the evening debut on May 24.

In the runup to the opening of the 1937 season, the ballpark survived a massive flood that swamped it in over 20 feet of water from nearby Mill Creek. A similar but lesser calamity two years later had a minimal impact on the field, yet the team in 1938 had turned a corner under new manager Bill McKechnie and emerged from its doldrums with a fourth-place finish and a record of 82–68–1. In 1939 the Reds took the NL pennant on the strength of 97 wins versus 57 losses, although they were swept by the New York Yankees in the World Series. The next season saw the team from the Queen City win 100 contests, lose 53, and vanquish the Detroit Tigers in a thrilling seven-game Fall Classic. The Series was played on seven consecutive days beginning October 2, with the last two games held at Crosley Field and the finale lasting a mere 1 hour and 47 minutes.

Ballpark historian Philip J. Lowry cited numerous changes in the distances along the foul lines and to centerfield, many of these implemented prior to 1940. The movement of home plate further from the backstop, the addition of sections of seats, and even the instance of when "the field was turned slightly" for the 1927 season factored into the geometric updates.[54] An additional dimension is most noteworthy:

> [S]urely the signature feature of Crosley Field was the Terrace in front of the left-field wall. It served the same purpose as a warning track, but warning tracks seldom trip the left fielder unfamiliar with their treachery. The Terrace was a 15-degree incline in front of the wall. Many a visiting left fielder found himself flat on the ground as he ran after a fly ball over his head.... York Street was four feet higher than the playing field and the steep incline eliminated the need to build a retaining wall to keep the street from falling into the field.[55]

Clubhouses were not incorporated within the stadium proper or otherwise connected to the dugout, but instead were located separately beyond the left field wall. This was also near the structure that was home to the Superior Towel and Linen Service, nicknamed "the Laundry," the roof of which was "where [Ernie] Lombardi and [Frank] McCormick belted

Noted for its slope near the outfield wall that served as a warning track of sorts, Crosley Field was home of the Cincinnati Reds through the opening of Riverfront Stadium in 1970. In the mid-1960s, Crosley briefly used Herculite glass in place of the typical screen behind home plate.

many a homer" and was "cleared" by the great slugger Jimmie Foxx.[56] Those batters capable of reaching this distance had the chance to add to their wardrobe courtesy of Siebler's, a local haberdashery: "Hit this sign—win a suit," read a placard atop the building.[57] With 11 suits to his credit, Wally Post, the Reds' longtime outfielder, was cited as the sartorial king before the sign was removed in 1965.

A gigantic scoreboard 58 feet tall was a combination of high- and low-tech: electric lights flashed the count on the batter, his uniform number, and the number of outs, while information on out-of-town games was manually posted to show the inning of play, score, numerical designations for each team's pitcher and catcher (the latter was eventually dropped), and score of the first game of a doubleheader, if applicable. The maintenance of this MacPhail-inspired creation was the duty of a five-man crew charged with putting all the numbers in the right places of the scoreboard's framework.

Another foible of the outfield wall—this was an amalgam of concrete and plywood sections—was its display of ground rules that were painted in plain view on its surface. Depending on the flight of the ball and the part of the wall in question, a home run would be counted if the ball went "on the fly to the right of white line," and another posting indicated a ground-rule double for a ball trapped underneath the scoreboard.[58]

Closer to home plate, the protective screen directly behind it was replaced in 1965 by a "glass backstop" that gave fans a clearer view of the action. "[I]t's a lot better than looking through the old wire screen we had," said the Reds' business manager, John Murdough.[59] The Herculite panels were durable and easier on the eye—"It's a lot better than looking through the wire screen. You don't hear the crack of the bat as well, but you can follow the ball much better," said the National League's assistant secretary, Fred Flieg—but the novelty dissipated when at least two incidents of the supposedly unbreakable glass occurred the following year in different baseball stadiums."[60]

There was no shortage of great moments in the history of Crosley Field besides the climactic 1940 World Series win: the first of Johnny Vander Meer's two consecutive no-hitters, the 1944 debut of 15-year-old pitcher Joe Nuxhall, two All-Star Games (1938 and 1953), the Reds' great run to the 1961 NL pennant, and a parade of talent across the decades by the men in uniform. "First there were Buck Herzog, Heinie Groh, and Joe Tinker. Then came Edd Roush. Next Eppa Rixey. In the middle pennant years, Ernie Lombardi, Ival Goodman, Bucky Walters, Paul Derringer, Frank McCormick, Bill Werber, and others. Then Ewell Blackwell, Ted Kluszewski, Gus Bell, Frank Robinson. And on to today's heroes."[61]

At the time this tribute was penned to commemorate the curtain call of Crosley Field in the summer of 1970, the contemporaneous luminaries included Johnny Bench, Tony Pérez, and Pete Rose. This trio of frontline Reds along with their teammates did well in the finale at Crosley Field on the evening of June 24, scoring two runs in the bottom of the eighth inning to edge the San Francisco Giants 5–4 before a crowd of 28,027.

The *Cincinnati Post* and *Cincinnati Enquirer* filled their sports pages the next day with coverage of the contest and a wide range of lookbacks and minutiae to delight any trivia buffs among the readership: "Pete Rose ran the last red light at Crosley Field, ignoring third base coach Alex Grammas' stop sign to score the Reds' third run in the fifth on Bobby Tolan's single. 'That wasn't a stop light, that [was] a caution light,' Pete said later."[62]

But the farewell to Crosley was heartfelt and civil, as "[m]ost fans came earlier than usual. They wanted to spend a lot of time in the old ball park," and when Bobby Bonds was retired on a "tap to the mound" grounder—Wayne Granger to Lee May—for the final out, "[s]ixty-five well-drilled policemen and ushers dashed onto the field ... taking positions along the foul lines to keep the fans off the grass." The crowd listened to organist Ronnie Dale play "Auld Lang Syne," "God Bless America," and "Good Night, Sweetheart."[63]

Some fans unabashedly wept when it was over—NL president Warren Giles did so before and after the game—and many lingered even when the large light towers were turned off while the concourses remained illuminated. There was little vandalism or carrying-on, but despite the security personnel on hand, two fans employed a clever means to succeed in collecting one last—and free—souvenir: "The police wouldn't let anyone walk on the field, so James Dever, Dayton, O., leaned over the fence. He scooped up some dirt in a paper cup and took it home. Dave Pfennig ... did the same."[64]

Graydon DeCamp, a reporter for the *Post*, waxed nostalgic a few days later. Admitting that he "paid less attention than usual to the game itself on that sweet, sad, last night at Crosley Field," he instead

> noticed little things which had never fully registered. The little metal number plaques on the lower grandstand railings that identify the boxes. The wishbone "C" [logo] cast in the metal frames of each seat. The disembodied hand from inside the scoreboard that puts the line-score numerals in place. The fact that the foul lines were really two-by-fours set flush in the turf. The smell of beer and brats. And tobacco juice.[65]

Relishing the unique aspect of the outfield terrace, he closed with the hope that his young son would someday be able see the final game played at the new Riverfront Stadium, whenever in the future that might take place.

Now abandoned by baseball, Crosley Field was used for the final two years of its existence as a lot for motor vehicles impounded by the city of Cincinnati before it was razed. Encroaching just to the east of the property was Interstate 75, and the automobiles that traversed it were emblematic of what contributed to the demise of the old ballpark. Situated near the city's Union Terminal railroad station and "among office buildings, shops, and houses on the West Side before most Americans owned cars, parking was an afterthought."[66]

And as the post–World War II lifestyle of citizens across much of the country found increasing numbers of them dependent on the automobile, the quaint ballparks that once satisfied the sporting public were now obsolete. The torch was being passed, for better or worse, to the next generation of stadiums that were sleek, and, like plastic and polyester, modern.

The three fields discussed in this chapter, with attention paid to their farewells, were emblematic of the transition from the humble ballpark to the contemporary stadium. Municipal Stadium in Kansas City was the next in line to fall, its service life ending in late 1972 as Royals Stadium was not just on the drawing board but actively under construction; it opened in April 1973 and remains the baseball half of the Truman Sports Complex.

But regarding the trio of past ballfields of special interest here, today only two of their architectural brethren survive: Boston's Fenway Park and Wrigley Field in Chicago continue to delight fans old and new, aged and young, and thanks to an assortment of adaptations and modernizations, these seem poised to endure for another generation. They have each rightfully earned their places in the hearts of admirers but also, perhaps as importantly, in the hearts of historians and preservationists.

As Connie Mack Stadium, Forbes Field, and Crosley Field met their inevitable appointments with the demolition crews, the sense of loss at the time was likely minimal: "Out with the old and in with the new" became the guiding principle that drove many post–World War II redevelopment projects across the country, not least being New York City's regretful decision to cast aside Pennsylvania Station in order to create its replacement and companion property, the conjoined fourth version of Madison Square Garden. Old ballparks—Fenway and Wrigley being the prime exceptions—constructed as they had been to meet the exigencies of the early 1900s, also became obsolete, and their stand-ins would run their courses as well: Only with the 1992 opening of Baltimore's Oriole Park at Camden Yards would there be a movement away from what is now historically mocked as the cookie-cutter stadiums.

In 2019, the architecture critic Paul Goldberger observed that "elegant

Forbes Field [was] one of many ballparks from the early years of the twentieth century ... [that] would in all likelihood be cherished icons had they managed to survive into the twenty-first century."[67] Unfortunately, the unavoidable costs of maintenance and the challenges of a baseball team to change the neighborhood in which it resided would have been daunting if not impossible to overcome. But nostalgia impresses as the great equalizer that allows us to dream of what might have been.

As the clock was running out at Crosley Field, Pat Harmon, the sports editor of the *Cincinnati Post & Times Star*, wrote a thoughtful look-back for the Reds 1970 yearbook as the team was about to relocate to Riverfront Stadium. His review encapsulated, in chronological order, what he felt were the events that most prominently marked the tenure of an old ballpark about to be consigned to the ash heap of history.

Harmon's closing comment spoke volumes of the sentiments that would always be with him and, certainly, many Reds fans for whom Crosley Field would never die, at least in spirit. "Those were the days, my friend," he signed off wistfully, yet that very feeling could apply to those who bade farewell to Forbes Field, Connie Mack Stadium, or any other baseball setting that conveyed the sense of belonging to—and reminding us of—a better time.[68]

9

Trends and Current Events

In its final issue of 1969, *Life* magazine placed the close of the 1960s in poignant perspective. "It is tempting for historians—and perhaps even more so for journalists—to paste a specific label on a decade.... And yet the significant movements of a decade rarely begin with the opening year and then stop neatly on calendar cue ten years later; men and events are not so tidy with time."[1] It would come as a great disappointment to those wishing to sweep away the untidiness of most recent times, especially so 1968, that the year 1970 would bring an enduring form of welcome relief.

Although chronologies had advanced to January 1970, the drag of items in the news weighed heavily on the American public. While the death toll of U.S. servicemen in the Vietnam War had dropped in 1969 from its peak the previous year, the program of turning over most of the fighting to South Vietnamese forces was barely 12 months into its implementation; protests against the war remained active despite the drawdown of American troops; and the bugbear of inflation was hindering the pocketbooks of households across the country. The effects of this last issue were forcing many families—not accustomed to such endeavors—to seek methods of self-sufficiency, for example, by learning to grow vegetable gardens or doing home repairs themselves, shopping in more thrifty manners—not least at flea markets—and generally avoiding unnecessary expenditures.

The NASA space program advanced in the wake of the inaugural landing of men on the moon, and race relations, which never ran far below the surface of American life, persisted in their stubbornness to reach a better degree of harmony between Blacks and Whites. Culturally, the landscape of the nation was continuing to evolve as cinema and television programming introduced increasing amounts of violence and sex, in the case of the former, as well as societal breakthrough elements, in the case of the latter. And the modernity of life, as manifest in fashion and product choices, carried through the early 1970s as an extension of the decade just concluded. "Plastics," the advisory word uttered by Mr. McGuire to

Benjamin Braddock, played by Dustin Hoffman in the classic 1967 film *The Graduate*, were an increasingly pervasive aspect of the nation's everyday life.

The world of baseball was swept along as these contemporaneous currents wended their way through American society. In the unfolding years ahead, nostalgia would soften the less attractive facets of the early 1970s or otherwise disregard their unpleasantness, and here follows a look at the times in which the national pastime was immersed as it moved forward in the earliest years of its second century as a professional enterprise.

As the Nixon Administration reduced the number of American combat troops in Vietnam from a peak of 543,000 to 340,000 by April 1970, "news from Saigon was mildly encouraging," but "[w]ar weariness was becoming increasingly evident in the United States, among the South Vietnamese, and in fighting units."[2] A constant thorn in the side of the American military was the use of Cambodia, a neutral country, by North Vietnamese forces as a sanctuary from enemy troops. In the aftermath of a mid–March coup that installed General Lon Nol as the head of Cambodia, the United States decided to invade South Vietnam's western neighbor in order to eliminate staging areas that had long been vital to Communist supply chains.

On April 30, President Richard Nixon addressed the nation to announce that military action had expanded into another country, and the fallout among antiwar protestors was predictable. Student strikes on college campuses, which were already smarting from earlier demonstrations, quickly took place as the spring semester was drawing to a close. "[T]he reaction eclipsed all previous protests. By the end of May 415 colleges and universities had been disrupted ... [by] the first general student strike in the country's history, and it was entirely spontaneous."[3]

The campus that became a touchstone for the antiwar movement was located at the state university in Kent, Ohio. The day after Nixon's revelation, "a rally had been openly announced for Monday noon, and invitations to attend it had been circulated on succeeding days; in fact, announcements for this rally had been scrawled on certain blackboards and were seen by students when they reported for classes on Monday."[4] When the ROTC building at Kent State University was put to the torch on May 2, Ohio Governor Jim Rhodes ordered the National Guard to the campus the next day and banned all gatherings.

Late on the morning of Monday May 4, the National Guard tried to head off the rally with announcements on the school's radio station and campus intercom system—the latter option had a very limited range of coverage—and it appeared "everyone knew ... except the students" that the assembly was now "forbidden."[5] As the number of attendees grew, by noon an order was given to break up the crowd, the Guard marching to strategic positions near Taylor Hall and using tear gas to disperse taunting students. With few implements at their disposal, protestors had "a few—not many—small stones and pebbles available" to hurl at the soldiers, and a later investigation "concluded that students would have required good right arms like Mickey Mantle's to have reached the Guardsmen."[6]

Subsequent forays by the youths had emboldened them to move closer to the Guard, some of whom were feeling hemmed in at various spots. But in spite of at least one open escape route being at their disposal, a phalanx of soldiers took positions near the south corner of Taylor and faced the throng. At 12:24, a 13-second period of gunfire erupted during which time "fifty-five M-1 bullets seem to have been discharged, plus five pistol shots and the single blast from a shotgun."[7] A large number of rounds did not make their mark, as many soldiers reluctant to fire on the crowd aimed above it to harmless effect, but those that did struck 11 young men and two women. The death toll came to three students who died at the scene and a fourth who perished after being taken to a nearby hospital.

At this point, the anger of May 1 fomented by the incursion into Cambodia unequivocally exploded across the campuses of America. Not only were U.S. servicemen dying in

In the aftermath of the deaths at Kent State and Jackson State as well as a riot in Augusta, Georgia, a student strike was declared for May 5, 1970, in Boston (Library of Congress).

Southeast Asia, but now an extension of the military, in the form of the Ohio National Guard, had killed American civilians on domestic soil. Student demonstrators, 100,000 strong, descended on the nation's capital the following weekend as the White House lay siege to the event.

The Tet Offensive of two years prior had shaken the confidence of an American public who had been given the impression by the military command that a light could be seen at the end of the Vietnam tunnel, only to be disabused of this notion. "The greatest damage wrought by the Cambodian adventure was its impact on the home front," especially now as signified by the bodies of the deceased college students.[8] The death toll increased shortly after the Kent State incident when two Black students died at Jackson State College in Mississippi after being shot by police during a racial disturbance along a public thoroughfare that passed through the school's property. While this affair was not related to the war—nor was another huge race riot in Augusta, Georgia—it nevertheless added to the prevailing angst that affected campuses nationwide.

One Major League player was greatly disturbed by the tragedy at Kent State, yet he found common ground with his empathetic manager. Reliever Tug McGraw, who helped the New York Mets to their first World Series championship just seven months before the shooting in Ohio, had a military connection through his service in the Marine Corps Reserve in the mid-1960s. Although the number of baseball players who served in Vietnam was a very small percentage of the troop total, many ballplayers were still called to duty at this time.[9] Through enlistments in the National Guard or various reserve units of the armed forces, the vast majority of players fulfilled their obligations, even when doing so entailed shuttling between their team and their military unit while the season was in progress.

The product of a broken home—McGraw's mother suffered from a bipolar disorder and his parents divorced when Tug was still a youngster—the pitcher nonetheless relished wearing his exuberant heart on his sleeve, but at times this demeanor cloaked his angst and inner emotions. In the aftermath of Kent State, a traumatized McGraw found himself retreating to a corner of the clubhouse to weep in private even when a successful outing on the mound would otherwise have been an occasion to be happy. Later he explained the distress that haunted him: "I never could believe that the country had reached the point where National Guard guys would have to shoot other people."[10]

McGraw's stoic manager, himself a combat veteran of Okinawa during World War II, became a shoulder for the pitcher to lean on. Gil Hodges was guided by a conservative mindset that did not necessarily jibe with the youthful attitudes of the day, but "he was surprisingly open-minded with McGraw" and understood what troubled him.[11] Hodges counseled McGraw by describing his own war-time circumstances: "I was in the service, too. I was younger and it was a different situation, a hell of a lot more clear-cut," the manager said in alluding to the differences between America's fight against fascism in the Second World War versus an undeclared conflict against communism in Southeast Asia. (Some antiwar activists further observed, with good reason, that Vietnam was engaged in a civil war to be decided only by its participants.) "Life can be bitter, the way it is today," Hodges continued, "Adversity comes and goes, bitterness comes and goes. But the thing that stays is your commitment to what's right…. If you let the worst in us ruin the best in us, you'll never find the answer." Taking Hodges's advice to heart, McGraw said, "There was never a time when he meant more to me."

However, the salve Hodges provided to one troubled player did not calm all the waters that had been roiled since the late 1960s by antiwar protests, the counterculture movement, and a willingness by young Americans to voice an opinion against authority of any sort. Just weeks before Kent State, the manager brought the issue of setting a post-game curfew time before a team meeting, giving the players the freedom to decide when that time would be. But when Hodges bristled at an unreasonable suggestion of three and a half hours, McGraw's teammate, outfielder Ron Swoboda, was quick to challenge Hodges. "Well, why don't you just tell us what time you want curfew to be and we'll get this bullshit meeting over with?"[12] This sass-laden comment would seem to be unthinkable, especially in the clubhouse of a defending champion and addressed to a manager who not too long previously had left the dugout in mid-inning to retrieve another outfielder, Cleon Jones, who he believed failed to give his best effort.

This was not to say that ballplayers were always fawning and obedient; their actions and reactions to authority were simply a reflection of the human condition and attitudes of the era. As Jim Bouton proved in his groundbreaking diary *Ball Four*—and much to the chagrin of the baseball establishment—a degree of innocence was lost and became a disappointment to those "who idealized ballplayers as role models for youth and who looked to baseball as one of the last strongholds of such traditional values as sexual morality and sobriety."[13]

Another manager deeply rooted in a conservative perspective was Walter Alston of the Los Angeles Dodgers, whose four World Series titles with the franchise spoke to his level of success. But a 21-year-old rookie named Bobby Valentine joined the team in 1971 and "was critical of Alston. Perhaps projecting his own outlook as a young man who came of age in the era of the late 1960s and early 1970s, Valentine described Alston as a man who 'tries to avoid confrontations, not because it is a way of smoothing things out, but because he doesn't know what to do in a crisis.'"[14]

When the outspoken youngster was traded after the 1972 season, "he believed Alston did not like him, or care for challenging questions or the general brashness that Valentine put forth."[15] Other prospects coursing through the Los Angeles farm system at that time apparently toed the line and gained favor in management's sight: Steve Garvey, Bill Russell, Bill Buckner, and Ron Cey would soon be wearing Dodger Blue and log substantial playing time to help re-establish the club as a perennial National League contender.

One of Valentine's teammates in 1971 was Dick Allen, whose relationship with Walter Alston was marked by a coexistence if not necessarily cordiality. The men shared a love of horses, and Alston never worried about the effort Allen gave on the field, even if the manager "stopped short of rolling out the red carpet for him."[16] When Allen became a member of the Chicago White Sox after his lone year in Los Angeles, future Hall-of-Famer Rich Gossage was generous in his praise for the slugger. "All the money in the world could not pay for the experience of having Dick talk to me about pitching," Gossage wrote years later. "He passed the torch to me and taught me everything. He drilled it into me."[17]

This mentoring of a white rookie pitcher barely old enough to legally drink by a Black veteran All-Star was one example of a shifting racial dynamic in baseball in the early years of the 1970s. Baseball's first Black umpire, Emmett Ashford, retired after the 1970 season, but this did not prevent the arbiter from continuing to serve the game. The flamboyant native of Los Angeles was hired by Bowie Kuhn's office as a public relations advisor based on the West Coast, and the popular Ashford—he had "severed all connections with the Hamm Brewing Company" as a concession to taking the new job—staged clinics and occasionally umpired minor league and college games as he was able.[18]

Kuhn also developed a very positive relationship with another Black baseball pioneer, Monte Irvin. After a stellar playing career that earned him induction to the Hall of Fame, Irvin found his way to public relations work for a brewery, Brooklyn-based Rheingold. In the wake of the assassination of Martin Luther King, Jr., in April 1968, Irvin segued to a public relations position under baseball commissioner William Eckert, becoming the first African American to work in that office. When Kuhn was named as Eckert's replacement in February 1969, he retained Irvin and was delighted to have him on his staff. "Monte was superior on special assignments, especially as pinch hitter for the commissioner," Kuhn

Monte Irvin (left) was an assistant to commissioner William Eckert and transitioned easily when Bowie Kuhn assumed the office in early 1969. Kuhn had high praise for the work of his valuable aide.

enthused in his memoir. "He flawlessly handled speaking engagements and other appearances I could not make," and importantly he "smoothed out public relations problems...."[19]

These advances for Blacks were steps in the right direction, yet in the early 1970s the idea of a manager, general manager, or front office executive was still years away. In a summer 1971 issue of *Black Sports*, the magazine featured a "rap session" in which it discussed "issues of Black ownership and management" with several prominent figures from the world of sports.[20] One of the panelists was New York Yankee president Michael Burke, who was asked this question: "What about Black people getting involved on a stock basis in a major franchise? Maybe that would precipitate Black management—Black control of a team." Burke replied, "I'm sure there's Black ownership of the New York Yankees. There's Black ownership because CBS has over 60,000 stockholders and among those stockholders are Black people. That's too indirect for this discussion, but I think that Black ownership of sports is devoutly to be wished."

Burke was oblique in admitting that owners of color could be found in his team's ownership, however minuscule this number may have been.

Yet, the remainder of his response tried to anticipate minority ownership of a sports franchise at some point in the future.

> I once had a conversation with Jackie Robinson, two or three years ago. It was not about any specific ownership but just on the general theory of how Blacks can be more involved with sports other than performance on the field. I simply wanted to get Jackie's views about this. I asked him about total Black ownership of a professional franchise—100 percent Black ownership of Cincinnati or any ball club. He was not in favor of that. He did not think there should be 100 percent Black ownership of a ball team; we were talking about baseball, of course. He thought that there should be some Black ownership—50-50, 60-40, 70-30 or something. There should be ideally Black and white ownership, with the Black representing, not one percent, but 25 percent or 40 percent, or something like that. I think this would be ideal: Black capitalists. Black businessmen as part owner, at least, of franchises.[21]

Frank Robinson was soon to serve a managerial apprenticeship in the Puerto Rican winter league, his first step in the long, slow process of clearing another of baseball's racial hurdles to become the Major Leagues' first Black skipper. But more than 50 years have passed since Michael Burke voiced his opinion on minority ownership, and the national pastime continues to struggle with the issue of decreasing participation by Blacks on the field and a proportionate lack of front office personnel.

Discrimination, whether overt or subtle, has lingered in various aspects of baseball. One academic study, referring to the Hall of Fame's Veterans Committee, found "no evidence of a voting bias against blacks" but concluded that "the black players nominated for the Hall of Fame have performance statistics that are much better than those for white players. This is consistent with the hypothesis that there is discrimination in the nominating process."[22] Another paper even linked this bias, dating to 1970, with its effect on the price of certain baseball cards, whereby "collectors treat black pitchers differently from white pitchers."[23]

Although gains, in a broad sense, have been made by Blacks, not all prejudices have disappeared from the national pastime or society in general—far from it. The barrier broken by Jackie Robinson in 1947 was a crucial springboard in fueling the post-war civil rights movement, and participation in baseball by Black players was still on the rise in 1970–1971, as about 15 percent of all players were African-American. (From 1973 to 1988, the level held at roughly 18 percent but began a decline into the new millennium. By 2024, this dropped to about six percent.)[24]

As Black athletes have drifted in growing numbers toward football and basketball, there has been an unmistakable impact on the demographic composition of baseball rosters in a trend that has not been reversed.

◆ ◆ ◆

9. Trends and Current Events

Baseball's rich history has had an abundance of larger-than-life characters of all persuasions, and the early 1970s proved no exception when Dock Ellis was establishing himself as a frontline starter for the Pittsburgh Pirates. The Black righthander from Los Angeles "both angered and amused ... his antics cut across racial and cultural lines, as he challenged old prejudices and 'normal' ways of doing things."[25] Feeling the sting of racism at an early age, Ellis took up the vices of alcohol and marijuana in high school, but his athletic ability shone through in dramatic fashion as his lively arm could not be ignored. A scout for the Pirates, Chet Brewer, also coached Ellis and enabled him to sign with Pittsburgh in 1964, one year before the creation of the amateur draft.

His minor league apprenticeship of four seasons was accompanied by alcohol and drug use, pep pills becoming part of his chemical diet. In March of 1968, Ellis felt slighted at not receiving a signing bonus and held out in spring training, quite a move by a player who had yet to appear in a Major League contest. Sent to Triple-A, he earned a call-up in mid–June and was used in starting and relief roles, but in subsequent seasons he was almost exclusively a starting pitcher. On June 10, 1970, Ellis threw a no-hitter against the Padres in San Diego while under the influence of LSD; he ingested the psychedelic drug but "lost track of the days" and thought that his system would be clean in time for his next pitching assignment.[26]

Also about this time, Ellis decided he was going to hold reporters at bay by refusing to speak to them. There was a small select group of players who were so inclined, the better to keep from being "misquoted and misunderstood." Columnist Jerome Holtzman informed readers of *The Sporting News* that Willie Horton of the Detroit Tigers was the latest ballplayer to take a vow of silence. "So far as I know, this makes Horton the third player who isn't talking to the writers. The two others are Dock Ellis of the Pirates and Alex Johnson of the Angels," wrote one of the deans of baseball scribes, who took a parting swipe by commenting, "Maybe every club should have a designated non-talker, along with designated pinch-batters and pinch-runners."[27]

Ellis's no-hit gem was one of his 13 victories in 1970, and the following season would turn out to be the best—statistically—of his eventual 12-year career. Posting a 19–9 record with a 3.06 ERA, Ellis earned his only All-Star berth while completing 11 of his 31 starts in 1971. In August, the Pirates' team physician disclosed that Ellis was afflicted with sickle cell trait, a non-fatal form of sickle cell anemia. Relieved that he was spared from a worse fate—"If I did [have sickle cell anemia], I'd probably be dead," he was quoted by the Associated Press—Ellis was in a charitable mood and joined over 30 other African-American athletes in donating $1000 to the Black Athlete Foundation for Sickle Cell Research.[28]

Weeks later when the Pirates won the National League East pennant and squared off against the San Francisco Giants for the right to play in the World Series, Ellis vented against his team's management when the Pirates' charter flight to the West Coast stopped in Omaha, Nebraska, for fuel. "It would have cost them $6000 to get a bigger plane," he groused, and upon arrival at the team hotel in the City by the Bay, he found the beds in his room to be too small, so he, his wife, and their infant found better lodging and "got the red carpet treatment" for an extra $50 per night that he footed himself.[29] While none of his teammates publicly thanked him for his outburst—several privately offered him kudos for taking management to task—he still defended the club as being one of the best on the field.

Talented, enigmatic, and battling addiction, Dock Ellis was a mainstay of the Pittsburgh Pirates pitching staff, especially during the team's championship season of 1971. He also served up Reggie Jackson's mammoth home run in that year's All-Star Game.

Just as the National League was more open to embracing racial diversity of players following the appearance of Jackie Robinson with the Brooklyn Dodgers, the Pirates in particular remained in the forefront of turning a blind eye to the skin color of their players. In 1967, among the more than two dozen players who logged the most time on Pittsburgh's active roster were a mix of whites (13), Blacks (5), and Latinos (8), the highest minority representation at the time.[30] After winning the World Series in 1960, the team performed inconsistently under manager Danny Murtaugh through 1964, and when Harry "the Hat" Walker took the helm in 1965 there was a rebound in the club's fortunes: a pair of third-place finishes, in Walker's first season thanks to a 90–72 record, and in 1966 on the strength of a 92–70 mark that had the Pirates just three games out of first place in the final NL standings.

However, one historian noted that Walker was born in Mississippi and raised in Alabama, and this exposure to the Deep South's culture and mores infused his personality with the prejudices inherent in many whites of the region. John N. Ingham cited three factors that put Walker at odds with a harmonious clubhouse that was populated by many players of color: his earlier stand against Robinson's joining the Dodgers; Harry's association with his brother, Dixie, who as a member of the Dodgers attempted to lead a revolt against having Robinson on the Brooklyn roster; and the bond that the Walker brothers had with Ben Chapman, the former manager of the Philadelphia Phillies, who made no secret of his disdain for the integration of baseball.[31]

In spite of this damning background, Harry Walker by the time of his arrival in Pittsburgh was credited by some, including columnist George Will, as having turned a page in his life's story. Walker had kindled a friendship with Bill White, the African American All-Star first baseman who, in his memoir, praised Walker for providing crucial batting tips in 1959 that "saved my major league career."[32] As the Bucs' manager, Walker had turned in a lineup card for one game in 1967 featuring minority players at all positions except pitcher. Yet, the stigma of his racism as perceived by many Black ballplayers persisted.

Walker was dismissed by the Pirates 84 games into the 1967 season, and in 1968, when he became a mid-season replacement as manager of the Houston Astros, second baseman Joe Morgan had been warned by Bill Mazeroski—the usually mild-mannered Pirate infielder "never had a bad word to say about anyone," according to Morgan—that Walker was "a bad guy."[33] In his later memoir, Morgan took Walker to task as "a fool because he undermined his team," often singling out outfielders Jimmy Wynn and Jesús Alou along with pitcher Don Wilson, all of them players of color, for unbecoming treatment. After a particularly galling loss, a perturbed Walker harshly griped in the clubhouse about his "damn starting pitchers on this ballclub [not having] any guts."[34] Wilson, whom Walker had removed in the eighth inning after walking the leadoff batter, was incensed at the comment and lunged at the manager.

Morgan was the first player among several to intervene before the confrontation grew worse, but incidents like this upheld Walker's poor reputation and contributed to Donn Clendenon's refusal to accept a trade to the Astros. For Morgan's part, his relationship with Walker curdled beyond repair when the second baseman was removed for a pinch-hitter in a 1971 game despite having singled against Tug McGraw of the Mets in his previous at-bat against the New York reliever. After the Astros lost, Morgan's passive-aggressive comment to Walker—"You know, you're not trying to win," Morgan said as he brushed by his manager—the second baseman "knew my days on any team Harry Walker was managing were numbered. I got the reputation of being a troublemaker," thereby giving management an excuse to part ways with him.[35]

As irksome as Walker may have been, Morgan was content in an Astro uniform because Houston was where he had put down roots, and he believed that in general the plusses there outweighed the minuses. But Morgan was traded to Cincinnati, a club just one year removed from playing in the World Series—he later claimed that he would have declined a rumored trade to the Phillies—and emerged as one of the best players in the game. "Because I was traded to a good team, I accepted the trade," he wrote, but he clearly fixed the blame on Harry Walker for his plight.[36]

Dock Ellis's outspokenness easily earned him the tag of malcontent—catcher Manny Sanguillen said the pitcher had "the biggest mouth" among the Pirates.[37] But when Danny Murtaugh was in his third stint as Pittsburgh's manager beginning in 1970, the pitcher had high praise for the skipper, calling the "Whistling Irishman" a "beautiful dude" because of his focus on winning as well as his fairness in treating players, "Black or white."[38] As Murtaugh assembled the lineup for his club's game on September 1, 1971, against Philadelphia, whether by accident or design, the nine players he penciled in were all of color.

With Ellis as that night's starting pitcher, the feat went one better than Harry Walker's eight-out-of-nine group, yet Pirate ace Steve Blass recalled that when "the baseball writers rushed in after the game and said, 'Danny, do you realize what happened?,'" Murtaugh demurred by defending his choice of players as being "the nine Pittsburgh Pirates that I [thought] had the best chance to win tonight."[39]

Perhaps Ellis reveled in the moment too much, lasting only 1.1 innings and charged with five runs, three of them earned, in a sloppy performance. But the incandescence of the lineup's breakthrough in the Bucs' eventual 10–7 victory became more than the answer to a future trivia question, and it may have diffused any question about the ability of minority players to coalesce on the field, Ellis's poor outing notwithstanding.

Yet, beyond his momentous use of LSD, the pitcher, whose later foibles included putting his hair in curlers as a pregame ritual, continued to be hounded by an unshakable drug addiction, and when the publication of *Ball Four* drew attention to the dispensation of pep pills in the trainer's room, the baseball commissioner's office was compelled to take measures in an attempt to curb the problem.

As the counterculture of the 1960s gained momentum, the historian James T. Patterson observed, "It reached a new efflorescence in January

1967, when some 20,000 people, most of them young, gathered at Golden Gate Park in San Francisco to celebrate their 'hippie' style of life. Timothy Leary was on hand to hail the wonders of LSD, a synthetic hallucinogenic, and other mind-enhancing drugs. He urged the crowd to 'turn on, tune in, drop out.'"[40]

By the summer of 1969, when the Woodstock Music and Art Fair in upstate New York drew a crowd of rock music fans estimated at close to a half-million, the feeling of great liberation may have reached a crescendo: Some in the gathering indulged their time in the country by stripping naked and "revel[ing] in their freedom," as "the vast majority smoked marijuana or used other drugs."[41] Trying to re-establish traditional values, the Nixon Administration was in an uphill battle against a youthful, antiauthoritarian movement that continued to be underpinned by protests against the Vietnam War.

Dock Ellis may not have embodied all of the sentiments coursing through the college-aged segment of the American population—"Don't trust anyone over 30," a popular catch-phrase coined in the mid–1960s by Jack Weinberg, was practically a directive for those younger than 30—but his issue with substance abuse and experience with LSD found common ground with many youth of the era.[42]

Upon his naming as baseball commissioner, Bowie Kuhn was predictably shocked to learn of the prevalent usage of "greenies" by players to give them a boost of energy, whether to surmount the problems of a hangover or simply to beat fatigue and be more alert for the coming game. As drug usage pervaded society, the world of sports was not immune, and in April 1971 the commissioner's office launched a drug education and prevention program to face the issue head-on. The plan, targeted to both Major and minor league organizations, was initiated with four objectives:

- To keep Baseball free from any drug problem
- To protect the health and safety of players
- To preserve the honesty, integrity and good name of Baseball
- To involve Baseball more fully in community action programs to combat the growing menace of drug abuse in our country, particularly as it applies to our youth[43]

The implementation took the form of seminars attended by team player representatives, coaches, managers, and administrative personnel. Other resulting action came in the form of a "Baseball vs. Drugs" booklet that was produced and given to public and school libraries; "[g]uidelines for trainers in dispensing *legal drugs* were adopted"; team physicians commenced a series of annual meetings to discuss substance issues; and a consultant for drug problems was appointed.[44] A glaring omission at the time was an attempt to confront alcohol abuse, which cut a far wider path for a longer period of time, but this was finally added seven years after the commencement of the program.

Material sourced from the U.S. Department of Health, Education, and Welfare as well the Department of Justice's Bureau of Narcotics and Dangerous Drugs was also furnished to all clubs. The initiative was paying close attention to an obvious demographic factor: "The Minor League phase of this program is of great significance because the incidence of drug abuse is greatest among an age group common to our Minor League players. Scouts should be thoroughly briefed to recognize indications of drug addiction or abuse in interviewing and evaluating prospects." "For your information," the program's documentation reminded, "the unprescribed possession or distribution of amphetamines and barbiturates (including 'greenies') is a violation of federal and state law."[45]

Umpires were also obliged to follow the protocol, and players, because of their status as role models with high public profiles, were encouraged to participate in community outreach programs and spread the anti-drug message. The commissioner's Security Division was charged with overseeing all aspects of the program, including following up with individual teams in order to address any problems.

On paper, this was a positive step of which Kuhn could be proud: "I felt that our drug program and the vigilance of our security personnel had alleviated the drug problem in baseball during the 1970s. By contrast with other sports, we looked pretty good, perhaps better than we deserved."[46] Unfortunately, this was the case of a favorable first impression that ultimately failed to gain a lasting foothold. Reaching the end of the 1970s and lacking a drug testing program as a means of enforcement, baseball by the early 1980s would drift into a cocaine scandal that shook the sports world. As player salaries escalated in the era of free agency, this economic phenomenon generated larger amounts of disposable income for players, and when conflated with cocaine gaining the cultural spotlight as a status symbol or "drug of choice," the temptation of this vice became too much to deny.

At the conclusion of his 12-year Major League career in 1979, Dock Ellis came full circle in his plight with substance abuse. Completing a rehabilitation stint at The Meadows, an Arizona treatment facility, he became a counselor in Los Angeles to assist others in their quest to kick drug addictions. Ellis adopted a stance that it was never too early to warn anyone about the perils of what he personally experienced, telling *USA Today*, "When I say young, I mean starting with kindergarten. That's the time when little bitty kids with little bitty eyes start watching and following adults."[47]

In the coming decades, more players, including those in other sports, would fall victim to the ills of substance abuse. This was part of the human condition that affected not only them but society at large, men and women, young and old, regardless of race. Through no fault of its own, the preventive effort of the national pastime fell short of solving a problem that would always be broader than its scope could handle.

An era punctuated by anger over the Vietnam War and the rising current of the counterculture was fertile ground for another movement. The idea to create an Equal Rights Amendment (ERA) for women dated to 1923 but gained little traction, and the stereotypical social attitude that females were to be consigned to a fate of home life and motherhood prevailed. "Women who rejected this kind of femininity were 'sick, unhappy, neurotic, wholly or partly incapable of dealing with life'" was a description that captured the mood reinforcing this bias.[48]

Equality issues abated somewhat because of labor demands during World War II, which saw women employed in many traditional male roles, especially in manufacturing. But the post-war trend quickly reverted to men resuming their places in the work force as soldiers returned to civilian life. Yet, women expecting equal rights beyond the ballot box were split into camps for and against an Equal Rights Amendment: those who believed that such legislation would codify what women were entitled to, and their counterparts who were against the bill based on a belief that women's equality was already in place and need no further safeguards or sanctions.

The journey of ERA's previous version through Congress came to naught in the early 1950s, and even the Presidential Commission on the Status of Women, established by John F. Kennedy in 1961, issued a report two years later that "advocated special training of young women to prepare them for marriage and proclaimed that motherhood was the major role of the American woman."[49] At nearly the same time of the release of the commission's findings, the publication of Betty Friedan's *The Feminine Mystique* revealed her own frustration with life as a woman (and wife) having to follow the day's prescribed, gender-skewed mores. That the book promoted the concept that women were entitled to an existence beyond home and hearth came at a time when the civil rights movement was gaining strength and soon to claim the 1964 Civil Rights Act and Voting Rights Act of 1965 as victories for minorities. The law of 1964 included Title VII, which outlawed employment discrimination based on sex.

Feminist activism moved more slowly, but in 1966 the National Organization for Women (NOW) was founded, with none other than Betty

Friedan named as its president. Coincidence or not, and as if to emphasize what was termed a "Rights Movement," that same year, the Major League Baseball Players Association began to coalesce in earnest under Marvin Miller. By the end of the decade, many formerly all-male colleges and universities were opening their doors to female students, and a renaissance of ERA came to the forefront.

Feminism reached another milestone in late August 1970 when a rally sponsored by NOW was held in New York City in commemoration of the 50th anniversary of the Nineteenth Amendment to the U.S. Constitution, which granted women the right to vote. Having already secured the franchise, women demanded access to free abortion and childcare in addition to equal employment and educational opportunities, and they further sought to dissolve legal bonds tethering them to their husbands. In many states at the time, there were restrictions on a woman's ability to own property, hold a credit card, or make a last will and testament without spousal consent.

As the women's breaking down of barriers continued through the new decade, baseball seemed to be stuck in a time warp of sorts both at the ballpark and away from it. During the 1970 World Series, the national pastime's preeminent team, the Baltimore Orioles, took a lighthearted approach in featuring a female member of the staff at Memorial Stadium. Four children of Jeannette and Ralph Warehime, Sr., served on the facility's ground crew—three boys between the ages of 16 and 19, but of particular interest was 14-year-old Linda, a pretty blonde tasked with using a team-color, black-and-orange broom to sweep off the bases during a break at the top of the fifth inning.

Whether with or without her parents' consent, the game program from that year's Fall Classic turned this "sweepy-time girl" into a sexualized—and certainly underaged—attraction that might well conflict with twenty-first century sensibilities.[50] Perhaps innocently enough, "[w]hen she sweeps the bases she also cleans the shoes of her Oriole basemen. She doesn't neglect the shortstop either," but near the end of her chores is when the "hot corner" may take on a different meaning: "At third base she is famous for her encounters with the rival coach." Linda decided to dust off the shoes of the visiting third-base coach and "now gives the opposing coach a kiss along with the shoe shine during his team's last game in Baltimore. She says unhesitatingly that the favorite part of her job is the 'third base coach.'" Tony Cuccinello of the White Sox accepted Linda's offer to sweep off her sneakers, after which "she kissed him on the cheek."

Joe Schultz, the manager of the Seattle Pilots who gained a large degree of notoriety in the narrative of Jim Bouton's recently published *Ball*

The wave of activism in the early 1970s included women's struggle for equality. This movement included an initiative for an Equal Rights Amendment to the U.S. Constitution (Library of Congress).

Four, presented her with a gift of flowers—and was bussed for his kind gesture. Mrs. Warehime even provided a behind-the-scenes look at Linda's routine at home, where doing the dishes and cleaning her room were part of her duties, but when "[s]he gets up in the morning and puts on her bikini ... [t]hen all the boys in the neighborhood who are going to drivers education classes drop by to talk to her brothers. But they stay longer if Linda is near."

In their yearbook for the following season, the Orioles further solidified the belief of where they believed women belonged. In a two-page spread titled, "Time out to eat.... You can't beat the Orioles.... Even in the kitchen," the wives of manager Earl Weaver, two coaches, the team equipment manager, and six players shared their favorite recipes. Each entry was introduced with a clever heading that related to the husband, such as the one for reserve infielder Chico Salmon—"This native dish of the Republic of Panama has great utility in any league's kitchen"—or Pete Richert's wife, Adele—"Here's the perfect pitch to better your e.r.a.—your excellent recipe average, that is...."[51]

During an interview for a magazine named *Jock*, Michael Burke was asked about the possibility of a female baseball player donning a Major League uniform. The Yankee president expressed his doubts, saying, "I think in sports, even such as baseball where the body contact is limited, but nevertheless there is some, you couldn't have women players. You know, going into second base and breaking up a double play and things like that."[52]

A safer haven for women was on offer from the Cleveland Indians, who sponsored a ladies' booster club known as the Basebelles. For a two-dollar annual fee—half that for Junior Basebelles—members could partake in a bus trip to a road game, and attend "a behind-the-fence dinner and luncheons including informal meetings with Indian players."[53] Also behind the fence, in a manner of speaking, in 1970 Nancy Faust, "leading candidate for rookie organist of the year," took her place "at the keyboard of the stadium Hammond, located in a canvas shed beneath the exploding scoreboard" at Comiskey Park in Chicago.[54] The 23-year-old musician had been playing the organ for most of her life, and she took her job with the White Sox with the utmost diligence, "consider[ing] the sports pages required reading as she works out a repertoire that includes a song for every baseball situation and a musical salute to every A.L. player."

Never far from the mind of marketing strategists, sex appeal was on display in 1970 when the Philadelphia Phillies released publicity photos of the club's new uniforms for players and stadium personnel. Although male ushers were to be clad in a mock-turtleneck with short sleeves and warm-up pants, their female counterparts, known as "Fillies," would be attired in high-collar, sleeveless tops that were paired with a miniskirt.

Where *Ball Four* had delivered a narrative that in several passages was scintillating, a milder version of that book's subtheme was published in *Sport Scene* that described Tony Conigliaro's lifestyle, with a firm nod to the outfielder's love life. The public figure who gave Tony C's story a head-turning aspect was the leading sex symbol of the 1960s, who in the new decade had hardly lost any of her appeal. When Conigliaro was traded from Boston to California weeks after the end of the 1970 season, he took up residence in a posh, two-story apartment near the ocean in Newport Beach. "I rented half a duplex on a cliff top overlooking the bay. I liked the layout," he explained. "After I paid the first month [rent] in advance, the landlady said to me, 'I guess I should tell you who the girl next door is. It's Raquel Welch.'"[55]

Sportswriter Bill Libby authored the piece by making good use of the macho-infused quality becoming of a handsome ballplayer juxtaposed with the beautiful women who were the quarry of said player. Mamie Van Doren, one of former Angel pitcher Bo Belinsky's old flames, makes an appearance by virtue of her "also dat[ing] Conig after meeting him on the Merv Griffin TV show," this tidbit coming after readers were introduced to Tony C on the article's opening page with this testosterone-laden boast: "I wore out 16 pairs of shoes my rookie year chasing broads. I don't have to anymore. They chase me."[56]

At the age of 26 and with a well-built physique of 200 pounds spread on a six-foot-three frame, Conigliaro admitted, "I don't think you can mix baseball and marriage." Yet he was also a man at odds with himself, stating, "I want to make the most of my baseball career first," while also declaring, "I want to get married. I'm dying to have children."[57] Libby's is a gender-affirming essay: a dapper bachelor still sowing his oats in the company of attractive women, and "relocated in glamorous surroundings [of Newport Beach], Conigliaro seems to have relaxed.... Now, contemplating babes in bikinis, he says, 'If I wasn't a ballplayer, I could spend my life very easily as a beach bum.'"[58]

Curiously, by the time the story was printed in the September issue of *Sport Scene*, its subject had long departed the playing field as well as his Southern California residence. Confessing that he was still plagued by headaches and eye problems—the fallout of his August 1967 beaning never completely cleared up, but he was also vexed by hamstring and rib-cage injuries—Conigliaro abruptly retired and retreated to the safety of his home and family near Boston after an extra-inning game on July 9 in which he went 0-for-8, fanning five times. This contest also saw him ejected after "a disputed strikeout" in the 19th inning, his manager, Lefty Phillips, saying after the game that Conigliaro was "ready for an insane asylum."[59]

In the early 1970s, women's roles remained delineated mostly by stereotype, whether they were housewives, workers in the labor force relegated to traditional occupations, or women on the receiving end of advances by men. A corner was turned on the evening of September 19, 1970, when a new television program, *The Mary Tyler Moore Show*, debuted on CBS, its lead character being a single woman who lands a job with a Minneapolis TV station. Although it was a situation comedy at bottom, the premise of the show was based on a youngish, 30-year-old lady who gains a new beginning after breaking up with a boyfriend and was "determined to make it on her own, ... [a] now-common concept [that] was rarely depicted on television in the early 1970s, despite some visible successes of the women's movement."[60]

The program's popularity was boosted by Mary Tyler Moore's earlier success on *The Dick Van Dyke Show*, but in her new series she was cast in the role of an independent woman. This became a small step—and important victory—toward the continued striving by women for equal rights as well as a means for them to move past the cultural norms—as represented above by domestication and sexual objectification—that had existed for centuries. Several years after the women's strike of 1970, equality—in this case, equal access in the workplace—took on a new form as female reporters sought entrée to men's locker rooms. This incursion to a male-only environment, once unthinkable, created a new dilemma and spawned legal challenges that took women like Melissa Ludtke and Claire Smith into uncharted territory as they tried simply to do their jobs as members of the media.

The creation of synthetic fibers dates to 1926 when efforts by DuPont, a giant in the chemical industry, and one of its chemists, Wallace Carothers, led to the development of nylon. Polyester polymers were used to form a new fabric, but it proved unreliable in holding its shape until the British chemists John Rex Whitfield and James Tennant Dickson developed a process that enabled them to be credited with inventing Terylene, the first polyester fiber, in 1941.[61]

Following an interruption in research due to the Second World War, Dupont bought the rights to manufacture polyester in the United States in 1946 and thereafter created Dacron. This new fabric was hailed for its durability and resistance to stains—to say nothing of the fact that it did not need to be ironed—and by the early 1950s was gaining acceptance as a material worthy of tailoring men's suits. In 1953, the Pittsburgh Pirates, under the auspices of general manager Branch Rickey, began using protective batting helmets that were molded from fiberglass and covered with a polyester resin. By the mid–1960s, artificial turf, the pile of which was "composed of grasslike nylon 'blades' ... knitted to a 15-ounce, polyester backing," gained increasing acceptance as a replacement for natural grass fields.[62]

Men's clothing was being revolutionized—Dodgers broadcaster Vin Scully said. "No more suit-carriers because you can pack the double knits without getting wrinkles"—and this movement carried over to what the players wore on the field.[63] The beginning years of the 1970s opened a new era in baseball fashion: The old flannel uniforms of a wool or cotton blend that were in use from around 1900 were supplanted by a wool/Orlon combination in the 1960s, and now this fabric was in turn being dropped in favor of polyester, the so-called miracle fabric.

"[T]he double-knit fabrics introduced in the early seventies provided so many more attractive and practical features over flannel: lighter, cooler, more comfortable, more durable, etc.," observed uniform expert Marc Okkonen. "Traditionalists insist that the tight-fitting stretchy double knit suits cannot compare with the well-tailored flannel look of the sixties, but the use of flannel materials for baseball uniforms is 'history.'"[64] There would be no turning back once the material divide was crossed, yet there was a most obvious downside to this sartorial transition: "Doubleknit fabric is well suited to form fitting garments that produce a streamlined look, which is fine in some cases but knits tell all; no more hiding excess flab under loose baggy suits."[65] Flattering or not, there began a gradual re-styling of uniforms in the 1970s.

Since 1963, the Cleveland Indians had worn vest-style uniforms with red-sleeved undershirts, but in 1970 the club switched to traditional, short-sleeve jerseys with pinstriping, and the formerly red caps were switched to blue. The Seattle Pilots had to quickly rework their uniforms when the team moved to Milwaukee just before the 1970 season commenced; their team colors of white, blue, and gold remained, as did the striping on the jersey sleeves, while the logos and lettering reflected the change in franchise.

Just as Cleveland underwent a full makeover, so did the Chicago White Sox in 1971. The Sox logos remained static but swapped out one traditional style for another: out was the blue-and-white scheme, along with the white stirrups and blue sanitary hose of the previous two seasons; in were red pinstripes for the home uniforms and powder-blue for away.

Chicago also added a new twist with its footwear: red cleats to match the red stirrups to be worn at Comiskey Park and on the road. And in what would be their final season in the nation's capital, the Washington Senators followed the lead of the Oakland Athletics by abandoning the usual black spikes and replacing them with white cleats.

Changes in venue courtesy of new stadiums prompted a few wardrobe updates. The Philadelphia Phillies anticipated moving from Connie Mack Stadium to Veterans Stadium in 1970, but even a one-year delay in that transfer did not prevent the team from introducing its new garb. "In preparing for the new stadium, the Phillies have changed their image by coming up with a new logo and uniforms," the club informed readers of its yearbook (if they had not already noticed how the players were now dressed). "Replacing the old cap with a baseball orbiting around it, the new symbol is a 'P' that grows out of the red stitches of a baseball and swirls into the letter with a ball in the middle. The new logotype spells out 'Phillies' in a unique lettering style and uses the 'P' symbol as an initial letter."[66]

Although the Cincinnati Reds enjoyed the new quarters at Riverfront Stadium, they held fast to their uniforms, but the same was not true in Pittsburgh. Upon moving out of Forbes Field, the Pirates, like the Indians, shed the tank-top jerseys they had worn since 1957 and became the first team to wear pullover jerseys. The team colors were slightly modified: the bright gold that augmented the usual black and white was replaced by a goldish mustard that was now the primary cap color.

Moving from 1970 into 1971, the California Angels underwent a change that bid farewell to its original—and very complicated—logo of an interconnected "CA," superimposed on a baseball with angel wings and a halo, which in turn were superimposed over a green infield. Greatly simplified, the new symbol was an outline of the state of California, with a small gold star placed in proximity to the location of the city of Anaheim, a small gold halo adorning the northwest corner of the state, and "angels" in all lower-case letters in an Arial-type font running diagonally from top to bottom within the state borders. The uniform lettering turned away from capital letters with serifs and used that of the new logo, and a lower-case "a" with small gold halo was on the cap. Now missing from the hat was the stitched halo that had made it unique in baseball fashion.

In 1971, the Houston Astros went from navy caps to bright orange and took on the nickname of "Orange Crush," but the Baltimore Orioles went even farther with that particular color. Wearing orange jerseys and pants to make for a combination perhaps as garish as the all-gold uniforms of the Oakland Athletics, the Orioles only brought those out for select dates that year and again in 1972.

By the early part of this decade, alterations to umpires' uniforms were being made as a concession to comfort. Having been outfitted in a dark blue suit for many years, "umpires relied on their uniform to establish a visual presence" and "the blue suit became the professional umpires' authority symbol until well into the 1960s.... Not until men's fashions underwent considerable changes in the 1960s was the readily identifiable suit dispensed with, although minor alterations adapted the suit to protective gear and made the arbiters more comfortable in extremely hot weather."[67] This last point was a huge consideration as modern outdoor stadiums installed AstroTurf, which retained heat more so than natural

9. Trends and Current Events 211

grass. Taking stock of "how hot AstroTurf is on the feet," Cincinnati general manager Bob Howsam opined, "I think some innersoles for shoes can be devised to solve the problem."[68]

White shirts for National League umpires were swapped for light blue beginning in the summer of 1970 in order to reduce their "overly formal" appearance.[69] The NL also started using a numbering system for umpires, with white numbers sewn on the right sleeve of the jacket or shirt. Both Major Leagues had switched to wash-and-wear fabrics for the new uniforms they supplied to the umpires every other season.

One final item of apparel gained currency through its adaptation to the realities of new field conditions. The profusion of artificial playing surfaces caused some players to reconsider their choice of footwear, and not just in terms of shoe color as dictated by their club. In the 1970 All-Star Game in Cincinnati, outfielder Pete Rose "wore a soccer-type shoe with rubber cleats for better traction on Riverfront Stadium's AstroTurf surface," the proof of which was visible in photographs taken of his collision with Ray Fosse.[70] A similar sighting occurred in the first game of the World Series a few months later when Rose's teammate, Bernie Carbo, tried to score on an infield chopper and, to much controversy, was called out at the plate. A quick inspection of a picture showing Carbo sliding toward home also confirms that he is shod with the same style of multi-studded cleats.

The turn of the calendar to the 1970s opened increasing possibilities as teams sought to refresh their on-field appearance. For all the attention devoted to the new double-knits, a certain amount of "what's old is new" could be detected by those who explored uniforms of years gone by. The navy-blue road togs of the 1902 Chicago White Sox or the 1936 "Palm Beach" bright red pants of the Cincinnati Reds foreshadowed what would be revived later in the 1970s by the ChiSox and the Cleveland Indians, respectively.

Updates to clothing were part of baseball's ever-changing optics that would very shortly be influenced by the players' attitudes about facial hair. The hirsute sprouting in the offseason was an indulgence for some, with the understanding that it would be removed in time for the opening of spring training because mustaches and beards were simply not allowed by baseball management. But as youth grew less reluctant to express themselves, their antiauthoritarian tendencies were in tandem with what the counterculture expounded, if not necessarily following Timothy Leary's dictum in the literal sense.

Irreverence was in vogue, and not just through the book *Ball Four*. In January 1970, the movie *M*A*S*H* was released to critical acclaim; Garry

Trudeau of *Doonesbury* comics fame called it "perfect for the times, the cacophony of American culture was reproduced on the screen."[71] A year later, the debut of *All in the Family* turned the television world upside down as the program's xenophobic lead—Archie Bunker, played by Carroll O'Connor—vents his middle-class spleen in unapologetically bigoted terms. The popularity of the TV show derived in part from the ability of working-class Americans to identify with Bunker and his straight-talking, blue-collar demeanor. *M*A*S*H* and *All in the Family* drew laughs from their audiences, but other matters in the real world were fully invested with far more gravity.

The response to the American invasion of Cambodia spawned a student uprising, but on May 8, 1970, the event that came to be known as the Hard-Hat Riot occurred in lower Manhattan. A confrontation between blue-collar patriots and antiwar demonstrators turned into a calamity when officials at City Hall learned that "Construction workers at the Twin Towers are going to take care of the protestors on Wall Street."[72] For the most part, the police stood by while the hardhats assaulted the antiwar crowd, thereby deepening the rift between hawks and doves over the Vietnam War. This round went to the hawks, but 13 months later, the antiwar movement received a vindication with the publication of the Pentagon Papers on June 13, 1971.

The work of Daniel Ellsberg, "whom [Nixon Administration official Henry] Kissinger had placed on the National Security Council staff as a consultant," the Papers were a series of documents culled from a top-secret study commissioned in 1967 by Secretary of Defense Robert McNamara regarding the history of the war in Vietnam.[73] Clandestinely copied by Ellsberg, the information was passed to the *New York Times*, which printed them to reveal ways in which the administration of President Lyndon Johnson "systematically lied, not only to the public but also to Congress" about how the conflict was being prosecuted.[74]

From the earliest days of the 1960s and then after U.S. troops landed in South Vietnam in March 1965, American officials soon understood that the war was a quagmire, yet continued to press on in the hope of somehow attaining victory in spite of a realization of an outcome not likely in favor of Western interests. The Pentagon Papers offered validation for the cause of the antiwar protestors.

War, the anger and protests against it, the division in the country born of the conflict as well as racially motivated disturbances contributed to a toxic aura in the United States. Violence seemed more and more an unavoidable attribute of American society: Kent State, the riot on Wall Street, the publication of *The Godfather*—the 1969 book was released as a motion picture three years later—the screening of *The French Connection*, the deadly Attica Prison riot of September 1971... There could be little wonder when Michael Burke lamented about violence appearing to rule the land. With fans rampaging at the closing of Forbes Field and Connie Mack Stadium in addition to the collision of Pete Rose and Ray Fosse, even baseball seemed to be infected at times.

Thankfully, those ballpark incidents and the jarring blow at Riverfront Stadium's home plate were anomalous. Baseball retained its pastoral qualities, and in addressing a meeting of the commissioner and the game's highest-ranking officials in August of 1971, Baltimore Oriole owner Jerry Hoffberger "stated that in his opinion the absence of violence was one of the touchstones which Baseball could offer."[75]

That same year, a coffee table-style book with the laudatory title of *This Great Game* was published "to make a statement of what baseball is really all about," and between its covers fans would discover "a new awareness, an insight into a sport that, without the violence of pro football or the speed of hockey, is both rough and graceful."[76] This tome was fully infused with the best that baseball's public relations could offer for every fan to enjoy: Commentary by Oriole manager Earl Weaver, who at the time had served but two full seasons at Baltimore's helm; analysis of pitching, fielding, and batting by noted baseball writers; a series of vintage photographs—and a firm nod to the historical aspects of the game—reproduced on heavy paper, as opposed to the glossy stock used elsewhere; a section of 12 specially commissioned works by contemporary artist LeRoy Neiman depicting 1970's best current players; arbiter Al Barlick's take on umpiring; a recap of the most significant plays in baseball history, courtesy of Joseph Reichler; and, resplendent throughout were scores of images in color and black-and-white depicting every aspect of the national pastime.

Although a majority of the pictures were supplied by just two photographers—San Francisco–based Fred Kaplan and Richard Raphael, who was from suburban Boston—they provided visual artistry that captured action, content, context, and, in some cases, the emotion that could be found on the diamond. Weighing in at over two pounds, *This Great Game* was a hard-cover celebration of baseball, not least being the most recent World Series that featured Brooks Robinson's seemingly single-handed cuffing of the Cincinnati Reds. Produced in conjunction with the commissioner's office, it was a book—to say nothing of a marketing tool—for the ages, even if its outsized cover price of $14.95 (over $100 in 2024 equivalent currency) may have been beyond the budget of many bibliophiles.

This earliest period of the 1970s showed the national pastime as rigorous but in a transitory state, as a new playoff system was taking root, and the MLBPA began to hit its stride in earnest. Baseball's uniformed personnel and front office staffs continued their unceasing arrivals and departures, a phenomenon seen in the abandoning of old ballparks as, for better or worse, the cookie-cutter stadiums opened their gates.

Baseball relishes hanging on to its past, as teammates Brooks Robinson and Frank Robinson, durable but now in their mid-30s, were accompanied by Willie Mays, Henry Aaron, and Harmon Killebrew among other aging stars approaching the twilight years of their storied careers. For some of them, the game would provide a paycheck beyond the playing field, and all of their endeavors would be carried by the stream of current events that shaped American culture and society.

There always exists a time when anyone can look back on a period of the game's history with fondness and nostalgia; the period of 1970 and 1971 is no different. Especially for Baby Boomers—perhaps accompanied by those a bit younger—now retired over two decades deep into the twenty-first century, a refrain of "those were the days" validates the memories, real or embellished, of an era once modern and now historic.

Chapter Notes

Works frequently cited have been identified by the following abbreviations:

PBKK Papers of Bowie K. Kuhn, BA MSS 100, National Baseball Hall of Fame and Museum, Cooperstown, NY.
TSN *The Sporting News*

Chapter 1

1. MLBPA Benefit Plan, Annual Reports for 1968, 1971, and 1972, PBKK, Series XI, Box 1, Folder 1.
2. Statement of World Series and League Championship Receipts and Distribution, October 31, 1970, PBKK, Series VI, Subseries 7, Box 25, Folder 1.
3. Balance Sheet, Office of the Commissioner, October 31, 1970, PBKK, Series VI, Subseries 7, Box 25, Folder 1.
4. Leonard Koppett, "New Agreement Will Cost Owners $4 Million," *Sporting News*, June 6, 1970, 6.
5. "N.L. Umps Organize, Seeking More Uniformity, Cooperation," *TSN*, October 23, 1963, 11.
6. Ed Edmonds and Frank Houdek, *Baseball Meets the Law* (Jefferson, NC: McFarland & Company, 2017), 121.
7. Brad Snyder, *A Well-Paid Slave: Curt Flood's Fight for Free Agency in Professional Sports* (New York: Plume, 2007), 206.
8. Jerome Holtzman, "Players, Umpires, Books, Law Suits…," in Paul MacFarlane, ed., et al., *Official Baseball Guide for 1971* (St. Louis: The Sporting News, 1971), 287–288. Three umpires were not available to participate in the voting.
9. Ralph Ray, "Unions Help Umps Settle Strike," *Sporting News*, October 17, 1970, 20.
10. Ralph Ray, "Unions Help Umps Settle Strike," *Sporting News*, October 17, 1970, 20.
11. Holtzman, "Players, Umpires, Books, Law Suits…," in Paul MacFarlane, ed., et al., *Official Baseball Guide for 1971*, 289.
12. Bowie Kuhn, *Hardball: The Education of a Baseball Commissioner* (New York: Times Books, 1987), 67.
13. Kuhn, *Hardball*, 67.
14. Bowie Kuhn, "Baseball 1970," n.d., PBKK, Series VI, Subseries 1, Box 1, Folder 5. Emphasis added. This document was likely a press release in the run-up to Opening Day.
15. Minutes of Joint Meeting of Major Leagues, May 15, 1970, PBKK, Series III, Subseries 2, Box 1, Folder 8.
16. Memo, Paul Porter to Bowie Kuhn, July 20, 1970, PBKK, Series 1, Subseries 2, Box 5, Folder 7. Emphasis added.
17. Minutes of the Major League Executive Council Meeting, October 19, 1970, PBKK, Series I, Subseries 1, Box 1, Folder 2.
18. Bill Francis, "A Classic Under the Lights," https://baseballhall.org/discover/-a-classic-under-the-lights. Viewed September 4, 2023.
19. Jack Craig, "SporTView," *TSN*, October 23, 1971, 41.
20. "Success with a Capital S," *TSN*, October 30, 1971, 14.
21. Jack Craig, "SporTView," *TSN*, November 6, 1971, 34.
22. Minutes of Joint Meeting of the Major Leagues, December 3, 1971, PBKK, Series III, Subseries 2, Box 1, Folder 8.
23. Minutes of the Major League Executive Council Meeting, October 19, 1970, PBKK, Series I, Subseries 1, Box 1, Folder 2.
24. Minutes of the Major League

Executive Council Meeting, November 30, 1971, PBKK, Series I, Subseries 1, Box 1, Folder 3.
25. Wharton Notes, PBKK, Series I: Subseries 2, Box 5, Folder 9.
26. Galbreath quoted in Kuhn, *Hardball*, 66.
27. Kuhn, *Hardball*, 66.
28. Kuhn, *Hardball*, 67.
29. Minutes of Joint Meeting of the Major Leagues, December 5, 1969, PBKK, Series III, Subseries 2, Box 1, Folder 7. Emphasis added.
30. Minutes of Joint Meeting of the Major Leagues, December 4, 1970, PBKK, Series III, Subseries 2, Box 1, Folder 8.
31. William D. Harsh to James T. Gallagher, December 15, 1971, PBKK, Series VI, Subseries 1, Box 10, Folder 10.
32. James T. Gallagher to Bowie Kuhn, et al., December 18, 1971, PBKK, Series VI, Subseries 1, Box 10, Folder 10.
33. Harry Dalton to Bowie Kuhn, September 8, 1971, PBKK, Series VI, Subseries 1, Box 10, Folder 11.
34. Alexander "Sandy" Hadden to Bowie Kuhn, January 8, 1971, PBKK, Series VI, Subseries 1, Box 10, Folder 11. Emphasis in original.
35. Cal Gauss to Bowie Kuhn, February 11, 1971, PBKK, Series VI, Subseries 1, Box 10, Folder 11.
36. "Wake-up Time for Baseball," *TSN*, April 17, 1971, 14.
37. Minutes of Joint Meeting of the Major Leagues, July 29, 1970, PBKK, Series III, Subseries 2, Box 1, Folder 8.
38. Cal Gauss to Bowie Kuhn, May 28, 1971, PBKK, Series VI, Subseries 3, Box 15, Folder 7.
39. Cal Gauss to Bowie Kuhn, May 28, 1971, PBKK, Series VI, Subseries 3, Box 15, Folder 7.
40. Cal Gauss to Bowie Kuhn, May 28, 1971, PBKK, Series VI, Subseries 3, Box 15, Folder 7.
41. Cal Gauss to Bowie Kuhn, May 28, 1971, PBKK, Series VI, Subseries 3, Box 15, Folder 7.
42. Minutes of Executive Meeting, May 6, 1971, PBKK, Series I, Subseries 1, Box 1, Folder 4.
43. Minutes of Executive Meeting, May 6, 1971, PBKK, Series I, Subseries 1, Box 1, Folder 4.
44. Minutes of Executive Meeting, May 15, 1971, PBKK, Series I, Subseries 1, Box 1, Folder 4.
45. Minutes of Executive Meeting, May 15, 1971, PBKK, Series I, Subseries 1, Box 1, Folder 4.
46. Minutes of Executive Meeting, May 15, 1971, PBKK, Series I, Subseries 1, Box 1, Folder 4.
47. Minutes of Executive Meeting, May 27, 1971, PBKK, Series I, Subseries 1, Box 1, Folder 4.
48. Minutes of Executive Meeting, May 27, 1971, PBKK, Series I, Subseries 1, Box 1, Folder 4.
49. Joe Reichler to Bowie Kuhn, January 4, 1971, PBKK, Series I, Subseries 2, Box 6, Folder 10.
50. Joe Reichler to Bowie Kuhn, January 4, 1971, PBKK, Series I, Subseries 2, Box 6, Folder 10.
51. Walter O'Malley to Charles Feeney, February 8, 1971, PBKK, Series I, Subseries 2, Box 6, Folder 10.
52. Walter O'Malley to Charles Feeney, February 8, 1971, PBKK, Series I, Subseries 2, Box 6, Folder 10.
53. Walter O'Malley to Charles Feeney, February 8, 1971, PBKK, Series I, Subseries 2, Box 6, Folder 10.
54. Harry Simmons to Bowie Kuhn, March 30, 1971, PBKK, Series I, Subseries 2, Box 6, Folder 10.
55. Joe Reichler to Bowie Kuhn, March 26, 1971, PBKK, Series I, Subseries 2, Box 6, Folder 10.
56. Minutes of Joint Meeting of the Major Leagues, August 4, 1971, PBKK, Series III, Subseries 2, Box 1, Folder 8.
57. Harry Simmons to Bowie Kuhn, December 7, 1971, PBKK, Series I, Subseries 2, Box 6, Folder 5.
58. William O. Cain, Jr., "A Technical Study of Three-League and Four League Play," n.d., PBKK, Series I, Subseries 2, Box 6, Folder 10. Based on its wording, the report seems to be from 1972.
59. Joe Reichler, "International World Series Problems," n.d., PBKK, Series VI, Subseries 1, Box 10, Folder 10. This document seems to be from December 1971.
60. Joe Reichler, "International World Series Problems," n.d., PBKK, Series VI, Subseries 1, Box 10, Folder 10. This document seems to be from December 1971.
61. Minutes of Joint Meeting of the

Major Leagues, May 15, 1970, PBKK, Series III, Subseries 2, Box 1, Folder 8.
62. Henry Fitzgibbon to Bowie Kuhn, February 5, 1971, PBKK, Series VI, Subseries 1, Box 3, Folder 5.
63. Post-trial memorandum of all defendants other than Bowie K. Kuhn, *Flood v. Kuhn*, 309 F. Supp. 793 No. 70 Civ. 202 (2nd Cir. 1970), found in PBKK, Series XI, Oversize Box 1. Emphasis in original.
64. Plaintiff's post-trial memorandum, *Flood v. Kuhn*, 309 F. Supp. 793 No. 70 Civ. 202 (2nd Cir. 1970), found in PBKK, Series XI, Oversize Box 1.
65. Marvin Miller, *A Whole Different Ball Game: The Sport and Business of Baseball* (New York: Birch Lane Press, 1991), 188.
66. Kuhn, *Hardball*, 88; Miller, *A Whole Different Ball Game*, 198.
67. Brad Snyder, *A Well-Paid Slave: Curt Flood's Fight for Free Agency in Professional Sports* (New York: Plume, 2007), 271.
68. Andy McCue, *Stumbling Around the Bases: The American League's Mismanagement in the Expansion Eras* (Lincoln: University of Nebraska Press, 2022), 40.
69. These events comprise only a part of the very complicated story of expansion and club movement. For an excellent survey of all the machinations at this time, see McCue, *Stumbling Around the Bases*.
70. Dissent quoted in Edmonds and Houdek, *Baseball Meets the Law*, 102. Emphasis added.
71. John J. McHale and Charles Bronfman, brief by Montreal baseball club, April 3, 1970, PBKK, Series IV, Subseries 1, Box 1, Folder 9. This quotation and those immediately following are from this same source.
72. Antitrust Exemption Materials, January 31, 1972, PBKK, Series IV, Subseries 1, Box 1, Folder 4.
73. Antitrust Exemption Materials, January 31, 1972, PBKK, Series IV, Subseries 1, Box 1, Folder 4.
74. Dale quoted in Antitrust Exemption Materials, January 31, 1972, PBKK, Series IV, Subseries 1, Box 1, Folder 4.
75. Paul A. Porter, "Organized Baseball and the Antitrust Laws," January 30, 1970, PBKK, Series IV, Subseries 1, Box 1, Folder 2.

Chapter 2

1. Jon Saraceno, "Denny McLain Q & A," *AARP Bulletin*, April 2018.
2. Jim Hawkins, *Al Kaline: The Biography of a Tigers Icon* (Chicago: Triumph Books, 2010), 198.
3. Denny McLain and Eli Zaret, *I Told You I Wasn't Perfect* (Chicago: Triumph Books, 2007), 65.
4. Hawkins, *Al Kaline*, 200.
5. McLain, *I Told You I Wasn't Perfect*, 144.
6. McLain, *I Told You I Wasn't Perfect*, 144. McLain wrote in his memoir that the amount was $446,000; contemporaneous stories in the press, such as one in *The Sporting News*, list various debts and obligations ranging from $209 to $25,000. However the calculations may be viewed, it suffices to say that McLain's financial entanglements were complicated and troublesome. See John F. Oppedahl, "McLain's Castle of Cards Collapsing," *TSN*, March 7, 1970, 3, 6.
7. Bowie Kuhn, *Hardball: The Education of a Baseball Commissioner* (New York: Times Books, 1987), 68.
8. Kuhn, *Hardball*, 69.
9. McLain, *I Told You I Wasn't Perfect*, 147.
10. Bowie Kuhn statement in Jerome Holtzman, "Players, Umpires, Books, Law Suits...," in Paul MacFarlane, ed., et al., *Official Baseball Guide for 1971* (St. Louis: The Sporting News, 1971), 265.
11. Freehan and McAuliffe quote in Holtzman, "Players, Umpires, Books, Law Suits...," in MacFarlane, *Official Baseball Guide for 1971*, 266.
12. McLain, *I Told You I Wasn't Perfect*, 154–155.
13. John F. Oppedahl, "McLain's Castle of Cards Collapsing," *TSN*, March 7, 1970, 6.
14. McLain, *I Told You I Wasn't Perfect*, 159.
15. Watson Spoelstra, "Raindrops Keep Falling on Denny's Head ... Crash," *TSN*, September 12, 1970, 5.
16. Joe Falls, "Kuhn Too Lenient? 'I Think I Was,'" *Detroit Free Press*, September 10, 1970. Emphasis added to differentiate ownership versus carrying the gun as a concealed weapon.
17. McLain, *I Told You I Wasn't Perfect*, 173.

18. Merrell Whittlesey, "Nats Nab McLain to Bolster Sagging Gate," *TSN*, October 24, 1970, 11.
19. McLain, *I Told You I Wasn't Perfect*, 177.
20. "Denny hits Washington—with his nightclub act," January 1971, Denny McLain file, National Baseball Hall of Fame Library.
21. Ben Bradlee, Jr., *The Kid: The Immortal Life of Ted Williams* (New York: Little, Brown, , 2013), 560.
22. Robinson quoted in Watson Spoelstra, "Tigers' Stock Rises on 'Steal-of-Year' Nat Deal," *TSN*, October 24, 1970, 11. Coleman would also suffer the effects of pitching for Billy Martin, who in 1971 kept the young pitcher on the mound for 286 innings, 280 more in 1972, and 288 in 1973. Martin was fired with less than one month left in the 1973 season but had established the troublesome pattern of burning out starters with heavy workloads.
23. McLain, *I Told You I Wasn't Perfect*, 208.
24. Jon Saraceno, "Denny McLain Q & A," *AARP Bulletin*, April 2018.
25. Brad Snyder, *A Well-Paid Slave: Curt Flood's Fight for Free Agency in Professional Sports* (New York: Plume, 2007), 52.
26. Curt Flood, baseball-reference.com. Viewed October 15, 2023.
27. Snyder, *A Well-Paid Slave*, 3.
28. Curt Flood and Richard Carter, *The Way It Is* (New York: Trident Press, 1971), 158.
29. Snyder, *A Well-Paid Slave*, 27.
30. Marvin Miller, *A Whole Different Ball Game: The Sport and Business of Baseball* (New York: Birch Lane Press, 1991), 175.
31. Flood quoted in Miller, *A Whole Different Ball Game*, 186.
32. Snyder, *A Well-Paid Slave*, 68.
33. Flood quoted in Kuhn, *Hardball*, 83.
34. Kuhn, *Hardball*, 83, 84.
35. Snyder, *A Well-Paid Slave*, 190. Delinquent alimony and child-support payments, fallout from his failed first marriage, were also contributing to Flood's personal implosion.
36. "Claim Flood's Pact Immune From Reserve Clause," *New York Daily News*, December 19, 1970.
37. George Resta quote in Snyder, *A Well-Paid Slave*, 216.
38. Red Foley, "Flood Quits Senators; Takes Off for Spain," *New York Daily News*, April 28, 1971, 104.
39. Snyder, *A Well-Paid Slave*, 231.
40. Snyder, *A Well-Paid Slave*, 233–234.
41. Jerome Holtzman, "The Year of the Player Strike," in Joe Marcin, ed., et al., *Official Baseball Guide for 1973* (St. Louis: The Sporting News, 1973), 281.
42. Kuhn, *Hardball*, 86.
43. Leonard Koppett, *TSN*, July 8, 1972, 6.
44. Miller, *A Whole Different Ball Game*, 199.
45. William J. Ryczek, "Loathed It: Ball Four," *NINE: A Journal of Baseball History and Culture*, Vol. 32, No. 1 (Fall 2023), 12, 13.
46. Jim Bouton, *I'm Glad You Didn't Take It Personally*, edited by Leonard Shecter (New York: William Morrow, 1971), 67.
47. Kuhn, *Hardball*, 73.
48. Mitchell Nathanson, *Bouton: The Life of a Baseball Original* (Lincoln: University of Nebraska Press, 2020), 156–157.
49. Kuhn quoted in Holtzman, "Players, Umpires, Books, Law Suits...," *Official Baseball Guide for 1971*, 302.
50. Bouton quoted in Nathanson, *Bouton*, 157.
51. Bouton, *I'm Glad You Didn't Take It Personally*, 71.
52. Bouton, *I'm Glad You Didn't Take It Personally*, 71.
53. Holtzman, "Players, Umpires, Books, Law Suits...," *Official Baseball Guide for 1971*, 302–303.
54. Curt Flood and Richard Carter, *The Way It Is* (New York: Trident Press, 1971), 88.
55. Nathanson, *Bouton*, 32.
56. Banks quoted in Ron Rapoport, *Let's Play Two: The Legend of Mr. Cub, The Life of Ernie Banks* (New York: Hachette Books, 2019), 352.
57. Catharine G. Eckert to Bowie Kuhn, May 2, 1971, PBKK, Series VII, Box 16, Folder 3.

Chapter 3

1. Paul Dickson, *The Dickson Baseball Dictionary* (New York: Facts on File, 1989), 358.

2. McLaughlin quoted in Terry Pluto, *The Earl of Baltimore: The Story of Earl Weaver, Baltimore Orioles Manager* (Piscataway, NJ: New Century, 1982), 14.
3. Pluto, *The Earl of Baltimore*, 26.
4. Pluto, *The Earl of Baltimore*, 30.
5. Pluto, *The Earl of Baltimore*, 56, 57.
6. Pluto, *The Earl of Baltimore*, 57.
7. Earl Weaver with Berry Stainback, *It's What You Learn After You Know It All That Counts* (New York: Fireside Books, 1983), 179.
8. Weaver with Stainback, *It's What You Learn After You Know It All That Counts*, 182.
9. Weaver quoted in Lowell Reidenbaugh, "Oh, What a Year for Beautiful Birds!" *TSN*, October 31, 1970, 33.
10. Weaver with Stainback, *It's What You Learn After You Know It All That Counts*, 186.
11. Weaver with Stainback, *It's What You Learn After You Know It All That Counts*, 187.
12. Weaver quoted in Phil Jackman, "Weaver Sets 1972 Goal—Record for 100 Wins," *The Sporting News*, October 16, 1971, 20.
13. Weaver with Stainback, *It's What You Learn After You Know It All That Counts*, 190. Emphasis in original.
14. Weaver quoted in Lowell Reidenbaugh, "Champ Bucs Batting 1.000 as Seers," *TSN*, October 30, 1971, 3.
15. The strike-plagued year of 1981 resulted in first- and second-half seasons because of the stoppage of play. The Orioles were in second place in the AL East when the strike began in June, and when play resumed two months later, they finished in fourth place in the second half. Coming after Weaver retired at the conclusion of the 1982 season, his ill-fated return to Baltimore in 1985 produced a 53–52 record, and in 1986 he retired for good when the Orioles sank to the basement of the AL East with 73 wins and 89 losses, twenty-two and one-half games behind Boston.
16. Earl Lawson, "Bristol, Deposed Red Boss, Victim of Pitching Letdown," *TSN*, October 25, 1969, 27.
17. Sparky Anderson and Dan Ewald, *Sparky!* (New York: Prentice-Hall, 1990), 54–55.
18. Anderson and Ewald, *Sparky!*, 59.

19. Sparky Anderson and Dan Ewald, *They Call Me Sparky* (Chelsea, MI: Sleeping Bear Press, 1998), 81.
20. Earl Lawson, "A View of the N. L. West," *TSN*, April 11, 1970, 10.
21. Anderson and Ewald, *Sparky!*, 72.
22. Cindy Thomson, "Sparky Anderson," Society for American Baseball Research, sabr.org/bioproj/person/sparky-anderson/. Viewed January 21, 2024.
23. Dick Williams with Bill Plaschke, *No More Mr. Nice Guy: A Life of Hardball* (New York: Harcourt Brace Jovanovich, 1990), 6.
24. Williams with Plaschke, *No More Mr. Nice Guy*, 29.
25. Jeff Angus, "Dick Williams," Society for American Baseball Research, sabr.org/bioproj/person/dick-williams/. Viewed January 22, 2024.
26. Williams with Plaschke, *No More Mr. Nice Guy*, 71, 73.
27. Williams with Plaschke, *No More Mr. Nice Guy*, 109–111.
28. Bill Nowlin, *Tom Yawkey: Patriarch of the Boston Red Sox* (Lincoln: University of Nebraska Press, 2018), 281.
29. Jeff Angus, "Dick Williams," Society for American Baseball Research, sabr.org/bioproj/person/dick-williams/. Viewed January 24, 2024.
30. McNamara quoted in Ron Bergman, "Dick Williams on Finley's Firing Line; McNamara Axing Blamed on Duncan," *TSN*, October 17, 1970, 25.
31. Williams quoted in *1971 Oakland Athletics Yearbook*, 11.
32. Jeff Angus, "Dick Williams," Society for American Baseball Research, sabr.org/bioproj/person/dick-williams/. Viewed January 25, 2024.
33. Todd Masters, *The 1972 Detroit Tigers: Billy Martin and the Half-Game Champs* (Jefferson, NC: McFarland, 2010), 20.
34. Jimmy Keenan and Frank Russo, "Billy Martin," Society for American Baseball Research, sabr.org/bioproj/person/billy-martin/. Viewed January 25, 2024.
35. Masters, *The 1972 Detroit Tigers*, 20.
36. Masters, *The 1972 Detroit Tigers*, 21.
37. Martin quoted in Peter Golenbock, *Wild, High, and Tight* (New York: St. Martin's Press, 1994), 177.
38. Golenbock, *Wild, High, and Tight*, 178.
39. Martin quoted in Watson Spoelstra,

"Martin to Visit His Tigers and Learn Their Problems," *TSN*, October 17, 1970, 34.

40. Willie Horton and Kevin Allen, *23: Detroit's Own Willie the Wonder, the Tigers' First Black Great* (Chicago: Triumph Books, 2022), 130, 131.

41. "Billy Martin—Born a Battler," *1971 Detroit Tigers Yearbook*, 7–8.

42. Kaline quoted in Jim Hawkins, *Al Kaline: The Biography of a Tigers Icon* (Chicago: Triumph Books, 2010), 207.

43. Bill Gallo Cartoons, BA MSS26, National Baseball Hall of Fame, Cooperstown, NY, Box 8, Folder 40.

44. Reese quoted in Mort Zachter, *Gil Hodges: A Hall of Fame Life* (Lincoln: University of Nebraska Press, 2015), 230.

45. Stengel quoted in Shirley Povich, "Nats Hand Get-Tough Policy to Nice-Guy Gil," *TSN*, June 1, 1963, 9.

46. Shirley Povich, "Nats Hand Get-Tough Policy to Nice-Guy Gil," *TSN*, June 1, 1963, 9.

47. Wayne R. Coffey, *They Said It Couldn't Be Done: The '69 Mets, New York City, and the Most Astounding Season in Baseball History* (New York: Crown Archetype, 2019), 22.

48. Jack Lang, "Simply Fantabulous, Those Mets," in Paul MacFarlane, ed., et al., *Official Baseball Guide for 1970* (St. Louis: The Sporting News, 1970), 117.

49. George Vecsey, *Joy in Mudville: Being a Complete Account of the Unparalleled History of the New York Mets from Their Most Perturbed Beginnings to Their Rise to Glory and Renown* (New York: McCall, 1970), 193.

50. "Gil Hodges," *1970 New York Mets Media Guide*, 27.

51. Tom Clavin and Danny Peary, *Gil Hodges: The Brooklyn Bums, the Miracle Mets, and the Extraordinary Life of a Baseball Legend* (New York: New American Library, 2012), 353–354.

52. Swoboda quoted in Clavin and Peary, *Gil Hodges*, 354.

53. Marino Amoruso, *Gil Hodges: The Quiet Man* (Middlebury, VT: Paul S. Eriksson, 1991), 118.

54. Colleen Hroncich, *The Whistling Irishman: Danny Murtaugh Remembered* (Philadelphia: Sports Challenge Network, 2010), 172.

55. Murtaugh quoted in Hroncich, *The Whistling Irishman*, 200.

56. Alan H. Levy, *Walter Alston: The Rise of a Manager from the Minors to the Baseball Hall of Fame* (Jefferson, NC: McFarland, 2021), 163.

57. Jon Barnes, "Bob Lemon," Society for American Baseball Research, sabr.org/bioproj/person/bob-lemon/. Viewed January 30, 2024.

Chapter 4

1. John Eisenberg, *From 33rd Street to Camden Yards: An Oral History of the Baltimore Orioles* (Chicago: Contemporary Books, 2001), 221.

2. Chan Keith, "It's a Whole New Ballgame," *1970 World Series Program*, 5.

3. *1971 Baltimore Orioles Media Guide*, 23.

4. Ray Scarborough to Harry Dalton, September 5, 1971, Harry Dalton collection, BA MSS 40, National Baseball Hall of Fame and Museum, Cooperstown, NY, Series I, Box 3, Folder 5. Emphasis in original. Scarborough was heading up the baseball program at Mount Olive College at the time that he wrote this memo.

5. Cal Ripken to Harry Dalton, October 28, 1971, Harry Dalton collection, BA MSS 40, National Baseball Hall of Fame and Museum, Cooperstown, NY, Series II, Box 5, Folder 4.

6. Frank Robinson quoted in Eisenberg, *From 33rd Street to Camden Yards*, 243.

7. Wells Twombly, "Finley Had a Great Idea," *TSN*, July 12, 1971, 14.

8. Williams quoted in Bill Libby and Vida Blue, *Vida: His Own Story* (Englewood Cliffs, NJ: Prentice-Hall, 1972), 171.

9. Herbert Michelson, *Charlie O: Charles Oscar Finley vs. the Baseball Establishment* (Indianapolis: Bobbs-Merrill, 1975), 171.

10. Williams quoted in Bruce Markusen, *A Baseball Dynasty: Charlie Finley's Swingin' A's* (Haworth, NJ: St. Johann Press, 2002), 7.

11. Mark Armour, "Charlie Finley," Society for American Baseball Research, sabr.org/bioproj/person/charlie-finley/. Viewed February 16, 2024.

12. Tom Clark, *Champagne and Baloney: The Rise and Fall of Finley's A's* (New York: Harper & Row, 1976), 80.

13. Coleman quoted in Earl Lawson, "A

Dynasty in Cincinnati?—Youth Is on Reds' Side," *TSN*, October 24, 1970, 23.

14. Bench quoted in Jim Ferguson, "Johnny Bench: A Portrait of Self-Confidence," *1970 Cincinnati Reds Yearbook*, 14.

15. Anderson quoted in Ritter Collett, "Sparky Anderson—That's Who!" *1970 Cincinnati Reds Yearbook*, 7.

16. Daryl Smith, *Making the Big Red Machine: Bob Howsam and the Cincinnati Reds of the 1970s* (Jefferson, NC: McFarland, 2009), 74.

17. Gregory L. Rhodes and John G. Erardi, *Big Red Dynasty: How Bob Howsam & Sparky Anderson Built the Big Red Machine* (Cincinnati: Road West, 1997), 82; Earl Lawson, "May, Perez Zero In on Reds' Lefty-Righty Homer Record," *TSN*, August 9, 1969, 19.

18. Earl Lawson, "Big Red Machine," *1970 World Series Program*, 69.

19. Smith, *Making the Big Red Machine*, 64.

20. Earl Lawson, "Reds Success Story: Instant Pitching!" *1970 All-Star Game Program*, 3.

21. Anderson quoted in Earl Lawson, "Reds Success Story: Instant Pitching!" *1970 All-Star Game Program*, 4.

22. *1971 Cincinnati Reds Media Guide*, 3.

23. Rhodes and Erardi, *Big Red Dynasty*, 107.

24. Bob Hunter, "Dodgers Regain Respectability in '69," in Paul MacFarlane, ed., et al., *Official Baseball Guide for 1970* (St. Louis: The Sporting News, 1970), 159.

25. Fred Claire, *Fred Claire: My 30 Years in Dodger Blue* (Champaign, IL: Sports Publishing, LLC, 2004), 27.

26. Campanis quoted in "Dodgers No. 1 Organization in Baseball," *1971 Los Angeles Dodgers Yearbook*, 50.

27. Tom Van Riper, *Cincinnati Red and Dodger Blue: Baseball's Greatest Forgotten Rivalry* (Lanham, MD: Rowman & Littlefield, 2017), 19.

28. "Your Dodgers of 1971," *1971 Los Angeles Dodgers Media Guide*, 3.

29. Mitchell Nathanson, *God Almighty Hisself: The Life and Legacy of Dick Allen* (Philadelphia: University of Pennsylvania Press, 2016), 203.

30. Nathanson, *God Almighty Hisself*, 213.

31. *1971 New York Yankees Media Guide*, 5.

32. Lee MacPhail, *My 9 Innings: An Autobiography of 50 Years in Baseball* (Westport, CT: Meckler Books, 1989), 108.

33. *1971 New York Yankees Yearbook*, 5.

34. *1971 New York Yankees Yearbook*, 6.

35. Philip Bashe, *Dog Days: The New York Yankees Fall From Grace and Return to Glory, 1964–1976* (New York: Random House, 1994), 212–213.

36. Bashe, *Dog Days*, 213.

37. Jack Lang, "Mets Close, But Lose 'Amazing' Tag," in MacFarlane, *Official Baseball Guide for 1971*, 121.

38. Bob Wirz, *The Passion of Baseball: A Journey to the Commissioner's Office of Major League Baseball* (Autryville, NC: Ravenswood, 2016), 104–105.

39. *1970 Kansas City Royals Yearbook*.

40. *1971 Kansas City Royals Media Guide*, 84.

41. Anne Morgan, *Prescription for Success: The Life and Values of Ewing Marion Kauffman* (Kansas City: Andrews and McMeel, 1995), 257.

42. Ted Blackman, "Expos Are Losers, But Loyal Montreal Fans Love 'Em," *TSN*, October 11, 1969, 20.

43. *1970 Montreal Expos Yearbook*, 1.

44. *1970 Montreal Expos Yearbook*, 3.

45. *1971 Montreal Expos Yearbook*, 57.

46. Ted Blackman, "Mauch Ate Words With Relish," in MacFarlane, *Official Baseball Guide for 1971*, 133.

Chapter 5

1. *1970 San Diego Padres Media Guide*, 2.
2. *1971 San Diego Padres Media Guide*, 3.
3. Bill Center, *Padres Essential: Everything You Need to Know to Be a Real Fan!* (Chicago: Triumph Books, 2007), 37.
4. William H. Mullins, *Becoming Big League: Seattle, the Pilots, and Stadium Politics* (Seattle: University of Washington Press, 2013), 21. The Mullins volume and the relevant portions of Andy McCue's *Stumbling Around the Bases* provide the best accounts of how the events played out to their conclusion.
5. Mullins, *Becoming Big League*, 86.
6. Mullins, *Becoming Big League*, 143.
7. Mullins, *Becoming Big League*, 62.
8. McCue, *Stumbling Around the Bases*, 94.

9. Memo on three-divisional play, June 19, 1969, PBKK, Series I, Subseries 2, Box 6, Folder 5.
10. Mullins, *Becoming Big League*, 231.
11. McCue, *Stumbling Around the Bases*, 97.
12. *1970 Milwaukee Brewers Yearbook*, 1.
13. "Deposition upon Oral Examination of Bowie K. Kuhn," September 21, 1973, PBKK, Series IV, Subseries 1, Box 5, Folder 5. The quotes in this section are from this same source.
14. Notes of Bowie Kuhn conversation with Bob Short, September 15, 1970, PBKK, Series VI, Subseries 2, Box 14, Folder 4.
15. Merrell Whittlesey, "Short Readies Bombshell for Nat Fans; First Negro Manager? It's Possibility," *TSN*, February 22, 1969, 39.
16. Howard quoted in "Insiders Say," *TSN*, March 21, 1970, 4.
17. Dave Brady, "Short Raps Business for Non-Support," *Washington Post*, March 4, 1970.
18. Notes of Bowie Kuhn telephone conversation with Bob Short, September 15, 1970, PBKK, Series VI, Subseries 2, Box 14, Folder 4. The broadcast-revenue ranking was reported in "Senators Need Help, But Franchise Shift Is Unlikely—Kuhn," *TSN*, October 24, 1970, 20.
19. "Senators Need Help, But Franchise Shift Is Unlikely—Kuhn," *TSN*, October 24, 1970, 20; "Short Spends to Lift Nats Despite Big Financial Losses," *Newark Star-Ledger*, December 9, 1970.
20. Francis J. Kane to Robert E. Short, March 5, 1971, PBKK, Series VI, Subseries 2, Box 14, Folder 4. Emphasis added.
21. Bowie Kuhn to Joe Cronin, March 23, 1971, PBKK, Series VI, Subseries 2, Box 14, Folder 5.
22. Leonard Shapiro, "Interior Opposes Stadium Transfer," *Washington Post*, March 24, 1971.
23. Notes of Bowie Kuhn telephone conversation with Bud Selig, March 30, 1971, PBKK, Series VI, Subseries 2, Box 14, Folder 5.
24. Sharon Blinco, "Short Buys Lowry, St. Paul Hotels, Adjacent Properties," unlisted publication, April 1, 1971, 1A. The story was likely from the *Minneapolis Star-Tribune*, and its appearance in the April Fool's Day edition might raise a bit of suspicion. See Robert Short file, National Baseball Hall of Library, Cooperstown, New York.
25. Shirley Povich, "This Morning...," *Washington Post*, June 14, 1971.
26. Arthur J. Bergman to Robert E. Short, June 16, 1971, PBKK, Series VI, Subseries 2, Box 14, Folder 4.
27. Notes of Bowie Kuhn telephone conversation with Ewing Kauffman, June 30, 1971, PBKK, Series VI, Subseries 2, Box 14, Folder 4.
28. "Owner Blamed for Current Dilemma of Nats," *Detroit Free Press*, July 14, 1971, 4-D.
29. Henry Fitzgibbon to Bowie Kuhn, August 24, 1971, PBKK, Series VI, Subseries 2, Box 14, Folder 4.
30. Kenneth Turan, "Senators Owner: 'What's a Suit Here or There?,'" *Washington Post*, August 25, 1971, E1.
31. John H. Johnson to Bowie Kuhn, September 7, 1971, PBKK, Series VI, Subseries 2, Box 14, Folder 4.
32. Morris Siegel, "Senators: 'There Is More Hope,'" *Washington Star*, September 16, 1971, C-1.
33. "$12 Million Called Bargain For Nats by Texas Mayor," *Washington Post*, September 14, 1971, D-1.
34. Thomas H. Dawson to Bowie Kuhn, September 10, 1971, PBKK, Series VI, Subseries 2, Box 14, Folder 4.
35. Jerome Holtzman, "'71 Saw Gate Up, Short Move, Alex Angry," in Paul MacFarlane, ed., et al., *Official Baseball Guide for 1972* (St. Louis: The Sporting News, 1972), 301.
36. American League Meeting Minutes, September 21, 1971, PBKK, Series IV, Subseries 1, Box 1, Folder 3.
37. Jerome Holtzman, "'71 Saw Gate Up, Short Move, Alex Angry," in Paul MacFarlane, ed., et al., *Official Baseball Guide for 1972* (St. Louis: The Sporting News, 1972), 301.
38. American League Meeting Minutes, September 21, 1971, PBKK, Series IV, Subseries 1, Box 1, Folder 3.
39. Joseph B. Danzansky remarks to American League owners, n.d., PBKK, Series I, Subseries 1, Box 1, Folder 1. Danzansky references the September 21, 1971, meeting, so his address seems to have taken place shortly thereafter.
40. Walter F. O'Malley to R.R.M.

Carpenter, Jr., September 22, 1971, PBKK, Series VI, Subseries 2, Box 13, Folder 7.

41. Dick Denham, "The Washington Senators Move," WRC980 editorial, September 23, 1971, PBKK, Series VI, Subseries 2, Box 13, Folder 7.

42. Norman Davis, "Senator's [sic] Lost For Many Reasons," WTOP editorial, September 22, 1971, PBKK, Series VI, Subseries 2, Box 13, Folder 7.

43. Merrell Whittlesey, "Senators Expire Amidst Love For Hondo, Hate—and Forfeit," *TSN*, October 16, 1971, 34,38.

44. Merrell Whittlesey, "Senators Expire Amidst Love For Hondo, Hate—and Forfeit," *TSN*, October 16, 1971, 34,38.

45. Allyn quoted in Jerome Holtzman column, *TSN*, October 9, 1971, 12.

46. Bob Addie, "Baseball Scrutiny Proposed," *Washington Post*, October 28, 1971; Gerald Ford news release, November 30, 1971, PBKK, Series VI, Subseries 2, Box 13, Folder 8. Celler would lose a New York Democratic primary in the summer of 1972, and his replacement on the House Judiciary Committee, Peter Rodino, was less enthusiastic about pursuing future antitrust initiatives.

47. *Congressional Record—Senate*, December 8, 1971, S20872, PBKK, Series VI, Subseries 2, Box 13, Folder 8.

48. "Baseball's Big Spender," *TSN*, January 15, 1972, 14.

49. Shelby Coffey III, "Into Majors with $1,000?" *Washington Post*., n.d., 1, 8. See Robert Short file, National Baseball Hall of Library, Cooperstown, New York.

50. Steve West, "Joe Burke," in Steve West and Bill Nowlin, eds., *The Team That Couldn't Hit: The 1972 Texas Rangers* (Phoenix: Society for American Baseball Research, 2019), 299.

51. Bob Whelan and Steve West, "Bob Short," Society for American Baseball Research, sabr.org/bioproj/person/bob-short/. Viewed February 29, 2024.

52. E.J. Bavasi to Bowie Kuhn, November 13, 1972, PBKK, Series VI, Subseries 2, Box 14, Folder 1.

Chapter 6

1. John N. Ingham, "Managing Integration: Clemente, Wills, 'Harry the Hat,' and the Pittsburgh Pirates' 1967 Season of Discontent," *NINE: A Journal of Baseball History & Culture*, Vol. 21, No. 1 (Fall 2012), 85. See also Joe Morgan and David Falkner, *Joe Morgan: A Life in Baseball* (New York: W.W. Norton, 1993), 111–123.

2. Jerome Holtzman, "Two Divisions, Rules, Player Demands, Etc.," in Paul MacFarlane, ed., et al., *Official Baseball Guide for 1970* (St. Louis: The Sporting News, 1970), 275.

3. Jerome Holtzman, "Two Divisions, Rules, Player Demands, Etc.," in Paul MacFarlane, ed., et al., *Official Baseball Guide for 1970* (St. Louis: The Sporting News, 1970), 277.

4. Harrelson quoted in Holtzman, "Two Divisions, Rules, Player Demands, Etc.," in MacFarlane, ed., et al., *Official Baseball Guide for 1970*, 277.

5. Mark Armour, "1969—Reorganization Talk," in Steve Weingarten and Bill Nowlin, eds., *Baseball's Business: The Winter Meetings, Volume 2, 1958–2016* (Phoenix: Society for American Baseball Research, 2017), 70.

6. Howsam quoted in Smith, *Making the Big Red Machine*, 70.

7. Shore quoted in Rhodes and Erardi, *Big Red Dynasty*, 111.

8. Don Merry, "A Stud Becomes a Phillie Overnight," in Jim Enright, ed., *Trade Him! 100 Years of Baseball's Greatest Deals* (Chicago: Follett, 1976), 62.

9. Merry, "A Stud Becomes a Phillie Overnight," in Enright, *Trade Him!*, 63.

10. Edwin Shrake, "The Richest Bonus Baby Ever," *Sports Illustrated*, July 6, 1964.

11. Reichardt, Fregosi, and Phillips quoted in John Wiebusch, "Rick Fires Parting Shot: 'The Angels Can't Win," *TSN*, May 9, 1970, 7.

12. A description of the Johnson–Conigliaro affair can be found in Paul Hensler, "Alex Johnson and Tony Conigliaro: The California Angels' Star-Crossed Teammates," *Baseball Research Journal*, Vol. 52, No. 2 (Fall 2023) (Phoenix: Society for American Baseball Research).

13. Mark Armour, Alex Johnson biography, Society for American Baseball Research, https://sabr.org/bioproj/person/alex-johnson/. Viewed May 3, 2024. Emphasis added. This was the earliest manifestation of Johnson's troubling attitude at the Major League level.

14. Sam McDowell with Martin Gitlin,

The Saga of Sudden Sam: The Rise, Fall, and Redemption of Sam McDowell (Lanham, MD: Rowman & Littlefield, 2022), 73.

15. McDowell, *The Saga of Sudden Sam*, 79.

16. Paul quoted in Fred Eisenhammer and Jim Binkley, *Baseball's Most Memorable Trades: Superstars Swapped, All-Stars Copped and Megadeals That Flopped* (Jefferson, NC: McFarland, 1997), 162.

17. Ron Bergman, "Monday Had to Go; A's Staff Depleted," *TSN*, December 18, 1971, 50.

18. *1972 Chicago White Sox Media Guide*, 8.

19. Bing Devine with Tom Wheatley, *The Memoirs of Bing Devine: Stealing Lou Brock and Other Winning Moves by a Master GM* (Champaign, IL: Sports Publishing, 2004), 105.

20. Larry Claflin, "Red Sox End Speculation With Deal," *TSN*, October 23, 1971, 17.

21. Larry Claflin, "Spirit of '76—Another Revolution in Boston," in Paul MacFarlane, ed., et al., *Official Baseball Guide for 1972* (St. Louis: The Sporting News, 1972), 129, 131.

Chapter 7

1. Barely a decade in existence, the contest was pre-empted by "inter-league war benefit games ... [d]uring the three-day period originally set aside for the All-Star Game." Commissioner Happy Chandler conceded that since the interleague games had already been scheduled in the spring of 1945, special considerations would need to be put in place to hold a regular All-Star Game later in the year. *The Sporting News* announced AL and NL roster selections in tribute to those players who likely would have been named to their respective squads and encouraged fans to envision how a "might have been" game could have played out. See Ed McAuley, "Promotion Director Post Set Up by Major Leagues," *TSN*, May 3, 1945, 2; J.G. Taylor Spink, "Chandler to Lead as Well as Police Game," *TSN*, May 3, 1945, 2; and Frederick G. Lieb, "All-Star Teams Selected for 'Dream' Game," *TSN*, July 12, 1945, 1.

2. Bill Center, "Looking back at the 1957 All-Star Game," https://www.mlb.com/news/looking-back-at-the-1957-all-star-game-c163192510. Viewed June 3, 2024.

3. "Revision of All-Star Voting Essential," *TSN*, July 10, 1957, 12.

4. Kuhn, *Hardball*, 52.

5. Kuhn, *Hardball*, 53.

6. "All-Star Balloting Is Returned to Fans," *TSN*, March 28, 1970, 23.

7. Gillette advertisement, *TSN*, June 6, 1970, 13.

8. "Fans to Begin Balloting For the All-Star Teams," *TSN*, May 23, 1970, 37.

9. Price quoted in "Fans to Begin Balloting For the All-Star Teams," *TSN*, May 23, 1970, 37.

10. Wynn Montgomery, Rico Carty biography, Society for American Baseball Research, https://sabr.org/bioproj/person/rico-carty/. Viewed June 6, 2024.

11. Dr. Israel Mizrahy quoted in "Rico Solid All-Star Choice in Florida Hospital," *TSN*, June 20, 1970, 30.

12. Ralph Ray, "All-Star Ballots Are a Joke, Critics Sneer," *TSN*, May 30, 1970, 12.

13. Daniel I. Schlossberg, letter to "Voice of the Fan," *TSN*, June 20, 1970, 4.

14. Larry Claflin, "Kasko Sends Rico Back to Shortstop," *TSN*, June 27, 1970, 12.

15. Oscar Kahan, "Two Million Fans Vote in All-Star Poll," *TSN*, July 18, 1970, 7; Ed Wilks, "Poll Is Bowie's Beaut—Not Bowie's Boo-Boo!" *TSN*, July 18, 1970, 6.

16. Oscar Kahan, "Two Million Fans Vote in All-Star Poll," *TSN*, July 18, 1970, 7.

17. Kuhn, *Hardball*, 53.

18. *All-Star Game Facts Book*, 1982, PBKK, Series VI, Subseries 3, Box 14, Folder 6.

19. Holds folder for All-Star Game voting, PBKK, Series VIII, Box 2, Folder 20.

20. Bob Addie column, *TSN*, July 25, 1970, 19.

21. Ross Newhan column, *TSN*, July 10, 1971, 21.

22. Joe McGuff "Injuries Shake Up Hot-Cold Royals," *TSN*, July 12, 1971, 28.

23. "Major Flashes," *TSN*, July 12, 1971, 49.

24. "Old School Stuffs Ballot Box for Ted," *TSN*, June 26, 1971, 28.

25. Memo, Thomas H. Dawson to Bowie Kuhn, PBKK, Series VI, Subseries 1, Box 10, Folder 11.

26. Hal Middlesworth, Tom Mee, Bob Fishel, Tom Seeberg, *A Working Manual*

for World Series, League Championship, All-Star Game, n.d., 15; BA MSS229 MLB All-Star Week Collection, National Baseball Hall of Fame, Cooperstown, NY. Based on its references to the 1970 All-Star Game, this booklet was likely published in late 1970 or 1971 by the American League office.

27. Middlesworth, et al., *A Working Manual for World Series, League Championship, All-Star Game*, 15.

28. Middlesworth, et al., *A Working Manual for World Series, League Championship, All-Star Game*, 17; Dave Bohmer email to author, June 12, 2024.

29. Middlesworth, et al., *A Working Manual for World Series, League Championship, All-Star Game*, 20.

30. Middlesworth, et al., *A Working Manual for World Series, League Championship, All-Star Game*, 20.

31. Middlesworth, et al., *A Working Manual for World Series, League Championship, All-Star Game*, 21. Emphasis in original.

32. Middlesworth, et al., *A Working Manual for World Series, League Championship, All-Star Game*, 22.

33. Staff meeting notes, December 16, 1971, PBKK, Series VI, Subseries 1, Box 10, Folder 10.

34. *1970 American League All-Star Team, Facts and Figures*, July 14, 1970, BA MSS229 MLB All-Star Week Collection, National Baseball Hall of Fame, Cooperstown, NY.

35. "About the Cover," *1970 All-Star Game Program*, 1.

36. Stan Isle, "Vagabond Hickman—All-Star Hero," *TSN*, July 25, 1970, 5.

37. Rose quoted in Robert Obojski, *All-Star Baseball Since 1933* (New York: Stein and Day, 1980), 93.

38. David Vincent, Lyle Spatz, and David W. Smith, *The Midsummer Classic: The Complete History of Baseball's All-Star Game* (Lincoln: University of Nebraska Press, 2001), 258.

39. Joseph Wancho, Ray Fosse biography, Society for American Baseball Research, https://sabr.org/bioproj/person/ray-fosse/. Viewed June 12, 2024.

40. Bob Talbert, "Detroit and Its People," *1971 All-Star Game Program*, 13, 66.

41. Bob Talbert, "Detroit and Its People," *1971 All-Star Game Program*, 13, 67.

42. Ellis quoted in "Pipeline Full of Chit-Chat," *TSN*, July 31, 1971, 8.

43. Vincent, Spatz, and Smith, *The Midsummer Classic*, 265.

44. Jackson quoted in Lowell Reidenbaugh, "Blue, Frank Robinson Contrast in A.L. Victory," *TSN*, July 31, 1971, 3.

45. Dick Young column, *TSN*, July 31, 1971, 17.

46. "Three Players, One Exec, Enter Hall," MacFarlane, ed., et al., *Official Baseball Guide for 1970*, 362.

47. "Three Players, One Exec, Enter Hall," MacFarlane, ed., et al., *Official Baseball Guide for 1970*, 363.

48. Jack Lang, "Frick, Combs and Haines New Hall of Famers," *TSN*, February 14, 1970, 29.

49. Minutes of Annual Meeting of the Board of Directors, Baseball Hall of Fame, July 26, 1970, PBKK, Series VI, Subseries 5, Box 21, Folder 6.

50. Daniel R. Levitt, George Weiss biography, Society for American Baseball Research, https://sabr.org/bioproj/person/geroge-weiss/. Viewed June 21, 2024.

51. Bill James, *The Politics of Glory: How Baseball's Hall of Fame Really Works* (New York: Macmillan, 1994), 162.

52. James, *The Politics of Glory*, 163.

53. Larry Tye, *Satchel: The Life and Tines of an American Legend* (New York: Random House, 2009), 268.

54. Larry Tye, Satchel Paige biography, Society for American Baseball Research, https://sabr.org/bioproj/person/satchel-paige/. Viewed June 21, 2024.

55. Tye, Satchel Paige biography, Society for American Baseball Research. Viewed June 21, 2024.

56. Bill Johnson, Josh Gibson biography, Society for American Baseball Research, https://sabr.org/bioproj/person/josh-gibson/. Viewed June 21, 2024.

57. Ted Williams, Hall of Fame induction speech, July 25, 1966, courtesy of National Baseball Hall of Fame and Museum, Cooperstown, NY.

58. Travis Smith, "A Generic Synthesis of Major League Baseball's Hall of Fame Speeches (1962–2003)" (Master of Arts thesis, Kansas State University, 2005), 75.

59. Bill Nowlin, *Ted Williams: First Latino in the Baseball Hall of Fame* (Cambridge, MA: Rounder Books, 2018), 7.

60. Nowlin, *Ted Williams*, 178.

61. Williams quoted in Jim Prime and Bill Nowlin, *Ted Williams: The Pursuit of Perfection* (Chicago: Sports Publishing, 2002), 239.
62. Leigh Montville, *Ted Williams: The Biography of an American Hero* (New York: Doubleday, 2004), 262.
63. Kuhn, *Hardball*, 109.
64. Leonard Koppett, "Baseball's Bias Is Subtle, Disturbing," *TSN*, March 23, 1970, 4.
65. Kuhn, *Hardball*, 110.
66. Kuhn, *Hardball*, 110. Emphasis added.
67. Tye, *Satchel*, 269.
68. Paige quoted in Jack Lang, "'Proud to Be in It!' Beams Satchel After Earning Shrine Spot," *TSN*, February 20, 1971, 42; Tye, *Satchel*, 269.
69. Satchel Paige, Hall of Fame induction speech, August 9, 1971, courtesy of National Baseball Hall of Fame and Museum, Cooperstown, NY.
70. *1971 Cleveland Indians Yearbook*, 38.
71. Paige quoted in Tye, *Satchel*, 269–270.
72. Steven R. Greenes, *Negro Leaguers and the Hall of Fame: The Case for Inducting 24 Overlooked Ballplayers* (Jefferson, NC: McFarland, 2020), 9.
73. Robert Peterson, "Josh Gibson Was the Equal of Babe Ruth, But...," in *The New York Times Book of Baseball History* (New York: Quadrangle/New York Times Book Co., 1975), 298.
74. Sheldon Curry, *Tell Me Again Why These (Mostly) Black Players Are Not in the Hall of Fame? Is It Racial?????* (Los Angeles: The Curry Pages, 2021), 314.
75. Greenes, *Negro Leaguers and the Hall of Fame*, 17.

Chapter 8

1. James Lincoln Ray, "Shibe Park / Connie Mack Stadium," Society for American Baseball Research, https://sabr.org/bioproj/park/connie-mack-stadium-philadelphia/. Viewed July 7, 2024.
2. James Lincoln Ray, "Shibe Park / Connie Mack Stadium," Society for American Baseball Research, https://sabr.org/bioproj/park/connie-mack-stadium-philadelphia/. Viewed July 7, 2024.
3. Bob Ryan, "Sweet Memories to Chew On," *Boston Globe*, June 14, 2009.
4. Bob Ryan, "Sweet Memories to Chew On," *Boston Globe*, June 14, 2009.
5. James Lincoln Ray, "Shibe Park / Connie Mack Stadium," Society for American Baseball Research, https://sabr.org/bioproj/park/connie-mack-stadium-philadelphia/. Viewed July 8, 2024.
6. Frank Brookhouser, "It's the Last Hurrah for Connie Mack Stadium," *Philadelphia Evening Bulletin*, September 21, 1969.
7. Philip J. Lowry, *Green Cathedrals: The Ultimate Collection of All 271 Major League and Negro League Ballparks and Present* (Reading, MA: Addison-Wesley, Inc., 1992), 211; James Lincoln Ray, "Shibe Park / Connie Mack Stadium," Society for American Baseball Research, https://sabr.org/bioproj/park/connie-mack-stadium-philadelphia/. Viewed July 8, 2024.
8. Lowry, *Green Cathedrals*, 212.
9. Bob Ryan, "Sweet Memories to Chew On," *Boston Globe*, June 14, 2009.
10. Doug Skipper, Connie Mack biography, Society for American Baseball Research, https://sabr.org/bioproj/person/-connie-mack/. Viewed July 12, 2024.
11. Doug Skipper, Connie Mack biography, Society for American Baseball Research, https://sabr.org/bioproj/person/-connie-mack/. Viewed July 12, 2024.
12. Rich Westcott, *Shibe Park—Connie Mack Stadium* (Charleston, SC: Arcadia, 2012), 105.
13. Bruce Kuklick, *To Every Thing a Season: Shibe Park and Urban Philadelphia, 1909–1976* (Princeton: Princeton University Press, 1991), 179.
14. *1971 Philadelphia Phillies Media Guide*, 8.
15. Westcott, *Shibe Park—Connie Mack Stadium*, 105.
16. Lucchesi quoted in Ross Newhan column, *TSN*, June 19, 1971, 32.
17. Frank Dolson, "Ball Park Cops Are Heroes, Too," *Philadelphia Inquirer*, October 2, 1970, 27.
18. John Dell, "It's 'Just Old Building' to Amos," *Philadelphia Inquirer*, October 1, 1970, 19, 21.
19. Kuklick, *To Every Thing a Season*, 180. Jerry Wolman, owner of the Eagles who had purchased the stadium in 1964, had the idea of selling off pieces of the ballpark, but this was not to happen.

20. Kuklick, *To Every Thing a Season*, 180.
21. "Phillies List Prize Winners," newspaper clipping, October 1970, in Connie Mack Stadium folder, A. Bartlett Giamatti Center, National Baseball Hall of Fame and Museum. The caption heading states, "Drawing for What Was Left."
22. Kuklick, *To Every Thing a Season*, 183.
23. "Old Stadium Hot Philadelphia Spot," AP story, August 21, 1971, in Connie Mack Stadium folder, A. Bartlett Giamatti Center, National Baseball Hall of Fame and Museum.
24. Ray W. Kelly, "Connie Mack Stadium," *Courier-Post* (Camden, New Jersey), June 22, 1974, 3, 5.
25. Ray W. Kelly, "Connie Mack Stadium," *Courier-Post* (Camden, New Jersey), June 22, 1974, 7.
26. Robert Trumpbour, "Forbes Field: Ahead of Its Time in 1909," *The National Pastime: Steel City Stories* (Phoenix: SABR Publications), https://sabr.org/journal/article/forbes-field-ahead-of-its-time-in-1909/. Viewed July 22, 2024.
27. Donald Lancaster, "Forbes Field: Construction and Opening Day," n.d., 1, in Forbes Field folder, A. Bartlett Giamatti Center, National Baseball Hall of Fame and Museum.
28. Lancaster, "Forbes Field: Construction and Opening Day," 3; Trumpbour, "Forbes Field: Ahead of Its Time in 1909."
29. This account is from Lancaster, "Forbes Field: Construction and Opening Day."
30. Lowry, *Green Cathedrals*, 217; Lancaster, "Forbes Field: Construction and Opening Day."
31. Lancaster, "Forbes Field: Construction and Opening Day."
32. Trumpbour, "Forbes Field: Ahead of Its Time in 1909."
33. Lancaster, "Forbes Field: Construction and Opening Day."
34. Distance data, incredibly varied, was derived from Lowry, *Green Cathedrals*, 216–217, and *1970 Pittsburgh Pirates Media Guide*, 11.
35. Daniel L. Bonk, "Ballpark Figures: The Story of Forbes Field," *Pittsburgh History*, Summer 1993, 66.
36. Bonk, "Ballpark Figures: The Story of Forbes Field," 66.
37. Andy McCue, Branch Rickey biography, Society for American Baseball Research, https://sabr.org/bioproj/person/branch-rickey/. Viewed July 22, 2024.
38. Bonk, "Ballpark Figures: The Story of Forbes Field," 67.
39. *1969 Pittsburgh Pirates Media Guide*, cover.
40. Nellie King quoted in David Cicotello and Angelo J. Louisa, eds., *Forbes Field: Essays and Memories of the Pirates' Historic Ballpark, 1909–1971* (Jefferson, NC: McFarland, 2007), 118.
41. Paul Ferrante, "Forbes Field," *Sports Collectors Digest*, June 25, 1999, 120.
42. Paul Ferrante, "Forbes Field," *Sports Collectors Digest*, June 25, 1999, 120.
43. Paul Ferrante, "Forbes Field," *Sports Collectors Digest*, June 25, 1999, 120.
44. Phil Musick, "Human Locusts Have Their Day," n.d., in Forbes Field folder, A. Bartlett Giamatti Center, National Baseball Hall of Fame and Museum. The column is likely from the *Pittsburgh Press* of June 29, 1970.
45. Musick, "Human Locusts Have Their Day."
46. Musick, "Human Locusts Have Their Day."
47. Paul Ferrante, "Forbes Field," *Sports Collectors Digest*, June 25, 1999, 121.
48. Bob Hoover, "Back, back, back … The Wall the Dedication ceremony," *Pittsburgh Post-Gazette*, July 6, 2006.
49. Bob Hoover, "Back, back, back … The Wall the Dedication ceremony.".
50. Pat Harmon, "Dawn of a New Era," *1970 Cincinnati Reds Yearbook*, 4.
51. Lon Garber, "Crosley Field," in Gregory H. Wolf, ed., *Cincinnati's Crosley Field: A Gem in the Queen City* (Phoenix: Society for American Baseball Research, 2018), 8.
52. Lon Garber, "Crosley Field," 9.
53. Charles F. Faber, Powel Crosley, Jr., biography, Society for American Baseball Research, https://sabr.org/bioproj/person/powel-crosley-jr/. Viewed July 5, 2024.
54. Lowry, *Green Cathedrals*, 138–139.
55. Lon Garber, "Crosley Field," 12.
56. Gene Mack cartoon, *1970 Cincinnati Reds Yearbook*, 5.
57. Lon Garber, "Crosley Field," 12.
58. Lon Garber, "Crosley Field," 12.
59. Earl Lawson, "Glass Backstop Makes Big Hit With Crosley Field Spectators," *TSN*, May 15, 1965, 9.

60. See notes in *TSN*, April 2, 1966, 25 and October 8, 1966, 49.
61. Pat Harmon, "Dawn of a New Era," *1970 Cincinnati Reds Yearbook*, 5.
62. Denny Dressman, "A List of Lasts For Crosley Field," *Cincinnati Enquirer*, June 25, 1970.
63. Pat Harmon, "Goodby to the old… and hello to the new," *Cincinnati Post*, June 25, 1970; Graydon DeCamp, "Memories," *Cincinnati Post*, June 30, 1970, 26.
64. Pat Harmon, "Goodby to the old … and hello to the new," *Cincinnati Post*, June 25, 1970.
65. Graydon DeCamp, "Memories," *Cincinnati Post*, June 30, 1970, 27.
66. Smith, *Making the Big Red Machine*, 96.
67. Paul Goldberger, *Ballpark: Baseball in the American City* (New York: Alfred A. Knopf, 2019), 181.
68. Pat Harmon, "Dawn of a New Era," *1970 Cincinnati Reds Yearbook*, 5.

Chapter 9

1. "A Divided Decade: The '60s," *Life*, December 26, 1969, 8.
2. William Manchester, *The Glory and the Dream: A Narrative History of America, 1932–1972* (New York: Bantam Books, 1973), 1208, 1209. April 1970 had quite an ebb and flow of major events: *Midnight Cowboy* won Best Picture at the 42nd Academy Awards ceremony, even though it initially drew an X-rating from the Motion Picture Association of America; The Beatles, the supergroup that had become riddled with strife, broke up; the ill-fated *Apollo 13* mission occurred (and had a dramatic but successful conclusion); and the inaugural Earth Day was held to begin an era of environmental awareness.
3. Manchester, *The Glory and the Dream*, 1211.
4. James A. Michener, "Kent, Ohio: May 1970," from *Kent State: What Happened and Why* in *Reporting Vietnam, Part Two: American Journalism, 1969–1975* (New York: The Library of America, 1998), 57.
5. Michener, "Kent, Ohio: May 1970," in *Reporting Vietnam*, 58.
6. Michener, "Kent, Ohio: May 1970," in *Reporting Vietnam*, 65, 66.
7. Michener, "Kent, Ohio: May 1970," in *Reporting Vietnam*, 70.
8. Manchester, *The Glory and the Dream*, 1211.
9. Charlie Bevis, "Vietnam-War Military Duty and Baseball," https://bevisbaseballresearch.wordpress.com/-research-archive/vietnam-war-military-duty-and-baseball/. Viewed August 18, 2024. Bevis cites "a confusing array of statistics about the number of Major-League ballplayers who served in the military during the Vietnam War," which ranged from 54 to 117. Regardless, when either figure is placed against the 8.6 million who served over the course of the war, the percentage is still minuscule.
10. Greg Prince, "A Trade Beyond Belief," faithandfearinflushing.com, September 8, 2020. Viewed August 17, 2024.
11. Quotes from McGraw and Hodges in this section are from Clavin and Peary, *Gil Hodges*, 352.
12. Swoboda quoted in Clavin and Peary, *Gil Hodges*, 351.
13. Philip Bashe, *Dog Days: The New York Yankees Fall From Grace and Return to Glory, 1964-1976* (New York: Random House, 1994), 188.
14. Levy, *Walter Alston*, 169.
15. Levy, *Walter Alston*, 169.
16. Mitchell Nathanson, *God Almighty Hisself: The Life and Legacy of Dick Allen* (Philadelphia: University of Pennsylvania Press, 2016), 206.
17. Goose Gossage, "City Rivals," *Memories and Dreams*, Vol. 44, No.5 (Fall 2022), 48.
18. Minutes of Executive Council Meeting, March 5, 1971, PBKK, Series I, Subseries 1, Box 1, Folder 3.
19. Kuhn, *Hardball*, 42.
20. Quotes in this section are from "Rap, Part II," *Black Sports*, July 1971, 32, 35, 51.
21. Burke quoted in "Rap, Part II," *Black Sports*, July 1971, 35, 51.
22. Arna Desser, James Monks, Michael Robinson, "Discrimination in Baseball Hall of Fame Voting," February 1997, Mount Holyoke College, Department of Economics, 7.
23. Torben Andersen, Ph.D., *Race Discrimination by Major League Baseball Fans* (Ann Arbor: UMI Dissertation Information Service, 1988), 302.

24. Mark Armour and Daniel R. Levitt, "Baseball Demographics, 1947–2016," Society for American Baseball Research, https://sabr.org/bioproj/topic/baseball-demographics-1947-2016/, viewed August 22, 2024; David Downey, "Why Does Major League Baseball Have So Few Black Players?" *Los Angeles Daily News*, April 17, 2024.
25. Paul Geisler, Jr., Dock Ellis biography, Society for American Baseball Research, sabr.org/bioproj/person/dock-ellis/. Viewed August 18, 2024.
26. Geisler, Jr., "Dock Ellis."
27. Jerome Holtzman column, *TSN*, June 20, 1970, 13.
28. "Ellis' Disease Nonfatal Form," Associated Press article, August 18, 1971, Dock Ellis folder, National Baseball Hall of Fame Library.
29. "Ellis Raps Pirates' Management," *Record American* (Boston), October 5, 1971, 39.
30. John N. Ingham, "Managing Integration: Clemente, Wills, 'Harry the Hat,' and the Pittsburgh Pirates' 1967 Season of Discontent," *NINE: A Journal of Baseball History & Culture*, Vol. 21, No. 1 (Fall 2012), 70.
31. Ingham, "Managing Integration," 81–82.
32. Bill White with Gordon Dillow, *Uppity: My Untold Story About the Games People Play* (New York: Grand Central, 2011), 64.
33. Joe Morgan and David Falkner, *Joe Morgan: A Life in Baseball* (New York: W.W. Norton, 1993), 113.
34. Morgan and Falkner, *Joe Morgan*, 115.
35. Morgan and Falkner, *Joe Morgan*, 121.
36. Morgan and Falkner, *Joe Morgan*, 123.
37. Sanguillen quoted in Hroncich, *The Whistling Irishman*, 178.
38. Bruce Markusen, *The Team That Changed Baseball: Roberto Clemente and the 1971 Pittsburgh Pirates* (Yardley, PA: Westholme, 2006), 12.
39. Blass quoted in Hroncich, *The Whistling Irishman*, 178.
40. James T. Patterson, *Grand Expectations: The United States, 1945–1974* (New York: Oxford University Press, 1996), 669.
41. Patterson, *Grand Expectations*, 710.
42. Nathaniel Moore, "Don't Trust Anyone Over the Age of 30," Youth Empowerment and Community Archives, https://www.freedomarchives.org/Documents/Finder/FreedomArchives.DontTrustAnyoneOver30.article.pdf. Viewed August 23, 2024.
43. "Baseball's Drug Education and Prevention Program," PBKK, Series II, Subseries 3, Box 8, Folder 8.
44. "Baseball's Drug Education and Prevention Program," PBKK, Series II, Subseries 3, Box 8, Folder 8. Emphasis added.
45. "Baseball's Drug Education and Prevention Program," Notice No. 12, April 5, 1971, PBKK, Series II, Subseries 3, Box 8, Folder 8.
46. Kuhn, *Hardball*, 304.
47. Mark Celender, "Dock Ellis Helping Drug Abusers Get Straight," *USA Today*, September 5, 1985.
48. Patterson, *Grand Expectations*, 36.
49. Patterson, *Grand Expectations*, 462.
50. Chris Schauble, "Sweepy-Time Girl," *1970 Baltimore Orioles World Series Program*, 87. Quotes in this section are from the same article.
51. "Time out to eat ... You can't beat the Orioles ... Even in the kitchen," *1971 Baltimore Orioles Yearbook*, 35–36.
52. Burke quoted in David Merrick, "Odd Couple," *Jock*, February 1970, 78.
53. *1970 Cleveland Indians Yearbook*.
54. Picture caption of Nancy Faust, *TSN*, May 23, 1970, 37.
55. Conigliaro quoted in Bill Libby, "Can Tony Conigliaro Keep His Mind On Baseball?" *Sport Scene*, September 1971, 35.
56. Libby, "Can Tony Conigliaro Keep His Mind On Baseball?" 38, 35. The "rookie year" quote does not exactly square with an account told to the author by a former employee at a renowned Boston nightclub. Lucifer's was lauded as the best club in the city and attracted a lively clientele of locals and out-of-towners such as ballplayers and airline stewardesses. John Dahle was a bouncer who witnessed Conigliaro, barely of legal drinking age, interacting with some of the women there, claiming that the Red Sox star was "like a babe in the woods" rather than the rake the player later claimed to be. Author conversation with John Dahle, April 9, 2023.

57. Conigliaro quoted in Libby, "Can Tony Conigliaro Keep His Mind On Baseball?" 36.

58. Libby, "Can Tony Conigliaro Keep His Mind On Baseball?" 80.

59. "Conigliaros in Uproar—Tony Quits, Billy Fumes," *TSN*, July 24, 1971, 35.

60. "The Mary Tyler Moore Show," Television Academy Foundation: The Interviews, https://interviews.televisionacademy.com/shows/mary-tyler-moore-show-the. Viewed August 27, 2024.

61. Wuman Textile, "History of Polyester Fabric," https://www.linkedin.com/pulse/history-polyester-fabric-wuman-textile-pl8yf/, May 27, 2024. Viewed August 28, 2024.

62. "Penn Selects AstroTurf—Ready in Fall," *TSN*, May 3, 1969, 56.

63. Ross Newhan column, *TSN*, May 15, 1971, 18.

64. Marc Okkonen, *Baseball Uniforms of the 20th Century: The Official Major League Guide* (New York: Sterling, 1991), 1.

65. Susan McCarthy, "Uniforms of the 1970s," in Bill James, *The New Bill James Historical Baseball Abstract* (New York: The Free Press, 2001), 293.

66. "The New Look of the Phillies," *1970 Philadelphia Phillies Yearbook*, 54.

67. Elizabeth K. Martin, "The Development of Baseball Umpires' Uniforms, 1846–1996," Master of Science thesis, University of Rhode Island, 1997, 4.

68. Howsam quoted in Earl Lawson, "Skeptics Silent As Cincy Park Opens on Time," *TSN*, July 18, 1970, 46.

69. Martin, "The Development of Baseball Umpires' Uniforms, 1846–1996," 39.

70. "All-Star Items," *TSN*, July 25, 1970, 8.

71. Trudeau quoted in "M*A*S*H—The Movie That Spoke Truth to War," The Attic, www.theattic.space/home-page-blogs/2020/2/8/test-draft. Viewed August 30, 2024.

72. David Paul Kuhn, *The Hardhat Riot: Nixon, New York City, and the Dawn of the White Working-Class Revolution* (New York: Oxford University Press, 2020), 135.

73. Patterson, *Grand Expectations*, 757.

74. R.W. Apple, Jr., "25 Years Later: Lessons From the Pentagon Papers," *New York Times*, June 23, 1996, Section 4, 5.

75. Summary of Commissioner's Meeting, August 3, 1971, PBKK, Series I, Subseries 1, Box 1, Folder 4.

76. End-flap comments, Doris Townsend, ed., *This Great Game* (New York: Rutledge Books, 1971).

Bibliography

Abbreviations

PBKK   Papers of Bowie K. Kuhn, BA MSS 100, National Baseball Hall of Fame and Museum, Cooperstown, NY.
TSN   *The Sporting News*

Special Collections

Harry Dalton collection, BA MSS 40, National Baseball Hall of Fame and Museum, Cooperstown, NY.
Bill Gallo cartoons, BA MSS 26, National Baseball Hall of Fame, Cooperstown, NY.
Bowie Kuhn collection, BA MSS 100, National Baseball Hall of Fame and Museum, Cooperstown, NY.
MLB All-Star Week collection, BA MSS 229, National Baseball Hall of Fame, Cooperstown, NY.
MLB All-Star ballots, BA MSS 231, National Baseball Hall of Fame, Cooperstown, NY.

Special Works

Andersen, Torben, *Race Discrimination by Major League Baseball Fans*. Ann Arbor: UMI Dissertation Information Service, 1988.
Desser, Arna, James Monks, and Michael Robinson, "Discrimination in Baseball Hall of Fame Voting," February 1997, Mount Holyoke College, Department of Economics.
Martin, Elizabeth K. "The Development of Baseball Umpires' Uniforms, 1846–1996," Master of Science thesis, University of Rhode Island, 1997.
Smith, Travis. "A Generic Synthesis of Major League Baseball's Hall of Fame Speeches (1962–2003)." Master of Arts thesis, Kansas State University, 2005.

Books

Amoruso, Marino. *Gil Hodges: The Quiet Man*. Middlebury, VT: Paul S. Eriksson, 1991.
Anderson, Sparky, and Dan Ewald. *Sparky!* New York: Prentice-Hall, 1990.
Anderson, Sparky, and Dan Ewald. *They Call Me Sparky*. Chelsea, MI: Sleeping Bear Press, 1998.
Anderson, Sparky, and Si Burick. *The Main Spark: Sparky Anderson and the Cincinnati Reds*. Garden City, NY: Doubleday & Company, 1978.
The Baseball Encyclopedia, 9th Edition. New York: Macmillan, 1993.
Bashe, Philip. *Dog Days: The New York Yankees Fall From Grace and Return to Glory, 1964–1976*. New York: Random House, 1994.
Bouton, Jim. *Ball Four*, Twentieth Anniversary Edition. New York: Wiley, 1990.
Bouton, Jim. *I'm Glad You Didn't Take It Personally*. Edited by Leonard Shecter. New York: William Morrow, 1971.
Bradlee, Ben, Jr. *The Kid: The Immortal Life of Ted Williams*. New York: Little, Brown, , 2013.
Cash, Jon David. *Boom and Bust in St. Louis: A Cardinals History, 1885 to the Present*. Jefferson, NC: McFarland, 2017.
Center, Bill. *Padres Essential: Everything You Need to Know to Be a Real Fan!* Chicago: Triumph Books, 2007.
Cicotello, David, and Angelo J. Louisa, eds. *Forbes Field: Essays and Memories of the Pirates' Historic Ballpark,*

1909–1971. Jefferson, NC: McFarland, 2007.

Claire, Fred. *Fred Claire: My 30 Years in Dodger Blue.* Champaign, IL: Sports Publishing, 2004.

Clark, Tom. *Champagne and Baloney: The Rise and Fall of Finley's A's.* New York: Harper & Row, 1976.

Clavin, Tom, and Danny Peary. *Gil Hodges: The Brooklyn Bums, the Miracle Mets, and the Extraordinary Life of a Baseball Legend.* New York: New American Library, 2012.

Coffey, Wayne R. *They Said It Couldn't Be Done: The '69 Mets, New York City, and the Most Astounding Season in Baseball History.* New York: Crown Archetype, 2019.

Cook, William A. *Gabe Paul: The Long Road to the Bronx Zoo.* Mechanicsburg, PA: Sunbury Press, 2022.

Corbett, Warren. *The Wizard of Waxahachie: Paul Richards and the End of Baseball as We Knew It.* Dallas: Southern Methodist University Press, 2009.

Corcoran, Dennis. *Induction Day at Cooperstown: A History of the Baseball Hall of Fame Ceremony.* Jefferson, NC: McFarland, 2011.

Curry, Sheldon. *Tell Me Again Why These (Mostly) Black Players Are Not in the Hall of Fame? Is It Racial?????* Los Angeles: The Curry Pages, 2021.

Devaney, John. *Gil Hodges: Baseball Miracle Man.* New York: G.P. Putnam's Sons, 1973.

Devine, Bing, with Tom Wheatley. *The Memoirs of Bing Devine: Stealing Lou Brock and Other Winning Moves by a Master GM.* Champaign, IL: Sports Publishing, 2004.

Dickson, Paul. *The Dickson Baseball Dictionary.* New York: Facts on File, 1989.

Edmonds, Ed, and Frank Houdek. *Baseball Meets the Law.* Jefferson, NC: McFarland, 2017.

Eisenberg, John. *From 33rd Street to Camden Yards: An Oral History of the Baltimore Orioles.* Chicago: Contemporary Books, 2001.

Eisenhammer, Fred, and Jim Binkley. *Baseball's Most Memorable Trades: Superstars Swapped, All-Stars Copped and Megadeals That Flopped.* Jefferson, NC: McFarland, 1997.

Enright, Jim, ed. *Trade Him! 100 Years of Baseball's Greatest Deals.* Chicago: Follett, 1976.

Flood, Curt, and Richard Carter. *The Way It Is.* New York: Trident Press, 1971.

Gallagher, Danny, and Bill Young. *Remembering the Montreal Expos.* Toronto: Scoop Press, 2005.

Goldberger, Paul. *Ballpark: Baseball in the American City.* New York: Alfred A. Knopf, 2019.

Golenbock, Peter, *Wild, High, and Tight: The Life and Death of Billy Martin.* New York: St. Martin's Press, 1994.

Greenes, Steven R. *Negro Leaguers and the Hall of Fame: The Case for Inducting 24 Overlooked Ballplayers.* Jefferson, NC: McFarland, 2020.

Hawkins, Jim. *Al Kaline: The Biography of a Tigers Icon.* Chicago: Triumph Books, 2010.

Helyar, John. *Lords of the Realm: The Real History of Baseball.* New York: Ballantine, 1994.

Hensler, Paul. *The New Boys of Summer: Baseball's Radical Transformation in the Late Sixties.* Lanham, MD: Rowman & Littlefield, 2017.

Horton, Willie, and Kevin Allen. *23: Detroit's Own Willie the Wonder, the Tigers' First Black Great.* Chicago: Triumph Books, 2022.

Hroncich, Colleen. *The Whistling Irishman: Danny Murtaugh Remembered.* Philadelphia: Sports Challenge Network, 2010.

James, Bill. *The New Bill James Historical Baseball Abstract.* New York: The Free Press, 2001.

James, Bill. *The Politics of Glory: How Baseball's Hall of Fame Really Works.* New York: Macmillan, 1994.

Kluck, Lee C. *Leave While the Party's Good: The Life and Legacy of Baseball Executive Harry Dalton.* Lincoln: University of Nebraska Press, 2024.

Kubik, Richard S. *Baseball Trades and Acquisitions, 1950–1979.* Smithtown, NY: Exposition Press, 1981.

Kuhn, Bowie. *Hardball: The Education of a Baseball Commissioner.* New York: Times Books, 1987.

Kuhn, David Paul. *The Hardhat Riot: Nixon, New York City, and the Dawn of the White Working-Class Revolution.* New York: Oxford University Press, 2020.

Kuklick, Bruce. *To Every Thing a Season: Shibe Park and Urban Philadelphia, 1909–1976.* Princeton: Princeton University Press, 1991.

Levy, Alan H. *Walter Alston: The Rise of a Manager from the Minors to the Baseball Hall of Fame.* Jefferson, NC: McFarland, 2021.

Libby, Bill, and Vida Blue. *Vida: His Own Story.* Englewood Cliffs, NJ: Prentice-Hall, 1972.

Lowry, Philip J. *Green Cathedrals: The Ultimate Collection of All 271 Major League and Negro League Ballparks and Present.* Reading, MA: Addison-Wesley, 1992.

MacFarlane, Paul, ed., et al. *Official Baseball Guide for 1970.* St. Louis: The Sporting News, 1970.

MacFarlane, Paul, ed., et al. *Official Baseball Guide for 1971.* St. Louis: The Sporting News, 1971.

MacFarlane, Paul, ed., et al. *Official Baseball Guide for 1972.* St. Louis: The Sporting News, 1972.

MacPhail, Lee. *My 9 Innings: An Autobiography of 50 Years in Baseball.* Westport, CT: Meckler Books, 1989.

Manchester, William. *The Glory and the Dream: A Narrative History of America, 1932–1972.* New York: Bantam Books, 1973.

Marcin, Joe, et al, ed. *Official Baseball Guide for 1973.* St. Louis: The Sporting News, 1973.

Markusen, Bruce. *A Baseball Dynasty: Charlie Finley's Swingin' A's.* Haworth, NJ: St. Johann Press, 2002.

Markusen, Bruce. *The Team That Changed Baseball: Roberto Clemente and the 1971 Pittsburgh Pirates.* Yardley, PA: Westholme, 2006.

Masters, Todd. *The 1972 Detroit Tigers: Billy Martin and the Half-Game Champs.* Jefferson, NC: McFarland, 2010.

McCue, Andy. *Stumbling Around the Bases: The American League's Mismanagement in the Expansion Eras.* Lincoln: University of Nebraska Press, 2022.

McDowell, Sam, with Martin Gitlin. *The Saga of Sudden Sam: The Rise, Fall, and Redemption of Sam McDowell.* Lanham, MD: Rowman & Littlefield, 2022.

McLain, Denny, and Eli Zaret. *I Told You I Wasn't Perfect.* Chicago: Triumph Books, 2007.

Michelson, Herbert. *Charlie O: Charles Oscar Finley vs. the Baseball Establishment.* Indianapolis: Bobbs-Merrill, 1975.

Miller, Marvin. *A Whole Different Ball Game: The Sport and Business of Baseball.* New York: Birch Lane Press, 1991.

Montville, Leigh. *Ted Williams: The Biography of an American Hero.* New York: Doubleday, 2004.

Morgan, Anne. *Prescription for Success: The Life and Values of Ewing Marion Kauffman.* Kansas City: Andrews and McMeel, 1995.

Morgan, Joe, and David Falkner. *Joe Morgan: A Life in Baseball.* New York: W.W. Norton, 1993.

Mullins, William H. *Becoming Big League: Seattle, the Pilots, and Stadium Politics.* Seattle: University of Washington Press, 2013.

Nathanson, Mitchell. *Bouton: The Life of a Baseball Original.* Lincoln: University of Nebraska Press, 2020.

Nathanson, Mitchell. *God Almighty Hisself: The Life and Legacy of Dick Allen.* Philadelphia: University of Pennsylvania Press, 2016.

The New York Times Book of Baseball History. New York: Quadrangle/New York Times Book Co., 1975.

Nowlin, Bill. *Ted Williams: First Latino in the Baseball Hall of Fame.* Cambridge, MA: Rounder Books, 2018.

Nowlin, Bill. *Tom Yawkey: Patriarch of the Boston Red Sox.* Lincoln: University of Nebraska Press, 2018.

Obojski, Robert. *All-Star Baseball Since 1933.* New York: Stein and Day, 1980.

Okkonen, Marc. *Baseball Uniforms of the 20th Century: The Official Major League Guide.* New York: Sterling, 1991.

Panzenhagen, Tom, and Barry Forbis, eds. *Sparky Anderson: The Life of a Baseball Legend.* Chicago: Triumph Books, 2010.

Patterson, James T. *Grand Expectations: The United States, 1945–1974.* New York: Oxford University Press, 1996.

Peterson, John E. *The Kansas City Athletics: A Baseball History, 1954–1967.* Jefferson, NC: McFarland, 2003.

Pluto, Terry. *The Earl of Baltimore: The Story of Earl Weaver, Baltimore Orioles Manager.* Piscataway, NJ: New Century Publishers, 1982.

Prime, Jim, and Bill Nowlin. *Ted Williams:*

The Pursuit of Perfection. Chicago: Sports Publishing, 2002.

Rapoport, Ron. *Let's Play Two: The Legend of Mr. Cub, The Life of Ernie Banks*. New York: Hachette Books, 2019.

Reichler, Joseph. *The Baseball Trade Register*. New York: Macmillan, 1984.

Reporting Vietnam, Part Two: American Journalism, 1969–1975. New York: The Library of America, 1998.

Rhodes, Gregory L., and John G. Erardi. *Big Red Dynasty: How Bob Howsam & Sparky Anderson Built the Big Red Machine*. Cincinnati: Road West, 1997.

Roewe, Chris, and Paul MacFarlane, eds. *Official Baseball Guide for 1969*. St. Louis: The Sporting News, 1969.

Simpson, Allan, ed. *The Baseball Draft: The First 25 Years*. Durham, NC: American Sports Publishing, Inc., 1990.

Smith, Daryl. *Making the Big Red Machine: Bob Howsam and the Cincinnati Reds of the 1970s*. Jefferson, NC: McFarland, 2009.

Snyder, Brad. *A Well-Paid Slave: Curt Flood's Fight for Free Agency in Professional Sports*. New York: Plume, 2007.

Townsend, Doris, ed. *This Great Game*. New York: Rutledge Books, 1971.

Tye, Larry. *Satchel: The Life and Tines of an American Legend*. New York: Random House, 2009.

Vanderberg, Bob. *Frantic Frank Lane: Baseball's Ultimate Wheeler-Dealer*. Jefferson, NC: McFarland, 2013.

Van Riper, Tom. *Cincinnati Red and Dodger Blue: Baseball's Greatest Forgotten Rivalry*. Lanham, MD: Rowman & Littlefield, 2017.

Vecsey, George. *Joy in Mudville: Being a Complete Account of the Unparalleled History of the New York Mets from Their Most Perturbed Beginnings to Their Rise to Glory and Renown*. New York: McCall, 1970.

Vincent, David, Lyle Spatz, and David W. Smith. *The Midsummer Classic: The Complete History of Baseball's All-Star Game*. Lincoln: University of Nebraska Press, 2001.

Weaver, Earl, with Berry Stainback. *It's What You Learn After You Know It All That Counts*. New York: Fireside Books, 1983.

Weingarten, Steve, and Bill Nowlin, eds. *Baseball's Business: The Winter Meetings, Volume 2, 1958–2016*. Phoenix: Society for American Baseball Research, 2017.

West, Steve, and Bill Nowlin, eds. *The Team That Couldn't Hit: The 1972 Texas Rangers*. Phoenix: Society for American Baseball Research, 2019.

Westcott, Rich. *Shibe Park—Connie Mack Stadium*. Charleston, SC: Arcadia, 2012.

White, Bill, with Gordon Dillow. *Uppity: My Untold Story About the Games People Play*. New York: Grand Central, 2011.

Williams, Dick, with Bill Plaschke. *No More Mr. Nice Guy: A Life of Hardball*. New York: Harcourt Brace Jovanovich, 1990.

Wirz, Bob. *The Passion of Baseball: A Journey to the Commissioner's Office of Major League Baseball*. Autryville, NC: Ravenswood Publishing, 2016.

Wolf, Gregory H., ed. *Cincinnati's Crosley Field: A Gem in the Queen City*. Phoenix: Society for American Baseball Research, 2018.

Zachter, Mort. *Gil Hodges: A Hall of Fame Life*. Lincoln: University of Nebraska Press, 2015.

Publications

AARP Bulletin
Black Sports
Boston Globe
Cincinnati Post
Cincinnati Post and Times Star
Courier-Post (Camden, New Jersey)
Detroit Free Press
Evening Star (Washington, D.C.)
Jock
Life
Los Angeles Daily News
Memories and Dreams
New York Daily News
New York Post
New York Times
Newark Star-Ledger
NINE: A Journal of Baseball History & Culture
Philadelphia Evening Bulletin
Philadelphia Inquirer
Pittsburgh History
Pittsburgh Post-Gazette
Pittsburgh Press
Record American (Boston)
Sport Scene
The Sporting News
Sports Collectors Digest

Sports Illustrated
USA Today
Washington Post
Washington Star

Baseball and Team Publications

1970 All-Star Game Program
1971 All-Star Game Program
1970 American League All-Star Team, Facts and Figures
1970 Baltimore Orioles World Series Program
1971 Baltimore Orioles Media Guide
1971 Baltimore Orioles Yearbook
1970 Cleveland Indians Yearbook
1971 Cleveland Indians Yearbook
1972 Chicago White Sox Media Guide
1971 Cincinnati Reds Media Guide
1970 Cincinnati Reds Yearbook
1971 Detroit Tigers Media Guide
1971 Detroit Tigers Yearbook
1971 Kansas City Royals Media Guide
1970 Kansas City Royals Yearbook
1971 Kansas City Royals Yearbook
1971 Los Angeles Dodgers Media Guide
1971 Los Angeles Dodgers Yearbook
1970 Milwaukee Brewers Yearbook
1970 Montreal Expos Yearbook
1971 Montreal Expos Yearbook
1970 New York Mets Media Guide
1971 New York Yankee Media Guide
1971 New York Yankee Yearbook
1970 Philadelphia Phillies Media Guide
1970 Philadelphia Phillies Yearbook
1971 Philadelphia Phillies Media Guide
1969 Pittsburgh Pirates Media Guide
1970 Pittsburgh Pirates Media Guide
1971 Oakland A's Media Guide
1971 Oakland A's Yearbook
1970 San Diego Padres Media Guide
1971 San Diego Padres Media Guide
A Working Manual for World Series, League Championship, All-Star Game [1970]

Web Sites

amortization.org
archives.gov
baseball-almanac.com
baseball-reference.com
baseballhall.org
bevisbaseballresearch.wordpress.com
case-law.vlex.com
en.wikipedia.org
faithandfearinflushing.com
freedomarchives.org
interviews.televisionacademy.com
linkedin.com
mijournalismhalloffame.org
sabr.org
theattic.space

Index

Aaron, Hank 144, 149, 151, 157, 214
ABC (media network) 14, 19
Adair, Jerry 133
Addie, Bob 150
Agee, Tommie 101
Alexander, Doyle 96, 139
All in the Family (TV show) 6, 212
All-Star Game: changes to ballot (1971) 150; computer card ballots 145–146; fan-voting scandal (1957) 143–144; French language ballot 150; game program (1970) 154; Pete Rose–Ray Fosse collision (1970) 155; Pitch, Hit & Throw contest 153; planning logistics 152–154; voting returned to fans 144–147; write-in option 145, 146, 149, 150
Allegheny Club (Three Rivers Stadium) 181
Allegheny (Pennsylvania) Conference for Community Development 178
Allen, Bernie 46
Allen, Dick 49, 83, 96, 97–98, 133, 138, 139, 140, 149, 194
Allison, Bob 57, 151
Allyn, John 123
Alou, Jesús 127, 199
Alston, Walter 83, 95, 96, 97, 193–194
Alvarado, Luis 14, 141, 148
American Football League 8
American League expansion 7, 26, 29, 34–35, 54, 83, 92, 102, 106, 109, 114, 152; *see also* Kansas City Royals; Seattle Pilots; Washington Senators
American Legion World Series 21
Anaheim Stadium 168
Anderson, George "Sparky" 65–68, 92, 93–95, 129, 156
Anderson, Lee Roy 65
Anderson, Shirley 65
Andrews, Mike 72, 141, 148
Aparicio, Luis 141, 148, 149, 151, 157
Apollo 13 4

Apollo 15 19
arbitration *see* labor issues
Arizona State University 138
Arlington Park Corporation 123
Arlington Stadium 123
Armbrister, Ed 129
Aronson, M.L. 181
Arthur Anderson & Company 123
Ashford, Emmett 194
AstroTurf 129, 210–211
Astrodome (Houston)
Atlanta Braves 17, 27, 34, 46, 57, 65, 66, 79, 81, 108, 111, 120, 126, 140, 146, 149, 150, 151
Atlanta Stadium 168
Attica Correctional Facility (New York) 5, 213
autograph policy 20–21, 31
Autry, Gene 88

Bahnsen, Stan 98
Baines, Harold 160
Baker, Frank 135
Baker Bowl (Philadelphia) 169, 171
Ball Four (book) 15, 31–32, 54–55, 193, 200, 206, 211
Baltimore Orioles 10, 16, 17, 18, 19–20, 21, 26, 28, 29–30, 44, 59–64, 67, 69, 72, 74, 76, 78, 79, 82, 85, 86–89, 95, 98, 111, 121, 124, 136, 139, 149, 151, 187, 204, 206, 210
Bamberger, George 86
Bancroft, Dave 159
Bando, Sal 90, 91
Banks, Ernie 57
Barber, Steve 55
Barlick, Al 213
Barnes, Eppie 164
Baseball Hall of Fame 143, 158–167; balloting (1970, 1971) 158, 159, 196; criticism of Veterans Committee 160
"Baseball vs. Drugs" booklet 201
Baseball Writers' Association of America (BBWAA) 158, 159, 164

Index

Bauer, Hank 60, 62
Bavasi, Buzzie 124
Baylor, Don 86, 88, 139
Beatles (rock group) 3, 4
Beckley, Jake 159
Behind the Mask: An Inside Baseball Diary (book) 31, 56
Belanger, Mark 151
Belinsky, Bo 57, 207
Bell, Gary 56, 133
Bell, Gus 144, 185
Belmont (NY) Race Track 175
Bench, Johnny 64, 92, 93, 94, 95, 149, 150, 151, 157, 186
Berra, Yogi 73, 81, 159
"Big Red Machine" (team nickname): origin 93
Biitner, Larry 119
Billingham, Jack 129
Billings, Dick 46, 119
Birmingham bus boycott 3
Black Sox Scandal 43, 182
Black Sports (magazine) 195
Blackwell, Ewell 185
Blair, Paul 62, 87
Blass, Steve 64, 88, 200
Blefary, Curt 86
Blue, Vida 52, 89–90, 91, 156, 158
Bonds, Bobby 186
Borbón, Pedro 92, 131
Bosman, Dick 45, 120
Boston Braves 159
Boston Red Sox 10, 26, 29, 30, 69, 70, 76, 133, 140–141, 148, 159, 169, 207; "Impossible Dream" (1967 team) 62, 69–70, 78, 130, 133
Boswell, Dave 74
Boudreau, Lou 158, 165
Bouton, Jim 15, 31–32, 54–56, 57, 193, 204
Bowa, Larry 14
Boyer, Clete 57
Bragan, Bobby 69, 81
Brecheen, Harry 86
Brett, Ken 140
Brewer, Chet 197
Brinkley, David 18
Brinkman, Ed 44, 45, 118, 119
Bristol, Dave 65, 134
Brock, Lou 139
Bronfman, Charles 35
Brooklyn Dodgers 66, 68, 69, 76–77, 83, 143, 159, 164, 165, 171, 178, 198, 199
Brown, Jim 166
Brown, Joe 82
Brown, Ollie 107
Brown v. Board of Education (court case) 3, 48

Buckner, Bill 14, 96, 194
Buford, Don 62, 86, 88
Bunker, Archie 6, 212
Bunker, Edith 6
Bunning, Jim 57, 174
Bureau of Narcotics and Dangerous Drugs (Department of Justice) 202
Burger, Warren 33
Burke, Joe 124
Burke, Michael 25, 99–100, 195–196, 206, 213
Burkett, Jesse 165
Burroughs, Jeff 120
Busch Stadium (St. Louis) 133, 168
Busch, August A. "Gussie," Jr. 139, 140

California Angels 1, 10, 43, 72, 80, 83, 88, 92, 122, 129, 131, 133–136, 139, 147, 154, 197, 210
Campanella, Roy 164, 165
Campaneris, Bert 90
Campanis, Al 96
Campbell, Jim 43, 44, 75
Candlestick Park (San Francisco) 168
Capra, Buzz 131
Carbo, Bernie 92, 94, 211
Cárdenas, Leo 131, 151
Carew, Rod 149, 151
Carlson, Ed 110, 112, 113
Carlton, Steve 140
Carnegie Technical Institute 179
Carothers, Wallace 208
Carpenter, Robert (Bob) 121, 172
Carroll, Clay 93, 94
Carty, Rico 146–147, 148, 149, 150, 155
Cash, Norm 146, 151
Cashen, Frank 88
Cater, Danny 141
CBS *see* Columbia Broadcasting System
Celler, Emanuel 123
Center Field Plaza (Pittsburgh) 181
Central Trust Company (Cincinnati) 183
Cepeda, Orlando 140
Cey, Ron 96, 98, 194
Chance, Dean 132
Chancellor, John 18
Chapman, Ben 199
Chicago Cubs 10, 36, 58, 79, 101, 138, 163, 174, 179
Chicago White Sox 36, 83, 92, 98, 113, 121, 138, 169, 194, 206, 209, 211
Cincinnati Enquirer 144, 186
Cincinnati Post & Times Star 188
Cincinnati Reds 10, 16–17, 19, 27, 47, 48, 63, 64–68, 83, 85, 86, 92–96, 98, 129, 134, 138, 139, 143–144, 154, 159, 182–187, 200, 210, 211, 213

Civil Rights Act (1964) 3, 48, 203
Claire, Fred 96
Clarke, Horace 122
Clemente, Roberto 64, 146, 158, 178, 180
Clendenon, Donn 101, 126–128, 142, 199
Cleveland Indians 25, 26, 29–30, 62, 69, 83, 96, 102, 108, 127, 129, 132, 135, 136, 138, 139, 141, 155, 158, 165, 172, 206, 209, 211; Basebelles 206; Junior Basebelles booster clubs 206
Cloninger, Tony 92
Colbert, Nate 107, 151
Cold War 3
Coleman, Gordy 93
Coleman, Joe 44, 46
Columbia Broadcasting System (CBS) 6, 99, 195, 208
Columbia Park (Philadelphia) 169
Combs, Earle 158
Comiskey Park (Chicago) 206, 209
competitive balance 23, 33, 36
Concepción, Dave 92, 129
Conigliaro, Billy 140, 141
Conigliaro, Tony 133–136, 206–207
Connecticut General Insurance Company 171
Connie Mack Stadium 168–175; final game 173–174; final Opening Day 172; "Spite Wall" 170
Cooper, Cecil 141
Cooper, Irving Ben 51
Copacabana (nightclub) 74
Corbett, Brad 124
counterculture (1960s) 4, 193, 200, 203, 211
Coveleski, Stanley 165
Craig, Jack 18
Crawford, Willie 95
Cronin, Joe 12, 20, 24, 27, 113, 119
Crosby, Bing 178
Crosley, Powel III 183
Crosley, Powel, Jr. 182–183
Crosley Field (Cincinnati) 95, 129, 168, 182–187; final game 186; glass backstop 185; ground rules 185; lighting system 183; outfield terrace 184
Crowe, George 144
Cuban Missile Crisis 3
Cuccinello, Tony 204
Cuellar, Mike 40, 62, 86, 88
Cullen, Tim 46

Dacron (polyester fiber) 208
Dale, Francis 37
Dale, Ronnie 186
Daley, William 109, 110
Dalton, Harry 21–22, 60, 61–62, 63, 86, 87, 88, 131, 136, 144

Daly, Ed 121
Danz, Fred 110
Danzansky, Joseph 107, 119–120, 121, 123
Davis, Willie 95, 150, 151
D.C. Stadium (Washington) see Robert F. Kennedy Stadium
Dean, James 4
Death Wish (movie) 100
DeCamp, Graydon 186
Dedeaux, Rod 65–66
Democratic National Committee 114–115
Democratic National Convention (1968) 4
Denehy, Bill 78
Derringer, Paul 185
Detroit Free Press 156
Detroit Tigers 14, 26, 28, 29–30, 31, 40, 41, 43–46, 56, 57, 62, 68, 70, 73–76, 87, 125, 133, 141, 146, 171, 176, 183, 197
Dever, James 186
Devine, Bing 49, 139–140
The Dick Van Dyke Show (TV program) 208
Dickson, James Tennant 208
Dickson, Paul 59
DiMaggio, Joe 166
Dobson, Chuck 91, 138
Dobson, Pat 87, 88
Doby, Larry 163
Dodger Stadium (Los Angeles) 96, 98, 168
Doonesbury (comic strip) 212
Doors (rock group) 5
Doubleday Field 167
Doyne, John 111
Dreyfuss, Barney 175–176, 177, 178, 181
Dreyfuss, Florence 178
Drug Abuse Prevention Week 15
drug education program 201
Drysdale, Don 95
Duffy, Frank 137
Duncan, Dave 71, 90, 91
DuPont Company 208
Duquesne University 179
Durocher, Leo 138
Dwyer, William 112

Earth Day 5
Ebbets Field (Brooklyn) 168
Eckert, William 38, 58, 114, 162, 163, 194, 195
Eisenberg, John 86
Ellis, Dock 156–157, 158, 179, 197–198, 200, 201, 202
Ellsberg, Daniel 212
Epstein, Mike 91, 100
Equal Rights Amendment (ERA) 203, 205
Erardi, John G. 93

240   Index

Ermer, Cal 74
Executive Council 20, 116
executive offices, relocation of AL and NL headquarters 20
Exposition Park (Pittsburgh) 175, 176, 178, 179

facial hair 67, 140, 211
Falls, Joe 44
Faust, Nancy 206
Federal Baseball Club of Baltimore, Inc. v. National League of Professional Baseball Clubs, Inc. (court case) 34, 50
Feeney, Chub 13, 20, 27
Feller, Bob 165
The Feminine Mystique (book) 203
Fenway Park (Boston) 20, 69, 70, 187
Ferguson, Joe 96
Figueroa, Ed 131
financial aspects (playoffs) 16–20
Fingers, Rollie 90
Finley, Charlie 18, 24–25, 71–72, 74, 89, 90, 91–92, 113, 115, 121, 162
Fisk, Carlton 141
Fitzgibbon, Henry 15, 31, 42, 119, 121
Flick, Elmer 165
Flieg, Fred 185
Flood, Curt 11, 32–34, 45, 47–57, 118, 133, 140
Foley, Red 53
footwear 209, 211
Forbes (magazine) 23
Forbes, Frank 164
Forbes, Gen. John 179
Forbes Field (Pittsburgh) 154, 168, 175–181, 187–188, 210, 213; amenities 176; "Crow's Nest" 176; final game 177, 179–181; "Greenberg Gardens" 177; "Kiner's Korner" 177; section of outfield wall 181
Ford, Gerald 123
Ford, Whitey 73
Fort Duquesne 176
Fort Pitt 176
Fosse, Ray 151, 155; and Pete Rose collision (1970) 155, 167, 211, 213
Foster, Alan 135
Foster, George 94, 95, 129, 138
Fowler, Bud 167
Fowler Way 167
Foxx, Jimmie 185
Foy, Joe 101, 130, 132, 133
Freedom Rides 3, 48
Freehan, Bill 31, 43, 56, 146, 149, 151
Fregosi, Jim 80, 131, 132, 133, 136
The French Connection (movie) 100, 212
Frick, Ford 143, 144, 158–159, 164, 165
Friedan, Betty 203, 204

Frisch, Frankie 160
Frisella, Danny 131

Galbreath, John W. 20, 178
Gallagher, James 21
Gallo, Bill 76
Gamble, Oscar 173
Gardella, Danny 37, 50, 54
Garr, Ralph 150, 151
Garvey, Steve 83, 96, 98, 194
Gaston, Clarence 107
Gauss, Cal 23, 24
Gentry, Gary 80. 131
Gerónimo, César 129
Giant Food, Inc. 119
Gibson, Bob 48, 154
Gibson, Josh 162, 163, 166
Giles, Warren 12, 186
Gillette Company 144
The Godfather (novel) 212
Goldberg, Arthur 33–34, 51, 53
Goldberger, Paul 187
Gómez, Preston 107
Goodman, Ival 185
Gorman, Lou 102
Gossage, Rich "Goose" 194
Gottlieb, Ed 164
Grabarkewitz, Billy 96, 97, 154
The Graduate (movie) 190
Grammas, Alex 93, 186
Granger, Wayne 93, 129, 186
Grant, M. Donald 25, 78
Green, Dick 91
Greenberg, Hank 177
Grich, Bobby 86, 88
Griffin, Doug 133
Griffith, Calvin 34, 74, 114
Griffith Stadium (Washington, D.C.) 114
Grimsley, Ross 93
Groat, Dick 140
Groh, Heinie 185
Grzenda, Joe 122
Gulf of Tonkin Incident 4
Gullett, Don 92

Haak, Howie 178
Hadden, Sandy 22, 25
Hafey, Chick 159, 160
Hahn, Gilbert 119–120
Haines, Jesse 158, 160
Hall of Fame 40, 59, 143, 159, 160–167, 182; Negro League candidacy 31, 143, 160–167; plaque placement 161, 164; Veterans Committee 57, 158–160, 196
Hamm Brewing Company 194
Hannan, Jim 44
Hard-Hat Riot (1970) 4, 212

Hardball (Bowie Kuhn memoir) 111, 149, 164, 194–195
Harmon, Pat 188
Harper, Tommy 134, 140, 141
Harrah, Toby 119
Harrelson, Bud 151
Harrelson, Ken "Hawk" 78, 127, 128, 133, 141, 142
Hawkins, Jim 44
Helms, Tommy 64, 92, 93, 129, 130
Hendrick, George 138
Hendrix, Jimi 4, 5
Henry Ford Hospital (Detroit) 44
Herzog, Buck 185
Hickman, Jim 154–155
Hodges, Gil 77–81, 84, 101, 114, 130, 160, 192–193
Hoffberger, Jerry 111, 213
Hoffman, Dustin 190
Holtzman, Jerome 56, 123, 197
Holtzman, Ken 92, 138
Hooper, Harry 159
Horton, Willie 75, 146, 197
Houk, Ralph 67
Houston Astrodome 129, 154, 168
Houston Astros 14, 57, 127, 129, 130, 132, 136, 199, 210
Howard, Elston 55, 115
Howard, Frank 52, 116, 120, 122, 149
Howsam, Bob 65, 66, 68, 93, 94–95, 129, 134, 211
Hoynes, Lou, Jr. 53
Hubbard, Cal 12
Hunter, Billy 62
Hunter, Bob 95
Hunter, Catfish 90, 91, 154
Huntz, Steve 138
Hutchinson, Fred 64

image of baseball 7, 8, 14–15, 16, 24–25, 99, 143, 210
Ingham, John N. 199
Instant Replay (book) 54
international World Series 31
Irvin, Monte 115, 164, 194–195

Jackson, Reggie 89, 90, 91, 138, 151, 157, 167, 198
Jackson State College (Mississippi) 192
James, Bill 160
Jarry Park 103–104
Jarvis, Ray 133
Jenkins, Fergie 179
Jobe, Dr. Frank 139
Jock (magazine) 206
John, Tommy 138–139
Johnson, Alex 134–136, 197

Johnson, Arnold 172
Johnson, Bob 130
Johnson, Davey 149
Johnson, Jack 166
Johnson, John H. 30, 120
Johnson, Judy 164
Johnson, Lyndon 4, 212
Johnstone, Jay 131
Jones, Cleon 79, 101, 193
Jones, Dalton 133
Jones, Mack 104
Joplin, Janis 4, 5
Jorgensen, Marian 49

Kaline, Al 76, 146
Kane, Francis 117
Kansas City Athletics 34, 69, 91, 108, 127, 138, 159, 162
Kansas City Royals 35, 72, 83, 92, 102–103, 106, 129, 130, 150, 155
Kansas City Royals Baseball Academy 102–103
Kaplan, Fred 213
Kasko, Eddie 148
Kauffman, Ewing 35, 102–103, 118
Keane, Johnny 48, 139
Keith, Chan 86
Kekich, Mike 56
Kennedy, John F. 3, 203
Kent State University 4, 190–192, 193, 212
Kerr, Paul 164
Kessinger, Don 149, 179
Killebrew, Harmon 149, 157, 214
Kiner, Ralph 177
King, Martin Luther, Jr. 49, 194
King, Nellie 179
Kison, Bruce 64
Kissinger, Henry 212
Kluszewski, Ted 93, 185
Koosman, Jerry 78, 80, 101, 131
Koppett, Leonard 54, 164
Koufax, Sandy 95, 136
Kramer, Jerry 54–55
Kranepool, Ed 127
Krausse, Lew 140, 141
Kroc, Ray 108
Kuhn, Bowie 9, 12, 13, 19, 21, 22, 58, 110, 124, 153, 194; addressing drug problem 201–202; and Alex Johnson 134–135; and bureaucratic re-organization 20; and Charlie Finley 18; and Clendenon/Harrelson trades 127–128; and Curt Flood 33, 51, 53; and Denny McLain 14–15, 42–44, 45; deposition in *State of Washington* case 111–114; desire to increase baseball's appeal 23–26, 31, 32; and fan All-Star voting 144, 149–150,

152; and Hall of Fame 161, 163–164; and Jim Bouton 32, 55–56; and Monte Irvin 194–195; and Washington Senators 116–120

labor issues (players): arbitration 12, 38; benefits (hotel, meal money) 11; Messersmith-McNally case 36, 54; 1969 MLBPA basic agreement 8, 11; 1970 MLBPA basic agreement 12; 1973 MLBPA basic agreement 12, 142; reserve clause and Curt Flood 47–54; reserve clause (Canadian aspect) 35; reserve system challenges 34, 35, 37, 50, 54
labor issues (umpires): umpire strike (1970) 13; umpires union 12–13
Laboy, Coco 104
Lacy, Sam 164
Lahoud, Joe 140
Lajoie, Nap 165
Landis, Kenesaw Mountain 43
Lane, Frank "Trader" 134
Lang, Jack 101, 164
Lasorda, Tom 96, 104
Lawson, Earl 66, 93–94
League Championship Series (attendance) 16, 17
Lear, Norman 6
Leary, Timothy 201, 211
Leavitt, Charles Wellford, Jr. 175
Lemon, Bob 83, 102
Lemon, James 114
Libby, Bill 207
Life (magazine) 189
Lindblad, Paul 120
Lindsay, John 100
logos 108, 154, 186, 209, 210
Lolich, Mickey 41
Lombardi, Ernie 184, 185
Lombardi, Vince 54, 55
Lonborg, Jim 70, 140, 141
Look (magazine) 31
Lopat, Ed 91
Lopes, Davey 96, 98
Lopez, Al 102
Los Angeles Angels *see* California Angels
Los Angeles Dodgers 10, 27, 64, 83, 95–98, 121, 133, 138, 139, 150, 154, 193–194
Los Angeles Lakers (NBA team) 114
Love Story (movie) 5
Lowry, Philip J. 183
Lucchesi, Frank 172–173
Ludtke, Melissa 208
Lyle, Sparky 141
Lynn, Fred 141

Mack, Connie 59, 169, 170, 171, 174
Mack, Earle 171
Mack, Roy 171
Macmillan *Baseball Encyclopedia* 166
MacPhail, Larry 183, 185
MacPhail, Lee, Jr. 25, 99
Maddox, Elliott 44, 119
Madison Square Garden (New York) 187
Major League Baseball: designated hitter proposal 23; drug abuse program 15, 201–202; league and divisional realignment proposal 26–27, 30; new playoff system 28; pitch clock 23; revenue sharing 37
Major League Baseball Players' Association (MLBPA) 7, 8, 9, 10–12, 14, 38, 50, 53–54, 204, 214
Major League Baseball Promotion Corporation 20
Major League Umpires Association 12–14
Maloney, Jim 65, 67
Man of La Mancha (musical) 70
Mangual, Angel 138
Mantle, Mickey 73, 191
Marquard, Rube 159
Martin, Billy 44, 72, 73–76. 124
The Mary Tyler Moore Show (TV program) 5, 208
M*A*S*H (movie) 5
Matlack, Jon 81, 101, 131
Mauch, Gene 70, 104, 134
May, Ed 42
May, Lee 64, 92, 129, 186
Mayberry, John 14
Mays, Willie 34, 80, 144, 146, 148, 149, 151, 214
Mazeroski, Bill 177, 178, 179, 180, 181, 199
McAndrew, Jim 131
McAuliffe, Dick 43, 146
McCarthy, Joe 59
McCarver, Tim 140, 173, 174
McCormick, Frank 184, 185
McCraw, Tom 46
McCue, Andy 35
McDowell, Sam 136–138, 154
McGee, Frank 18
McGlothlin, Jim 92, 94
McGraw, John 59
McGraw, Tug 131, 192–193, 199
McHale, John 35
McKechnie, Bill 183
McLain, Denny 14–15, 31, 33, 40–47, 52, 56, 57, 75, 86, 118, 119, 120, 125, 133
McLain, Sharon 47
McLaughlin, Jim 60, 63
McMullen, Ken 133
McNally, Dave 36, 54, 62, 86, 87–88

McNamara, John 71, 72
McNamara, Robert 212
McRae, Hal 92
McRae, Norm 44
The Meadows (drug treatment facility) 202
Mele, Sam 74
Melton, Bill 138
Menke, Denis 129
Merritt, Jim 92, 94, 154
Merv Griffin (TV show) 207
Messersmith-McNally case 36, 54
Metro, Charlie 83, 102,
Middlesworth, Hal 153
Millán, Félix 81
Miller, Marvin 8, 11–12, 33–34, 38, 50, 51, 53–54, 55, 204
Miller, Rick 141
Miller, Robert L. 132–133
Milner, John 81, 101
Milwaukee Braves 34, 81
Milwaukee Brewers 14, 26, 29, 30, 35, 87, 92, 108, 110–112, 114, 116–117, 134, 140, 209
Milwaukee County Stadium 111, 118
Minnesota Twins 10, 35, 36, 57, 62–63, 72, 74, 75, 92, 114, 132, 149, 151, 154
minority franchise ownership 195–196
MLBPA *see* Major League Baseball Players' Association
The Mod Squad (TV program) 14, 95
Monday, Rick 91, 138
Monday Night Football 5, 19
Monday Night Movie 18
Montgomery (Alabama) bus boycott 3, 48
Montreal Expos 14, 27, 35–36, 70, 71, 80, 103–104, 106, 126, 127, 173
Montreal Royals 66
Montville, Leigh 163
Morgan, Joe 95, 129, 130, 136–137, 199–200
Morgan, Tom 131
Morrison, Jim 5
Moses, Jerry 133, 135
Moss, Dick 55
Mullins, William 108
Municipal Stadium (Kansas City) 187
Munson, Thurman 14, 98
Murcer, Bobby 99, 151
Murray, Jim 51
Murtaugh, Danny 67, 81–82, 198, 200
Musial, Stan 144
Musick, Phil 180

NASA space program 4, 189
Nathanson, Mitchell 55, 97, 98
National Football League (NFL) 18–19, 26, 28, 29, 150; and rising popularity of pro football 35, 58
National Hot Stove Baseball League 21
National Labor Relations Board (NLRB) 12
National League expansion 7, 26, 35, 64, 66, 77, 103, 105, 106, 108, 126, 152, 158
National Organization for Women (NOW) 203–204
Naugatuck (CT) High School 22
NBC (network) 18, 19, 121, 157
NBC Game of the Week 19
NBC Monday Movie 18
NBC Nightly News 18
Negro League panel *see* Hall of Fame
Neiman, LeRoy 213
Nelson, Dave 119
Nelson, Jim 179
Nettles, Graig 133
New York Central System 5; Pennsylvania Railroad 5
New York Giants (baseball team) 35, 36, 159, 160, 164, 171, 178
New York Giants (NFL team) 100
New York Mets 7, 10, 14, 16, 25, 34, 35, 36, 62, 67, 72, 77, 78–81, 86, 101, 102, 104, 126, 130–132, 148, 192
New York Times 5, 166, 212
New York Yankees 10, 25, 35, 36–37, 50, 54, 64, 73, 81, 82, 98–101, 104, 122, 132, 141, 164, 171, 177, 178, 183, 195
NFL Films 35
Nicola Building Company 175
1961 Freedom Rides 3, 48
1964 Civil Rights Act 3, 48, 203
1965 Voting Rights Act 3, 48, 203
19th Amendment (U.S. Constitution) 204
Nixon, Richard 4, 122, 154, 190
Nixon Administration 15, 190, 201, 212
Nol, General Lon 190
Nolan, Gary 65, 92, 94
Noll, Roger 123
Northrup, Jim 146
Nowlin, Bill 70, 163
Nuxhall, Joe 185

Oakland-Alameda County Coliseum 168
Oakland Athletics 10, 34, 46, 71–72, 88, 89–92, 102, 104, 113, 138, 155, 209, 210
O'Brien, Bob 139
O'Connell, Dick 133, 141
O'Connor, Carroll 6, 212
The Odd Couple 5
Odom, John "Blue Moon" 90, 91, 138
Oglivie, Ben 141
Ohio National Guard 190–191, 192
Okkonen, Marc 209

Index

Okner, Benjamin 123
Oliphant, Dave 37
O'Malley, Walter 27–28, 121
orange-colored baseball 25
Osborn, Gene 179
Osteen, Claude 95
Otis, Amos 130, 155
Oyler, Ray 56

Pacific Northwest Sports, Inc. 109, 111
Paciorek, Tom 96
Paige, Leroy "Satchel" 160–167
Paley, William 99
Palmer, Jim 62, 87, 88, 154
Pan Am World Airways 52
Parc Jarry see Jarry Park
Parker, Wes 95, 97
Parks, Rosa 48
Pascual, Camilo 57
Patterson, James T. 200
Pattin, Marty 140, 141
Paul, Gabe 136, 137
Pavletich, Don 140
Penn Central Transportation Company 5
Pennsylvania Historical and Museum Commission 181
Pennsylvania Station (New York) 187
Pentagon Papers 5, 212
Pepitone, Joe 100, 132
Pérez, Tony 64, 92, 94, 129, 149, 186
Perry, Gaylord 137–138, 154
Perry, Jim 154
Peters, Gary 141
Peterson, Fritz 56, 99
Petrocelli, Rico 141, 148–149
Pfennig, Dave 186
Philadelphia Athletics 159, 169–172
Philadelphia Eagles (NFL) 172
Philadelphia Phillies 33, 36, 49, 51, 52, 57, 58, 66, 93, 97, 121, 134, 169–174, 200, 206, 209–210
Phillips, Harold "Lefty" 66, 133, 136, 207
Phoebus, Tom 62
Piersall, Jimmy 77
Pinson, Vada 47, 129, 135
Pittsburgh Civic Light Opera 179
Pittsburgh Pirates 10, 16, 18, 36, 49, 60, 63–64, 67, 81–82, 88, 175–181, 197–200, 208, 210
Pittsburgh Pirates Radio Network 179
Pittsburgh Post-Gazette 181
Pittsburgh Steelers (NFL team) 179
Pittsburgh Symphony 179
Player Relations Committee 20
player uniform style 206, 209–211
Playing Rules Committee 24
playoff system 28

PNC Park (Pittsburgh) 181
Polo Grounds (New York) 168
Pompez, Alex 184
Porter, Paul 37
Post, Wally 144, 185
Posvar Hall (University of Pittsburgh) 181
Povich, Shirley 118
Powell, Boog 62, 87, 149, 151
Powles, George 47
Presidential Commission on the Status of Women 203
Presley, Elvis 4
Price, Jim 44, 146
Prince, Bob 180

Quinn, Bob 49–50

race relations 50, 156, 189, 192
Rader, Doug 146
Randle, Lenny 119
Raphael, Richard 213
Redland Field (Cincinnati) *see* Crosley Field
Reese, Pee Wee 77
Reform School for Juvenile Negro Law-Breakers (Alabama) 160
Reichardt, Rick 133
Reichler, Joseph 26, 27, 28, 30, 31, 53, 213
Reiner, Rob 6
reserve clause *see* labor issues (players)
Resinger, Grover 56
Rettenmund, Merv 86, 87, 139
Reuss, Jerry 140
revenue-sharing system 37
RFK Stadium (Washington, DC) 45, 107, 115, 117, 118, 119, 121, 122, 123, 124
Rheingold Brewery 194
Rhodes, Gregory L. 93
Rhodes, Jim 190
Rice, Jim 141
Richards, Paul 126
Richert, Pete 139, 206
Rickey, Branch 178, 208
Ringling Brothers Circus 99
Ripken, Cal, Sr. 88
Riverfront Stadium (Cincinnati) 63, 95, 129, 153, 154, 168, 186, 210, 211
Rixey, Eppa 185
Robert F. Kennedy Stadium (Washington, DC) *see* RFK Stadium
Robinson, Brooks 19, 46, 62, 63, 67, 85, 86, 87, 88, 151, 154, 213
Robinson, Frank 47, 62, 86, 88, 89, 98, 139, 149, 151, 157, 185, 196, 214
Robinson, Jackie 48, 49, 51, 115, 143, 158, 159, 163, 164, 196, 198–199
Robinson, Wilbert 59

Robles, Sergio 139
Rockefeller, Nelson 34
Rodríguez, Aurelio 44, 118, 119, 131, 133, 147
Rojas, Cookie 150, 151
Ron Kramer Trio 45
Roosevelt, Franklin D. 183
Rose, Pete 14, 64, 92, 93, 94, 146, 154–155, 167, 186, 211, 213
Roseboro, John 57
Roush, Edd 185
Rowan & Martin's Laugh-In (TV program) 18
Royals Stadium (Kansas City) 187
Rudi, Joe 90, 91, 138
Russell, Bill 83, 95, 96, 98, 194
Ruth, Babe 158, 166
Ryan, Bob 169
Ryan, Nolan 78, 80, 131, 132
Ryczek, Bill 55

Sadecki, Ray 131
St. Louis Browns 36, 60, 162, 169
St. Louis Cardinals 33, 36, 37, 48, 49, 56, 60, 66, 70, 97, 129, 134, 139, 140, 159, 160, 179
Salerno, Al 12–13
Salmon, Chico 206
Salvon, Ralph 86
San Diego Padres 14, 27, 66, 72–73, 105, 106–108, 124, 173, 197
San Diego Stadium 106, 107, 108, 168
San Francisco Giants 10, 27, 28, 82, 83, 98, 111, 129, 137, 186, 198
Sanguillen, Manny 82, 150, 151, 200
Saratoga (NY) Race Track 175
Scarborough, Ray 87
Scheffing, Bob 131
Schenley Park (Pittsburgh) 175, 176, 180
Scherger, George 93
Schlossberg, Daniel 148
Schoendienst, Red 60
Schofield, Dick 57
Schuerholz, John 102
Schultz, Joe 55, 204
Schwab, Matty 182
Scott, George 140
Scully, Vin 209
Seattle Pilots 35, 54, 92, 106, 108–114, 204, 209
Seattle Rainiers 108
Seattle Seahawks (NFL team) 111
Seaver, Tom 78, 131, 154
Security Department (Commissioner's office) 14–15, 119, 202
Segar, Charles 15
Seghi, Phil 25

Segui, Diego 91
Seibert, Sonny 141
Seitz ruling 36, 91, 142
Selig, Allan H. "Bud" 110, 111, 114, 117–118
Selkirk, George 77
Serpico (movie) 100
Shannon, Mike 147
Shea Stadium (New York) 78, 79, 80, 101, 104, 131, 132, 168
Shepard, Larry 93
Sherman Antitrust Act 33, 50
Shibe, Benjamin 169, 170
Shibe, Jack 170
Shibe Park *see* Connie Mack Stadium
Shore, Ray 129
Short, Robert E. (Bob) 33, 44–46, 52–53, 113, 114–124, 126, 133
Sicks' Stadium 108–109, 110, 113
Simmons, Harry 29
Simmons, Ted 151
Simpson, Wayne 92, 94
Singer, Bill 95
Singleton, Ken 80
Sisler, Dick 64
Sizemore, Ted 95, 133
Skrable, Pat 140
Smith, C. Arnholt 107–108
Smith, Claire 208
Smith, Mayo 41, 44, 56, 74, 75
Smith, Red 51
Smith, Reggie 141
Smith, Wendell 164
Snyder, Brad 34, 49
Society for American Baseball Research (SABR) 1, 124
Soriano, Dewey 109, 110
Soriano, Max 109, 110, 112
Southeast Florida Tuberculosis Hospital 146
Southfield (Michigan) High School 151
Sparma, Joe 42
Speaker, Tris 165
Spencer, Jim 131
Spoelstra, Watson 44
Sport Scene (magazine) 207
The Sporting News 18, 23, 44, 54, 65, 66, 67, 82, 89, 93, 94, 103, 123, 133, 140, 144, 145, 148, 149
Sports Illustrated 14, 42, 56, 80
Sportservice (concessionaire) 109–110
Sputnik 3
Stanley, Mickey 146
Stapleton, Jean 6
Stargell, Willie 151, 157
The State of Washington, the County of King, and the City of Seattle v. The American League of Professional

Baseball Clubs, et al (court case) 111–113
Staub, Rusty 80, 104, 127
Steelworkers Union 33
Steinbrenner, George 99, 101
Stengel, Casey 73, 77, 81
Stewart, Jimmy 129
Stillman, Royle 139
Stinson, Bob 133
Stone, George 81
Stottlemyre, Mel 99, 154
Strunk, Amos 173
Sudakis, Bill 95
Swoboda, Ron 80, 193
Symington, Stuart 34
synthetic fabric 208–209

Talbert, Bob 156
Tallis, Cedric 102
Tatum, Jarvis 133
Tatum, Ken 133
Taylor, Ron 131
Taylor, Tony 174–175
The Team That Couldn't Hit: The 1972 Texas Rangers (book) 124
Teamsters and Building Services unions (Pittsburgh) 13
Terry, Bill 160
Terylene (polyester fiber) 208
This Great Game (book) 213
Three Rivers Stadium (Pittsburgh) 13, 168, 178–179, 181
Thrift, Syd 102
Tiant, Luis 132, 133
Tiger Stadium 43, 76, 153, 156
Till, Emmett 3
Tinker, Joe 185
Title VII (legislation) 203,
Tolan, Bobby 68, 92, 94, 129, 186
"Tommy John surgery" 139
Toolson v. New York Yankees (court case) 35, 37, 50, 54
Toolson, George 37, 54
Topping, Daniel 99
Toronto Globe & Mail 66
Torre, Joe 140, 151
Trudeau, Garry 211–212
Truman Sports Complex (Kansas City) 103, 187
26th Amendment (U.S. Constitution) 5
Twombly, Wells 89
Tye, Larry 160
Tyler Moore, Mary 208

Uhlaender, Ted 133
Umont, Frank 157
umpire uniforms 210

Underminers' Club (Washington Senators) 46
Union Terminal (Cincinnati railroad station) 187
U.S. Department of Health, Education, and Welfare 202
U.S. Interior Department 116, 117
United States Supreme Court 13, 33, 34, 35, 50, 51, 52, 53, 54
University of Pittsburgh 178, 181
University of Southern California 65
University of Washington 108
Unser, Del 120
USA Today 202

Valentine, Bill 12–13
Valentine, Bobby 96, 98, 193–194
Vance, Sandy 96
Vander Meer, Johnny 185
Van Doren, Mamie 207
Veeck, Bill 83, 165
Veterans Stadium (Philadelphia) 168, 170, 172, 174, 209
Vietnam War 4, 5, 67, 189, 190, 192–193, 201, 203, 212
violence in society 22, 23, 25, 189, 212–213
Virdon, Bill 82
Voting Rights Act of 1965 3–4, 48, 203

Walker, Dixie 199
Walker, Harry "the Hat" 82, 127, 198–200
Walker, Rube 78
Walsh, Dick 131, 134–135
Walt Disney World 5
Walters, Bucky 185
Warehime, Jeannette 204, 205–206
Warehime, Linda 204–206
Warehime, Ralph, Sr. 204
Washington Board of Trade 121
Washington D.C. Armory Board 117–119, 120
Washington Post 118, 124
Washington Redskins (NFL team) 117
Washington Senators (American League expansion team) 26, 29, 33, 35, 44, 45, 46, 52, 56, 62, 70, 77, 78, 89, 100, 107, 111, 113, 130, 133; final game 122; transfer to Texas 114–124
Washington Senators (original American League team) 34, 35, 114, 177
Washington Star 120
Waxahachie (TX) High School 22
The Way It Is (book) 56
Weaver, Earl 59–64, 68, 84, 85, 87, 88, 157, 206, 213
Webb, Del 99
Weil, Sidney 183

Index

Weinberg, Jack 201
Weiss, George 159, 165
Welch, Raquel 207
Werber, Bill 185
Wert, Don 44
Westcott, Rich 172, 173
Western Union 153
Wharton School of Business 19–20
White, Bill 48, 199
White, Roy 99
Whitfield, John Rex 208
Wilcox, Milt 92
Will, George 199
Williams, Billy 163
Williams, Charlie 131
Williams, Dick 68–73, 89, 90, 91, 104, 133
Williams, Edward Bennett 117
Williams, Ellery 68
Williams, Harvey 68
Williams, Stan 132
Williams, Ted 22, 45–46, 52, 115, 119, 124, 162–163, 164
Wills, Maury 115, 150, 151
Wilson, Don 199
Winter Meetings 24, 39, 78, 95, 126, 128, 131, 142
Wirz, Bob 102
Wise, Rick 140
WLW (Cincinnati radio station) 183
Wolman, Jerry 174
women's issues 203–208; Women's Strike for Equality 5; *see also* Equal Rights Amendment
Woodstock Music and Art Fair (New York) 201
Woodward, Woody 93
World Airways, Inc. 121
World Baseball Classic 31
World Series 18–19, 88
World Trade Center 5
WRC 980AM (Washington, DC radio station) 121
Wright, Clyde 136, 154
Wrigley Field (Chicago) 20, 57, 187
WTOP-TV (Washington, DC) 119
WWDC (Washington, DC radio station) 119
Wynn, Early 159
Wynn, Jimmy 136, 199

Yancey, Bill 164
Yankee Stadium 100–101, 155, 166
Yastrzemski, Carl 70, 72, 133, 134, 141, 149, 151
"Yastrzemski Theory" 24
Yawkey, Tom 70, 72, 133
Yorkin, Bud 6
Young, Cy 165
Young, Dick 157, 164

Zahn, Geoff 96
Zerman, Allan 49, 50

www.ingramcontent.com/pod-product-compliance
Lightning Source LLC
Chambersburg PA
CBHW032036300426
44117CB00009B/1083